CW01375903

The Diversity of Nonreligion

This is a timely work that considerably furthers our understanding of nonreligious identities in regions that hitherto have seen little scholarly attention. The authors provide researchers with an invaluable toolbox for and illuminating examples of thorough and multidimensional analysis of contemporary nonreligion vis-à-vis its societal others.

Tom Kaden, *University of Bayreuth, Germany*

This book explores the relational dynamic of religious and nonreligious positions as well as the tensions between competing modes of nonreligion. Across the globe, individuals and communities are seeking to distinguish themselves in different ways from religion as they take on an identity unaffiliated to any particular faith. The resulting diversity of nonreligion has until recently been largely ignored in academia.

Conceptually, the book advances a relational approach to nonreligion, which is inspired by Pierre Bourdieu's field theory. It also offers further analytical distinctions that help to identify and delineate different modes of nonreligion with respect to actors' values, objectives, and their relations with relevant religious others. The significance of this conceptual frame is illustrated by three empirical studies, on organized humanism in Sweden, atheism and freethought in the Philippines, and secular politics in the Netherlands. These studies analyze the normativities and changing positions of different groups against the background of both institutionalized religious practice and changing religious fields more generally.

This is a fascinating exploration of how nonreligion and secularities are developing across the world. It complements existing approaches to the study of religion, secularity, and secularism and will, therefore, be of great value to scholars of religious studies as well as the anthropology, history, and sociology of religion more generally.

Johannes Quack is Assistant Professor of Social Anthropology at the University of Zurich, Switzerland. He is the author of *Disenchanting India: Organized Rationalism and Criticism of Religion in India* (2012).

Cora Schuh is a PhD student at the Institute for the Study of Culture, University of Leipzig, Germany.

Susanne Kind is a PhD student at the Institute for the Study of Culture, University of Leipzig, Germany.

Routledge Studies in Religion

Religion and Human Security in Africa
Edited by Ezra Chitando and Joram Tarusarira

The Paranormal and Popular Culture
A Postmodern Religious Landscape
Edited by Darryl Caterine and John W. Morehead

Religion and Politics Under Capitalism
A Humanistic Approach to the Terminology
Stefan Arvidsson

American Catholic Bishops and the Politics of Scandal
Rhetoric of Authority
Meaghan O'Keefe

Celebrity Morals and the Loss of Religious Authority
John Portmann

Reimagining God and Resacralisation
Alexa Blonner

Said Nursi and Science in Islam
Character Building through Nursi's Mana-i harfi
Necati Aydin

The Diversity of Nonreligion
Normativities and Contested Relations
Johannes Quack, Cora Schuh, and Susanne Kind

The Role of Religion in Gender-Based Violence, Immigration, and Human Rights
Edited by Mary Nyangweso and Jacob K. Olupona

For more information about this series, please visit: www.routledge.com/religion/series/SE0669

The Diversity of Nonreligion
Normativities and Contested Relations

Johannes Quack, Cora Schuh,
and Susanne Kind

Routledge
Taylor & Francis Group
LONDON AND NEW YORK

First published 2020
by Routledge
2 Park Square, Milton Park, Abingdon, Oxon OX14 4RN

and by Routledge
52 Vanderbilt Avenue, New York, NY 10017

Routledge is an imprint of the Taylor & Francis Group, an informa business

© 2020 selection and editorial matter, Johannes Quack, Cora Schuh, and Susanne Kind; individual chapters, the contributors

The right of Johannes Quack, Cora Schuh, and Susanne Kind to be identified as the authors of the editorial material, and of the authors for their individual chapters, has been asserted in accordance with sections 77 and 78 of the Copyright, Designs and Patents Act 1988.

All rights reserved. No part of this book may be reprinted or reproduced or utilised in any form or by any electronic, mechanical, or other means, now known or hereafter invented, including photocopying and recording, or in any information storage or retrieval system, without permission in writing from the publishers.

Trademark notice: Product or corporate names may be trademarks or registered trademarks, and are used only for identification and explanation without intent to infringe.

British Library Cataloguing-in-Publication Data
A catalogue record for this book is available from the British Library

Library of Congress Cataloging-in-Publication Data
A catalog record for this book has been requested

ISBN: 978-0-367-18548-0 (hbk)
ISBN: 978-0-429-19679-9 (ebk)

Typeset in Sabon
by Apex CoVantage, LLC

Contents

List of tables		vi
Acknowledgments		vii
List of abbreviations		ix
1	Introduction: researching the diversity of nonreligion	1
2	Concept: non/religious constructions and contestations	7
3	Contested humanist identities in Sweden	35
4	Collective nonreligiosities in the Philippines	77
5	Secularizing politics in the Netherlands	105
6	Comparison: normativities and contested relations	143
	Bibliography	168
	Index	184

Tables

5.1	*Non-church affiliation; party comparison*	132
5.2	*Relatedness with humanism; party comparison*	132
5.3	*Religion and politics; party comparison*	133
5.4	*Perceived religious-nonreligious conflict*	133
5.5	*Satisfaction with Dutch democracy*	134
5.6	*Election results, Second Chamber*	134
5.7	*D66 electoral strength and government participation*	134

Acknowledgments

There are many people whom we wish to thank here. Most importantly, our gratitude is owed to our interlocutors, interview partners, and contact persons. Thank you for your time, trust, interest, and your general support for our research.

We would further like to thank some institutions and our respective colleagues for their support, dialogue, and constructive criticism. In this respect, we would like to thank the Department of Social and Cultural Anthropology at the University of Frankfurt, the Department of Social Anthropology and Cultural Studies (ISEK) at the University of Zurich, the Uppsala Religion and Society Research Centre (CRS) at the University of Uppsala, and our colleagues at the Nonreligion and Secularity Research Network (NSRN).

Monika Wohlrab-Sahr and Peter Bräunlein have provided guidance regarding the individual research studies as well as the overall project at various stages. Their profound assessments, comments, and criticism have provided inspiration at decisive points and have significantly influenced the quality of the individual studies. We thank them for their constant encouragement and experienced eye for relevance and structure.

Special gratitude also goes to Per Pettersson, Anders Sjöborg, and Anders Bäckström for providing a great research environment at the CRS Uppsala, not only in terms of their invaluable feedback and advice but also for the insights they offered into the Swedish context more generally. Many thanks for the welcoming atmosphere and the exciting conversations over fika also go to the inspiring colleagues at CRS and beyond: Marta Axner, Maria Klingenberg, Annette Leis-Peters, Jonas Lindberg, Martha Middlemiss Lé Mon, Oriol Poveda, Josephine Sundqvist, Anneli Winell, Hans-Georg Ziebertz, Pelle Nilsson, Magnus Hedelind, Mia Lövheim, and Grace Davie.

Within the framework of the project, productive and inspiring workshops were held with Matthew Engelke, Michaela Köttig, and Jens Kugele. Their respective inputs are greatly appreciated. Furthermore, we thank all the participants of our workshop on nonreligion: Stefan Binder, Serina Heinen, Petra Klug, Björn Mastiaux, David Schneider, Stefan Schröder, and Mascha Schulz.

Beyond that, we wish to thank those who helped during the overall project and in the process of writing this book, Stefan Schröder and Björn Mastiaux for reading and commenting on earlier versions, our incredibly flexible and efficient English proofreader, Janine Murphy, as well as the different student research assistants that were involved at various stages in the process, Cornelia Aufmuth, Eva Brandl, Martin Jägel, Kora Kruse, Julianne Lehmann, Alexandra Jugelt, Andrei Stoinescu, and Rivana Cerullo, for their helpful support at the stage of proposal-writing, and our colleagues Sandra Bärnreuther, Anne Breubeck, Esther Horat, and Mascha Schulz, who have strengthened the overall project with helpful criticism.

Special gratitude also goes to all the people in our personal lives. We wish to thank our families and friends for being supportive and distractive. Most importantly though, we thank our partners for the various ways in which they contributed to making this project possible; their assistance, patience, care, as well as their interferences.

This book is the outcome of the research project "The Diversity of Nonreligion," funded by the German Research Foundation (DFG) from 2012 to 2016. We wish to thank the DFG for generously funding the project as well as its flexibility.

And last, but not least, we wish to cordially thank Alexander Blechschmidt for his contribution and his companionship throughout the whole project!

Abbreviations

ANiS   Andhashraddha Nirmulan Samiti (Organization for the Eradication of Superstition)
ARP   Anti-Revolutionaire Partij (Anti-Revolutionary Party)
CDA   Christen-Democratisch Appèl (Christian Democratic Appeal)
CHU   Christelijk-Historische Unie (Christian Historic Union)
CPN   Communistische Partij van Nederland (Communist Party Netherlands)
CU   ChristenUnie (Christian Union)
D66   Democraten 66 (Democrats 66)
FF   Filipino Freethinkers
GL   GroenLinks (GreenLeft)
KVP   Katholieke Volkspartij (Catholic People's Party)
LPF   Lijst Pim Fortuyn (List Pim Fortuyn)
LSH   life stance humanism
MP   member of parliament
OMH   opinion-making humanism
PATAS The Philippine Atheists and Agnostics Society
PSP   Pacifistisch Socialistische Partij (Pacifist Socialist Party)
PvdA   Partij van de Arbeid (Labor Party)
PVV   Partij voor de Vrijheid (Party for Freedom)
RKSP   Rooms-Katholieke Staatspartij (Roman Catholic State Party)
SDAP   Sociaal-Democratische Arbeiderspartij (Social-Democratic Workers' Party)
SGP   Staatkundig Gereformeerde Partij (Reformed Political Party)
SHA   Swedish Humanist Association
SP   Socialistische Partij (Socialist Party)
VVD   Volkspartij voor Vrijheid en Democratie (People's Party for Freedom and Democracy)

1 Introduction

Researching the diversity of nonreligion[1]

Johannes Quack, Cora Schuh, and Susanne Kind[2]

Labels like atheist, freethinker, humanist, or secular refer to people who explicitly or implicitly distance themselves from certain religious traditions and ways of life or from religion as such. They refer to important but certainly not to all possible ways of being nonreligious.

The notion, "nonreligion," signals a tension between a distinction from and relatedness to religion. Nonreligious positions thereby take different forms. Indifference to religion on the one hand and the criticism of religion on the other hand exemplify different ways of being nonreligious. The same holds for claims of independence or differentiation from religion, for neutrality, or even ignorance towards it, as opposed to aims for controlling, competing, or cooperating with religious others from a position that is not seen as religious in itself.

One *locus classicus* for diverging nonreligious positions is the historical debate between the secularist, George Holyoke, and the atheist, Charles Bradlaugh, on whether an attempt to ignore religion necessarily implies a denial of religion (Holyoake and Bradlaugh [1870] 1987; Quack 2011). The empirical case studies in this book analyze the religion-related positionings of and related internal discussions among humanists in Sweden, between atheists and freethinkers in the Philippines, and within a secular political party in the Netherlands.[3] These case studies explore questions about when, where, and how these actors should engage with religious issues, and – for some – the degree to which such engagement implies becoming "religion-like." For others, the question is whether they should move away from certain kinds or, indeed, all kinds of "religion-relatedness."

A detailed discussion of these matters is not only important to better understand the socio-political debates around religion in contemporary societies; variations of this tension are also evident in academia, for instance, in the study of religion, secularity, and nonreligion (Quack 2014). Ever since its "emancipation," the academic study of religion has attempted to move away from religion-likeness, debating what forms of religion-relatedness are permissible under, e.g., the headings of "methodological agnosticism" and "methodological atheism." Similar concerns are explicit in the academic study of nonreligion when Matthew Engelke, as an example, argues that the notion "nonreligion" pulls us back to what we are trying to get away from: religion (Engelke 2015). Finally, the genealogy of the concept "secularity" also signals such tension, since it has been understood as both "differentiation" or "independence of religion" (what we call *third space*) as well as a "transformation of religion."

To address such tensions, we conceptualize, empirically illustrate, and comparatively discuss the fruitfulness of a relational study of religion and nonreligion. The book has six chapters; in the second chapter, we introduce our conceptual frame for analyzing nonreligion: a relational approach to nonreligion. In Chapters 3, 4, and 5, we apply our concepts to three empirical case studies of organizations self-positioning as nonreligious in different ways: humanists in Sweden, organized atheists and freethinkers in the Philippines, and the secular party, D66, in the Netherlands. Against the backdrop of our conceptual frame, Chapter 6 comparatively brings together the different findings.

Taken together, the book introduces a relational study of nonreligion understood as the study of a variety of claims, contestations, and positions with respect to religion in a religion-related surrounding (German: *Umfeld*). It focuses on positions that seek to transform religion, reject and deny its claims, or to explicitly compete, cooperate, or criticize religion as well as on positions that aim for a degree of independence from religion, something to be overcome, and self-describing as indifferent, ignorant, differentiated from, or neutral to religion.

A relational approach to nonreligion

The idea of the project, "The Diversity of Nonreligion," on which this book is based, emerged from previous research on organized rationalism in India with a focus on the group *Andhashraddha Nirmulan Samiti* (Organization for the Eradication of Superstition – ANiS) in Maharashtra (Quack 2012). This ethnography describes and analyzes the group's steadfast ambition to disenchant India. Later, Quack (2013, 2014) conceptualized a more general notion of nonreligion: positions considered by relevant agents to be both distinct from but also related to religion. This relational approach to nonreligion shifts the focus from opposing religion and nonreligion to the discourses and practices that constitute a certain phenomenon as religion-related or not. The actors' perspective and the field perspective are thereby both of importance, although they have to be distinguished analytically.

Obviously, Quack has not been alone with his interest in nonreligion; on the contrary, scholarly interest in the phenomena has constantly risen. Influential contributions on contemporary phenomena were made by, e.g., Amarasingam (2010), Beaman and Tomlins (2015), Blankholm (2014), Cimino and Smith (2014), Cotter (2015), LeDrew (2016), Lee (2015), Zuckerman (2009, 2011, 2014), Zuckerman, Galen, and Pasquale (2016). However, methodological approaches and theoretical conceptualizations in this area differ, especially as they are rooted in different scientific disciplines and traditions. This book serves to demarcate a particular conceptual position in the wider field of studies of secularity and nonreligion. We elaborate upon a relational approach to nonreligion to analyze the complex ways in which positions distinct from religion are related to religious positions. Furthermore, we explore contestations about what constitutes religion and its others. By looking at nonreligious activism with a relational approach, we gain new insights into the respective society at large and how it deals with religion. Potentially more important, this research sheds light on the different ideas about the envisioned or dreaded religious others.

One aim of the project, "The Diversity of Nonreligion," was to identify and analyze diverse modes of nonreligion against the backdrop of their societal context. Beyond that, this book seeks to delineate nonreligion as a heuristically broad concept, which can also fruitfully be applied to, e.g., the academic study of religion, secularity, and nonreligion.

To describe distinctive modes of nonreligion, we focus on the different values, objectives, and dominant relations that characterize certain religion-related perspectives. The activism we research is motivated by different themes, including but not limited to social justice, individual liberty, truth, and rationality. Some actors are looking to counter the apparently privileged status and norm-giving role of religion while collaborating with other religious actors for that sake, while others focus on criticism and others still on competition. This is interrelated, e.g., with the question whether they see what they produce in their organizational frame (e.g., the formation of a distinct community) as a value in itself, or as a means to influence the respective society at large.

The book presents three case studies of groups that are located in different social context and that define their collective identity and self-position in relation to different religious others. We highlight both differences and similarities between groups and countries. The dynamics of distinction and relatedness central to a relational definition of nonreligion play a role in all three case studies, albeit to differing degrees.

Case studies: actors and relations to religion

Across the globe, people relate to phenomena that are commonly understood to be religious on a daily basis in their respective contexts. Some of those relations and references are very explicit, while others occur rather inconspicuously. Some might, for example, express what they understand as their nonreligious view of the world as part of larger groups, organizations, or movements. Such people and groups in the diverse settings of Sweden, the Philippines, and the Netherlands are at the center of our research.

In contemporary Sweden, the site of the first case study (Chapter 3), a self-understanding as nonreligious is no minority position. The country is commonly described as one of the most secularized countries in the world.

At the same time, the traditionally dominant position of the Church of Sweden is often emphasized in the country. In this book, the ambivalent status of secularity as well as the Church of Sweden is illustrated using an analysis of the Swedish Humanist Association (SHA) and the different nonreligious positions therein. SHA members are fighting passionately over the role of humanist ceremonies in their organizational activism. Two different idealtypical understandings of secular humanism, which some members perceive as partly contradictory, are identified in the case study. On one hand, the proponents of the concept of "life stance humanism" emphasize nonreligious social practices like humanist ceremonies as well as social gatherings as an important part of a humanist community. On the other hand, advocates of "opinion-making humanism" want to abandon or at least minimize such social humanist practices within the organization's frame, which are part of humanist traditions in several countries, preferring instead to focus on strengthening their position as a professional and critical actor and participant in public debate and political decision-making. The debated status of the ceremonies and related issues stands for a more general debate over the identity and aims of the organization as a whole. This (re-)orientation process of the organization can partly be explained by but also sheds light on significant changes in the religious field in Sweden at large.

At almost the other side of the globe in the mainly Catholic context of the second case study (Chapter 4) on the Philippines, parliament has not only recently accepted a much-contested bill regarding reproductive rights, but the new president has also massively attacked the Church and challenged its authority. Other examples of challenges to the hegemony of Catholicism could be named: the discussion about a reproductive health bill, sexual orientation, and self-determination for example, or the already older Marxist tradition of religious critique that still echoes throughout current-day academia. More recently, two groups in Manila, partly emerging from atheist online networks, were founded to advertise free-thought as well as atheism: the Philippine Atheists and Agnostics Society (PATAS) and the Filipino Freethinkers (FF). While both are primarily comprised of atheists, the two groups have taken different paths, have different agendas in their activism, and position themselves differently in relation to the Catholic Church in particular and religion in general. These examples not only sketch a broad variety of positions opposed to the Catholic Church but also express that such opposition can take divergent directions. Accordingly, the comparison of these two organizations highlights similarities and differences when it comes to membership demographics as well as the emancipative and sociopolitical objectives and projects of these actors.

The third case study (Chapter 5) on the Dutch social liberal party, D66, shifts the focus from civil society actors to the field of party politics, a perspective that both fits and extends the framework that has been established in the other case studies. In its self-understanding as nonreligious, it is not religious institutions but parties with a religious base that comprise the central other for D66. The differentiation between politics and religion is central to what nonreligion means in that case. Such differentiation, on the other hand, has always been a contested notion of politics, challenged by Christian and socialist parties alike. Against the background of the emergence of the religion-related political field in the 19th century, the case study focuses on the party's struggle against the religion-relatedness of politics. The chapter sketches the party's emergence in the late 1960s, a time of a widespread cultural and institutional break with the pluralist-confessional past, and its successful push for a secularization of politics, state, and law in the 1990s and the early 21st century. In their most recent articulation of a moral and epistemic standpoint, they construe politics and democracy as distinct from religion. The party's positioning as differentiated from religion matches the profile of its voters.

The questions that guide our research pertain to individuals and subgroups within the organizations at hand, the organizations themselves, as well as their broader social embeddedness and roles. Accordingly, we ask: how do actors define their activism and organizational identity? What do such groups try to achieve? How are they perceived by other actors in the respective society? What do these actors understand as religion? In what ways are actors individually as well as a group related to religion? What are the aspects and themes that inform such relatedness? What do we learn about the Philippines, Sweden, and the Netherlands in general and the role of religion in these countries in particular by researching such groups? Finally, on a much broader scale, what do we learn about the diversity of nonreligion across the globe through these actors and positions?

Religio-normativity and modes of nonreligion

The concluding chapter (Chapter 6) discusses the central themes and findings of the three case studies explored in the previous chapters in a comparative perspective and in relation to the conceptual frame that lies at their foundation. The chapter's focus on the described groups' diverse forms of activism provides insight, first, into the role of religion in each of the respective societies. This not only refers to the various forms of religious establishment but also to the means by which religion is experienced as carrying certain social orders and normativities – something we label "religio-normativity." The respective activism counters both stigmatized nonreligious identities as well as conservative (religious) moralities, especially with respect to matters around sexuality and the beginning and end of life. Secondly, we discuss how debates around religion frequently function to both uphold and challenge established symbolic orders regarding notions of gender, sexuality, race, class, age, etc.

In this respect, the sixth chapter emphasizes that the divide between religious and nonreligious actors is sometimes not as clear-cut as it might look at first sight. Religious-nonreligious divides partly intersect with divides between different values and norms, and, respectively, debates about morality can also take the form of an assertion of religious orthodoxy or that of an antireligious critique. Similarly, while religion can be a carrier of emancipation and liberty, it can also conflict with the emancipation and liberty of other groups or subjects. This might lead to movements both in the name of as well as opposed to religion. Therefore, we discuss examples where nonreligious actors share interests with certain religious actors, all the while opposing other actors deemed nonreligious.

Against this background, the concluding chapter underlines the conceptual arguments made in the first and illustrated in the empirical chapters of this book. Of importance here are thus the tensions between different nonreligious positions, particularly in relation to two overarching aims that we introduce in the second chapter: the aim of moving away from religion-likeness and the aim of moving away from religion-relatedness. We encounter these two moves in different empirical settings, not only in our three case studies, but also in the debate between Bradlaugh and Holyoake on whether to ignore religion means to deny religion (Holyoake and Bradlaugh [1870] 1987; Quack 2011) as well as academic debates in the study of religion concerning, e.g., ideas of methodological agnosticism or atheism (Quack 2014). In all these cases, the notion of religion is a placeholder for many different aims and arguments. The competing modes of nonreligion we observe imply a negotiation of what constitutes religion and its respective other. Indeed, struggles between competing modes of nonreligion can be framed as contestations of the borders of the religious field in the sense that what seems a mode of nonreligion to some is rendered a mode of religion by others.

Notes

1 The work on this book was generously funded by the German Research Council (DFG) as part of the Emmy Noether Project (QU 338/1–1), "The Diversity of Nonreligion." This book was written in part with the support of a grant by the Kolleg-Forschergruppe (KFG) "Multiple Secularities – Beyond the West, Beyond Modernities" at Leipzig University. The KFG is funded by the German Research Foundation (DFG).
2 The Introduction, Chapter 2, and Chapter 6 of this book were jointly written by Kind, Quack, and Schuh, and all three authors have made more or less similar contributions to the different chapters. Rather than listing the authors always in alphabetical order we decided, however, to mix the order of authors.
3 The three case study chapters are excerpts from the dissertation projects of Susanne Kind, "Secular Humanism in Sweden: Non-Religious Activism in 'One of the Most Secularized Countries in the World'" (in preparation), Alexander Blechschmidt, "The Secular Movement in the Philippines: Atheism and Activism in a Catholic Country" (submitted and defended September 2018), and Cora Schuh, "Politics of Secularity: Dutch Social-Liberalism after Confessionalism" (in preparation).

2 Concept

Non/religious constructions and contestations

Cora Schuh, Johannes Quack, and Susanne Kind[1]

The study of irreligion and nonreligion

The study of nonreligion is still an emerging research field and it is approached with diverging interests and conceptualizations. Our research on the diversity of nonreligion engages with the different ways people, groups, or institutions position themselves or are positioned by others as not being religious while they are in relevant ways entangled with and thus related to religion. In our use of the term (Quack 2014), nonreligion refers to positions considered by relevant agents to be distinct from, but related to religion – with Bourdieu, one can speak of positions outside a religious field that are in relevant ways related to such a field. As a concept, nonreligion is not identical with the self-identification of people, even if it is still based on such. It is distinguished from heterodox religious positions (even if they might be considered nonreligious by others) as well as from areligious phenomena.[2]

Our question is not what is and what is not religion or nonreligion, but is instead (see Quack 2014, 458): how is a particular group or agent related to particular positions in a religious field? How do representatives of a religious field and other observers react to such positions, and how do all actors mutually shape each other's positions? How are the borders between the religious and other fields constituted as well as negotiated, challenged, subverted, or undermined in such relations?

The aim of this chapter is to add to the overall understanding of the concept and the empirical phenomena it describes, and to further the understanding of different starting points and directions taken in this endeavor. Building on our prior work and that of others, we suggest that the diversity of nonreligion ought to be conceptualized through studying its relations with different religious and nonreligious others as well as the different values, themes, and objectives that orient such relations.

In order to do so, the chapter is separated into two parts: the first part introduces a relational approach to nonreligion, which we developed further in the context of our project and in the light of our empirical research. We trace the emergence of the concept nonreligion via Campbell's (1971) earlier concept of "irreligion" and engage with the related-but-somewhat-distinct notion of nonreligion suggested by Lois Lee (2012, 2015). We then suggest the adoption of a relational approach to nonreligion based on Bourdieu's methodological relationalism and his notion of fields by introducing and discussing the concept of a religion-related surrounding (German: *Umfeld*). We sketch different possible field-positions of nonreligion and the different ways in which religious-nonreligious relations can transform the borders of a religious field.

The second part of this chapter offers conceptual tools for analyzing and differentiating different modes of nonreligion. This concept, as well, was coined by Quack (2012) and further elaborated in the course of our research. It stands for a specific conglomerate of different conceptual factors, such as the religious (and nonreligious) others they relate to, the foci that orient these relations, and the different kinds of relations that are established. We further introduce the concept of assemblages as a means of understanding the complex webs of different relations that mark individual nonreligious positions. We then focus on tensions between competing nonreligious positions and introduce two particular themes that such critique can take: that of moving away from religion-likeness and that of moving away from religion-relatedness. Concludingly, we outline how these aspects collude with regard to the diversity of modes of nonreligion from a relational perspective.

A relational approach to nonreligion

After briefly introducing the concept of nonreligion, its prior sibling irreligion, and the way in which these terms are used by other authors, this part outlines a relational approach to nonreligion. It first provides a general idea of what we mean by relationality, and suggests a relational definition of nonreligion. It then introduces the notion of a religion-related surrounding comprising that which is related to and co-constitutive of a religious field and how actors seek to influence the borders and rules of a religious field. The part closes with a brief discussion of the concept of religio-normativities.

Irreligion and nonreligion: emergence of a research field

In 1971, Colin Campbell published a book under the programmatic title, *Towards a Sociology of Irreligion*. Empirically, his book focuses on several 19th and early 20th century groups, which for the first time turned critiques of religion into organized mass and protest movements. His focus was on freethinkers, positivists, ethical societies, and humanists. Beyond this empirical focus, a major aim of Campbell's book was to introduce and conceptualize irreligion as a new field of sociological research. As "irreligion," Campbell understands "those beliefs and actions which are expressive of attitudes of hostility or indifference toward the prevailing religion, together with indications of the rejection of its demands" (1971, 21). Such irreligious responses may be "latent, manifest or covert, organized or unorganized, a minority or majority tradition in relation to the structure of religious orthodoxy" (Campbell 1971, 21). For Campbell, irreligion is different from religious radicalism or religious prejudice (1971, 29). Further, as an ideal type, irreligion is a "'primary' response" towards religion and not a derivate of "more general world-view[s]" and "secular ideologies or philosophies," such as communism, positivism, utilitarianism, idealism, rationalism, humanism, nationalism, and existentialism, although it commonly appears in association with such (Campbell 1971, 36–7).

Campbell's promotion of a genuinely new field of study, labeled irreligion, found late support in the study of nonreligion, for example in the "Nonreligion and Secularity Research Network" (founded 2008, see www.nsrn.net). His definition of irreligion as a primary response in direct relation to religion was echoed by Lois Lee's early work. She defined nonreligion as "[s]omething which is defined *primarily* by the way it differs from religion" (Lee 2011, 2, emphasis in original). In her more recent work, she understands nonreligion as "philosophies and cultures developed in contradistinction from religious ones," thus explicitly understanding it as something substantive beyond the mere rejection of religion (Lee 2015, 32). We highly appreciate Lee's inspiring work. We wonder, however, whether her aim to identify nonreligion as a distinct social object might be understood as constituting a conceptually problematic reification.

Such a reifying tendency may be read, e.g., into her early definition of nonreligion, which did not include phenomena such as humanism, some forms of naturalism, or rationalism, as all these examples "may have nonreligious aspects, but are usually defined by their own core principles and practices, [with] differentiation from religion being a secondary rather than primary consideration" (Lee 2012, 131). As such they would be "ontologically autonomous from religion" (Lee 2012, 131). In her more recent work, she continues to struggle with the fact that such "cultures," at least in part, exist in religious and nonreligious versions (Lee 2015, 34–5). In our understanding, the question whether something really is religious or nonreligious threatens to lead research into an essentialist direction.

When we speak of nonreligious agents or phenomena, the intention is not to make claims on their nature. Nonreligion denotes a position in a field rather than an essentialist characteristic of people. If a position changes, many of the other relations change as well. If the constitutive elements of a religious field are transformed, the borders of the religion-related field have to be reassessed. If the "rules of the game" change, the whole structure of the field changes. In all such cases, fields and relations are construed, preserved, or challenged by actors, and it is concrete individual and collective actors that our empirical research focuses on, actors that are of interest to us because of their positions and relations with regards to positions or phenomena deemed religious. This is the perspective we wish to capture when speaking about nonreligious actors or groups.

Aside from academic definitions, also actors in the field operate with different notions of nonreligion. Campbell (1971, 130–2), e.g., noted that irreligious activists were in part divided over whether their movements constituted something similar to religion, while religious nonconformists might be classified as irreligious by some (e.g., the orthodoxy). Lee (2015, 131–3) observes that some interview partners self-positioning as religiously indifferent had implicit but strong religion-related commitments. In our writing, we seek to understand competing perspectives from the field-positions and relations of different actors. Rather than seeking a clear-cut demarcation between things religious, nonreligious, and areligious, we aim at researching the ambivalence and contestedness at stake.

Of importance for us are the tensions, differentiations, and conflict lines between positions deemed religious and nonreligious, as well as the self-positionings and ascriptions that are used in such situations. No a priori understanding of religion is thereby applied; assessments of what is associated with religion have to be made on a case-by-case basis (Quack 2014, 448–50). Our perspective takes contestations about the borders of a specific religious field and the cultural embeddedness of those positioned within, at, or outside its borders as central to understanding nonreligion.

Moreover, our relational definition widens the conceptual scope of nonreligion when compared to those of Lee and Campbell. Nonreligion in our understanding might also include, e.g., particular scientific or political positions (Quack 2014, 458–9). The study of nonreligion should include phenomena like the study of religion, which claims neutral knowledge on religion and understands itself to be based on a "methodological agnosticism, atheism, and naturalism" while also being historically related to avowed nonreligious groups (Quack 2014; see also: Krech and Tyrell 1995, 15f). Nonreligion thus implies a reflexive perspective on the political and epistemological entanglements of academic studies of religion with their object of research. In the same line of reasoning, the study of nonreligion can also be considered a form of nonreligion. Moreover, two of us suggested elsewhere that also indifferent positions might at least be indirectly or situationally related to religion and thus (indirectly) seen as part of the study of nonreligion (Quack and Schuh 2017).

Subsequently, we illustrate the fruitfulness of a widened conceptual and empirical scope by complementing the research of groups like those that drew the attention of Campbell (the SHA in Sweden and FF and PATAS in the Philippines) with the study of a secular political party (D66 in the Netherlands). This helps us to illustrate that the frame of nonreligion is not only fruitful for understanding nonreligious worldviews or antireligious activists, but also for understanding conflicts and positions within the political field (or any other field, for that matter).

Defining and understanding nonreligion relationally

Talal Asad famously noted that "[a]ny discipline that seeks to understand 'religion' must also try to understand its other" (Asad 2003, 22). Our initial emphasis on the diversity of nonreligious positions was also a reply to such a focus on the secular that is common in post-colonial studies and arguably most prominently the work of Asad (2003). Asad's work, similar to Charles Taylor's work (2007), gave insufficient attention to the diversity of religion's others – a critique which has also been raised by Weir (2015).

If we speak of a relational approach to nonreligion, we follow Bourdieu by conceptualizing "the real as relational," a position that is opposed to "substantialist" philosophies of the social world (Bourdieu and Wacquant 1992, 15–19). Such relationalism shifts the focus from the question of whether something should be considered religious or nonreligious, to the discourses and practices that constitute a certain phenomenon in relation to or distinction from religion. We draw on Bourdieu's methodological relationalism to indicate that (non/religious) identities, borders, and positions are not given but depend on relational assemblages. Attempts to position oneself differently have to work on the respective relations that constitute the position. Positions in or outside a given field can only be located via relations, while relations can also only be understood as the links between positions.

Bourdieu's conceptualization of "fields" can be seen as an operationalization of this relational mode of thought (Vandenberghe 1999). Bourdieu's metaphor of the field as playing field is illustrative here: an observer does not understand the actions of a football player if his focus is placed exclusively on a single player. Instead, the observer ought to focus on relational factors such as the position of teammates and opponents, the position of the ball, the score, the remaining time, the ambitions of the players, and their physical conditions. If the position of the ball changes, many of the other relations change as well. What we add is the idea that factors apparently outside the game might still be in determinable ways related to it, and as such, should be taken into consideration as well. Within the given example, we might think of referees, supporters, league ranks, but also of the place of the game, the transfer-market, practices of sponsoring and marketing, the bribing-mafia, doping, the hooligans, police reactions, etc.

In line with such relationalism, we understand nonreligion to include any outside position that stands in determinable relation with positions in a specific religious field (Quack 2014, 445–6). Those nonreligious positions that are constituted by a binary opposition to religious positions or to religion (as such) we label "irreligious," i.e. "irreligion" refers to a specific subgroup of "nonreligion." All nonreligious positions taken together constitute what we designate below as a religion-related surrounding (*Umfeld*). It is the relatedness that distinguishes nonreligion from areligion. In other words, nonreligion means to capture the simultaneous distinctness and relatedness of nonreligious phenomena from (aspects of) religion at stake in a specific case study, being positioned as not religious, while standing in a mutual (often co-determining) relation with religion. As research objects, they be understood only in limited ways without taking such relatedness account. What is constituted as nonreligion depends on the context. In contexts, shopping on a Sunday will conflict with religious norms and thus be regarded as a religion-related practice, while in other contexts it might be considered unrelated to religious traditions and thus areligious. The question regarding if something is related to religion or not itself is often contested within a social context.

Relatedness – as will be exemplified later – can result from an unsuccessful disentanglement, when actors wish to cut relations with religion, while remaining entangled for various reasons (the debates between theology, the "academic study of religion," and the "scientific study of religion" is a good example). In that sense, the determinable relatedness with religion might contrast with the position that actors wish for and work towards, be they politicians trying to manage religion, scholars trying to study religion, or secular humanists trying to supplement, destroy, or ignore religion. Indeed, by proposing a relational understanding of nonreligion, we also propose that religion-related concerns that seem quite distinct at first sight can and should be located in the same conceptual framework. To illustrate this point, we take up the notion of "homology," suggesting that relationships between positions in different fields might follow similar patterns.

> ... once the generative and unifying principles of a system of relations are codified and formalized in the theoretical model, this model can be transposed to, and compared with, other fields of practices so as to uncover functional and structural homologies.
>
> (Vandenberghe 1999, 45)

Although this book does not explicitly trace such homologies, we want to highlight the heuristic potential of taking the oppositions and relations central to the case studies presented in this book as homologous to other oppositions and relations in religion-related fields. Specific discussions amongst atheists, humanists, and secularists (such as the one between Holyoke and Bradlaugh regarding whether to ignore religion means to deny religion) will be generalized in what follows with respect to "moving away from religion-relatedness" and "moving away from religion-likeness." Arguably, these generalizations also apply to other fields, e.g., the discussions concerning methodological agnosticism and methodological atheism in the academic study of religion.

To give a brief example: Matthew Engelke (2015, 136) questions in an important intervention the analytical usefulness of the notion "nonreligion," which makes him "frustrated" because it is always beholden to "religion." Moreover, he also points to the trouble of negation that comes along with the notion nonreligion (Engelke 2015, 135). These two arguments of Engelke are in many ways comparable to the arguments e.g. of the humanists that he himself studied in the UK. Some humanists do not find acceptable that "religion as a concept" defines the space they are located in by researchers. The same is the case for Engelke in particular and many colleagues in the academic study of religion in general (see the largely unsuccessful scholarly attempts to move away from "religion," e.g., Fitzgerald 2003).

In our understanding, the notion nonreligion points to uneasy and contested relationships with "religion" which are crucial for many people and groups. These include scholars of religion (such as Engelke and ourselves), atheists, secularists, and humanists (such as those in Sweden and the Philippines), political parties (such as D66), as well as e.g. evangelical Christians (see Engelke 2015, 142). Indeed, as argued by Engelke (2015, 142): "For a host of social, political, and theological reasons, 'religion' is often abandoned by those whom we might least expect, even as it is simultaneously embraced." A relational study of nonreligion studies such tensions and the respective contestations. Its field approach allows us to ask the heuristic question regarding whether a system of relations in one case study can be transposed to, and compared with, other fields of practice so as to uncover functional and structural homologies.

We consider such tensions, contestations, and ambivalences between e.g. differentiation and relationality as crucial for the very concept of nonreligion. What counts as religion, areligion, and nonreligion is not defined a priori but analyzed instead as an object and outcome of social (including scholarly) constructions and contestations. Therefore, it is such constructions and contestations that we are interested in. The resulting contestedness of positions and borders is at the heart of the study of nonreligion. Thereby we also contribute to existing research on secularity and secularization, particularly that focusing not on an alleged religious decline but on "culturally and symbolically as well as institutionally anchored forms and arrangements of differentiation between religion and other social spheres" (Wohlrab-Sahr and Burchardt 2012, 881). Our concept of nonreligion supplements such a concept of secularity by putting emphasis on exploring the complexities of religion-related phenomena, their features and associated forms of relationships, and the contestedness of both, relations and differentiations.

In order to further explore such a contribution, we further discuss in what follows the notion of a religion-related surrounding (*Umfeld*), examine possible positions of nonreligion from a field-based perspective, and sketch ways in which actors transform the borders of a religious field.

*The religion-related surrounding (*Umfeld)

Taken together, all nonreligious positions in a given context can be conceptualized as part of a religion-related surrounding (*Umfeld*). In the two subsequent sections, we first explain how such a surrounding builds on and relates to Bourdieu's work on the religious field. Then we focus on how the religion-related surrounding relates to other fields outside the religious field, in what ways a religious field can be extended to include nonreligious positions, and how the religion-related surrounding might take the features of a field itself.

In our earlier work, we have conceptualized the space of multiple nonreligious positions in a respective context as a heterogeneous surrounding of a religious field, comprising all positions that are in some way distinct from but related to the latter (Quack 2013; Quack 2014, 448–51). The concept of a religion-related surrounding was introduced to label a research field comprising all that which nonreligious-studies are about as well as to denote the various positions partly (co-)constituted by the religious field in a specific social setting. If understood in a Bourdieu-inspired conceptual way, the religion-related surrounding is neither a genuine part of the religious field, nor is it completely separate from it. It marks a borderland of the religious field, a realm of ambiguity or contestation. Neither positions in the religious field, nor those in its surrounding, are thereby static but are in a constant dynamic.

The concept of a (religion-related) surrounding builds on but also goes beyond Bourdieu's notion of the (religious) field. Bourdieu first coined the notion of a religious field following a particular reading of Weber's sociology of religion ([1971] 2000). His focus is on the genesis and structure of the religious field and the competition between different actors about the accumulation of capital via the mobilization of lay populations. In contrast to Bourdieu, our focus is not (only) on power struggles within the religious field but on those taking place at the field's borders and its outside. In this regard, our contribution to field theory is part of those few studies which put emphasis on the surroundings of fields.[3]

To reconstruct any kind of Bourdieusian field, four things are necessary: relative autonomy; field-inherent rules or "logics"; objectively defined positions and positionings; and, goods at stake (Bourdieu usually speaks of "capital").[4] In a field, there usually are struggles for domination, e.g. between experts and the laity or between different religious groups and offers, or (drawing on Weber's typology of the actors in a religious field taken up by Bourdieu) between priest, prophet, and sorcerer. In many empirical cases, however, there is no homogenous and autonomous religious field. Even with regard to France, Bourdieu noted the difficulties once he reflected on his bias towards institutionalized religion with clear hierarchical distinctions between religious experts and lay people. He therefore moved from suggesting a clearly definable religious field (Bourdieu [1971] 2000) to the other extreme by attesting to "the dissolution of the religious field" with respect to the various ways in which people fuse questions about health, wholeness, and salvation (Bourdieu 1987). In contrast to Bourdieu, we seek in our case studies a middle way between the two extremes of an autonomous or diffused religious field, and focus on the interrelations at its borders.

The religion-related surrounding of a religious field does not constitute a field in the sense of Bourdieu.[5] Still, we think that also the contestedness and ambivalences with respect to borders and peripheries of Bourdieusian fields can be analyzed with the different metaphors with which Bourdieu conceptualized field dynamics: a field can be imagined as a battlefield to highlight conflicts and contestations. Our case studies focus on positions (in a religious field and its surrounding) struggling about the borders of religion and terms that constitute being considered in- or outside the respective religious field; a field is a playing-field based on certain rules and logics which have to be followed by those who want to play along. This directed our empirical work to questions about the rules that orient the relations between religious and nonreligious positions. Accordingly, we were interested in e.g. the degree to which nonreligious positions are willing to play according to the rules of a religious field. Furthermore, the metaphor of a field as magnetic field implies the idea of certain structuring forces implicit in any field (Martin 2003, 3–7), and second that the religious field might function to either attract or repel phenomena. We come back to this in the conceptual chapter as well as in the case studies by discussing attempts to move away from religion-likeness and religion-relatedness.

While this perspective focuses on the relations between religious and nonreligious positions, a field-based approach to nonreligion can be further refined in several ways. For example, understanding nonreligious positions as located less on the margins of the religious field and more as positions within (emerging) fields differentiated from, but related to a religious field, and second, by focusing on relations and struggles between different nonreligious positions. This leaves one to understand a religion-related surrounding as heterogeneous and as comprising different logics, as the following section illustrates.

Borderlands, inter-field relations, and the transformation of fields

In this section we discuss how the notion of a religion-related surrounding relates to other fields surrounding a religious field, ways in which borders of a religious field can be transformed, as well as the extent to which a religion-related surrounding can show features of a genuine field. In order to do so, we present four interrelated arguments which allow us to understand a religion-related surrounding as a heterogeneous space comprising different logics and open to further transformations: (1) Nonreligious positions can be located on the periphery of a religious field but also in other fields than the religious one. This points us to understanding religious-nonreligious entanglements as taking place at the level of inter-field relations. (2) An aspect of inter-field relations are struggles about the relative weight of different fields,[6] including struggles about the relative weight of religious and nonreligious forms of capital. Respective power struggles can take place at the borders of the religious field, but also in other (related) fields, as well as in the field of power. (3) Field borders and relations depend on continuous preservation, and might be challenged and undergo transformations. We discuss ways in which borders of the religious field can change in relation to religious-nonreligious entanglements. (4) Struggles and differentiations cannot only take place between religious and nonreligious positions, but also between different nonreligious positions.

(1) In our conceptualization of the outside of a field as a surrounding (*Umfeld*), we also take other fields into account, in the sense that nonreligious positions might not simply be in a borderland of the religious field, but located in other fields while being related to the religious one in different ways. Examples are positions in the scientific or political field that are both differentiated as well as related to religion through e.g. researching or governing it. This allows us to understand other fields as religion-related as well as to focus on religious-nonreligious struggles as an aspect of inter-field relations.

(2) Regarding inter-field relations, we only wish to stress that the relative weight of different fields and types of capital can be an object of struggles between actors with different kinds of capital in the field of power as well as possibly also other fields. According to Bourdieu, the field of power is a meta-field in which the relative weight of different fields, and thus the generalization of their capital, is determined, including the relative position of the religious field compared to other fields (Mangez and Liénard 2014, 182).[7] Bourdieu illustrates that the field of power is often centrally determined by the opposition of cultural and economic capital. Complementing Bourdieu's work, others have argued that the field of power might be co-structured by a religious-secular divide (Mangez and Liénard 2014, 184). With respect to the case of Belgium, these authors argue for understanding the field of power not as a bipolar space, but as shaped by different divides, including that of religion and secular positions, and this perspective seems also beneficial for the Dutch case (see Chapter 5).

This perspective of a more general importance of religious and religion-related divides also allows to understand other fields as co-determined by respective struggles about the relative weight of religious capital. According to Bourdieu, fields are autonomous to various degrees, depending on the way in which they are determined by other fields and capitals (Mangez and Liénard 2014, 182). The religious field – as is any other field – is to some degree influenced by and influences other fields. This means that by illustration, the political or scientific field can become arenas for struggles over the adequate relation with religion (see Chapter 5). Different actors are thereby invested to varying degrees in, e.g., differentiating or un-differentiating certain fields from the religious one. While some construe a field's objective (e.g., science or politics) as religious or irreligious and thus render the political field religion-related, others might insist on its differentiated, third-space character. While these positionings can be understood as homologous to the realm of religious and nonreligious positions more generally, also from the perspective of certain religious positions, differentiation can be an aspiration.

(3) Field borders and relations are not static but depend on continuous preservation, are challenged, and are potentially transformed through interaction and in struggles over power. Fields emerge from the interaction between actors and the consequential institutionalization of rules, relations, and positions. Borders of and between fields are not fixed and stable, they

need constant work and might be changed and transformed in such interaction and struggle.[8] From such a dynamic perspective, there are different scenarios of how nonreligious positions relate to and potentially transform the religious field: in some cases, a nonreligious position results from a process of excluding a certain position from the religious field. We can speak of a reduction of the religious field when, for example, heterodox or subdominant positions are excluded from the religious field (Bourdieu [1971] 2000, 102). In other cases, a nonreligious position might be integrated into the religious field – in both cases, this transforms the rules and borders of the religious field. An example would be when nonreligious organizations successfully establish themselves in the (hitherto religious) field of pastoral care and thereby transform it into a religious-nonreligious field of counseling. The recent foundation of atheist congregations is a further example, given that they compete with established religion over creating spiritual and ritualistic communities. A religious-nonreligious field can further emerge from the fusion of the religious field with another, formerly differentiated field (see also Karstein 2012). Whenever the religious field is extended into a religious-nonreligious one, the question arises regarding to what extent the emerging field is based on rules similar to those of the old religious field. Labeling such an emerging field obviously depends on whatever is at stake in a specific case of religious-nonreligious entanglements. In her study on the GDR, Karstein (2012) e.g. speaks of a "religious-ideological field" in which religious and nonreligious truth claims are placed against each other.

(4) Last but not least, nonreligious positions are not only constituted by their relations with religious others but also by relations with nonreligious others. Respectively, we might also think of the realm of religion-related positions as not merely a surrounding to the religious field, but as having features of a field as such – structured by positions and relations. In such a field or realm, further differentiations based on competing notions of what constitutes an adequate notion of and relation to religion are possible.

An example for tensions between different modes of nonreligion is that nonreligious activists might render mere indifference to religion as problematic and criticize those deemed indifferent as apathetic or implicitly religious (Burchardt 2017). This can be seen as an attempt to draw indifferent populations into more explicit relations with the religious field (Quack and Schuh 2017). Another example stressed by Campbell (1971, 31–2) is that some nonreligious actors seek to discredit others by denigrating them as, e.g., crypto-religious – which happens to be a common accusation in the study of religion.

All case studies in this volume point to competing modes of nonreligion and show that, within a realm of nonreligious positions, particular differentiations might be drawn and changed, which not only affect the border of a religious field but also re-constitute existing fields as such. Differentiations between modes of nonreligion might, but do not necessarily have to, find institutional expression.

18 *Cora Schuh, Johannes Quack, and Susanne Kind*

The next section complements these field-centered elaborations by focusing on the social orders at stake in religious-nonreligious struggles, regardless of the fields in which they are located.

Nonreligion, social orders, and religio-normativities

Bourdieu ([1971] 2000, 96–8) argued that the religious field would support the established symbolic order and its power relations. In contrast to that, Karstein (2012) argued that the religious field might also initiate a change of the dominant symbolic order. In order to conclude this first introduction into our relational approach to nonreligion, this section engages in more detail with the question regarding how religion and nonreligious responses relate to more general social hierarchies and symbolic orders, such as those regulating gender, sexuality, and the social space and role of religion.

At a very fundamental level, the point of whether in a given society state and church, respectively, legal rights and religious belonging, are differentiated greatly influences nonreligious actors' social position and their scope of action. Respectively it is no surprise that nonreligious activists, like religious dissenters, have been important agents of secularization (Campbell 1971, 7, 122). They e.g. struggle for democratic rights and the social acceptance of nonreligious people, the separation of Church and state, the abolition of religious privileges, and the secularization of education. Going beyond state and legal regulations in the strict sense, we suggest speaking of religio-normativity for the various ways in which religion can be part of normative orders. We thereby wish to stress two interrelated dimensions, both of which will be taken up in more detail in the comparison chapter (Chapter 6): (1) A first point starts out with the observation that religion can carry and undermine a dominant symbolic-cultural order in a given society. Further, we might find both religious and nonreligious actors on the conservative or liberal side with respect to matters of gender and sexuality – this giving way to both tensions and commonalities between religious and nonreligious actors. The divide between conservative and liberal positions, as will become clear throughout the book, constitutes a central one for the case studies while also competing with that between religion and nonreligion. (2) A second point to raise is that also particular forms of religiosity, or being religious as such, might constitute a social norm and orient ways of belonging, status, chances, and liberties in a given society, with negative effects on the deviantly religious and the nonreligious.

The idea of religio-normativity thereby functions analogously to the notion of hetero-normativity and implies that normative orders can be established at a very basic level and be part of what is perceived as natural and taken for granted. The concept religio-normativity allows us to understand why individuals and groups experience religion as a normative force within their lives and societies, which limits their freedom. The enforcing aspects of this normativity are often difficult to grasp by those who fit in easily. In different ways – and to different degrees – nonreligious activism can be understood as a reaction to experienced religio-normativities. Similar arguments can of course be made with respect to the normativities carried by secular or nonreligion, respectively, that of being secular or nonreligious. We do not discuss the impacts of secular normative orders in symmetry with religio-normativities for several interrelated reasons. First, secular-normativities have received considerable attention within the last years (most prominently by Asad 2003; Mahmood 2005). Moreover, the dominant perspective on the normative implications of religion(s) is generally researched with respect to the people and practices at the core of a religious tradition or field. In this perspective religion is presented, for example, as socially cohesive, or as helping to deal with the contingencies of life, or as making life meaningful (one could list, of course, more such "functionalist" understandings of "religion"). In contrast to this, we try to look through the eyes of people who would not locate themselves within a religious tradition or field. While Asad and Mahmood show how secular normative orders restructure religious traditions, we focus on the religious normativities experiences by secular actors. This perspective, we argue, does not correct but complements perspectives that arguably gained more attention in the more recent past.

To sum up: the previous sections introduced our relational notion of nonreligion with a particular focus on a Bourdieu-inspired field approach. While principally based on a relational perspective of the social, we particularly focus on the related outsides of a religious field. Under the caption of a religion-related surrounding, we discussed the ways in which nonreligious positions are related to certain positions in the religious field. We further discussed the relation of a surrounding with other "nonreligious" fields and the possible transformations of a religious field with respect to nonreligious positions. Finally, we introduced the concept of religio-normativity as a concept that helps to understand nonreligious activism. Taking up the notion of diverse modes of nonreligion, we go on to discuss the parameters along which such diversity can be sketched.

Different modes of nonreligion

A central aim of this research project is to document and analyze the diversity of nonreligion. We highlight the concept *modes of nonreligion* to distinguish between different empirical manifestations of nonreligion.

There are four aspects we consider most central for understanding modes of nonreligion. First, understanding nonreligion means to explain what the *non* is referring to in each specific case: pointing to the various religious others whom nonreligious actors relate to as well as the different notions of religion that they use. Second, nonreligious actors can have different foci, in the sense that their activism can be rooted in different values and refer to different discourses, as well as in the sense that they might have different collective objectives. Third, nonreligious actors can stand in different kinds of relations with religious others. We distinguish four ideal-typical relations between nonreligious actors and their others: conflict, competition, dialogue, and cooperation.

In this context, we introduce the concept of assemblages in order to take into account that nonreligious positions are embedded in a complex network of different relations with different positions in a religious field and beyond. Building on what has been said regarding potential tensions between different nonreligious positions as well as the idea of webs of complex relations, we then introduce two themes with which actors might counter-distinguish themselves from a competing mode of nonreligion: the aim to move away from religion-likeness and that to move away from religion-relatedness. The four different conceptual tools offered here facilitate understanding and enable the comparison of different case studies with regard to respective modes of nonreligion. Other factors that generally are of central importance for the formation of modes of nonreligion, either understood as distinct empirical manifestations or as ideal types, are milieu, class, and the established orders of secularity. On the basis of such different categories, ideal-typical modes of nonreligion can be construed. Ideal-types in the Weberian sense offer conceptual frames for understanding and analyzing social reality, but they are not identical with empirical reality (Weber [1922] 1980a, I.I. 6, 11). In the individual case studies, some of us developed specific ideal-types (Chapter 3), but in the context of the comparison of all three case studies, we do not go as far as construing common ideal-types. The subordinate concepts, though, already help to analyze and compare different cases with respect to the nonreligious positions adapted by different actors.

Different religious others: what the "non" refers to

Nonreligious actors refer and relate to different religious others on the basis of different understandings and perspectives on religion. In this sense, the *non* in nonreligion may, for example, refer to: distinct religious traditions or institutions, like Buddhism or the Catholic Church, or aspects of religion or religious traditions, such as the belief in God or certain rituals, religiously endorsed ways of life and behavior or religion-based forms of belonging, community, and identities, as well as generalized notions of religion (as a collective singular). Moreover, in a religiously diverse and globalized world in which news and people travel fast and many societies are characterized by religious diversity, nonreligious actors might also refer to religious traditions of migrants and cultural minorities as well as to foreign or global religious others beyond their immediate living realities. Different religious others can be relevant for different aspects of the identity construction of nonreligious activists or in the focus of diverse forms of social activism.

Even if a nonreligious position stands in tension with a distinct religious other and a particular idea of religion, conflict lines with and notions of religion might be generalized (as e.g. something irrational, exclusive, unjust, illiberal, or communal). Such generalized notions of religion do not only stand in a certain tension to empirical religious diversities (see Campbell 1971, 32–3), but they may also alienate likeminded religious actors. Changes within a religious field as well as immigration challenge institutionalized notions of nonreligion and secularity, which might be asserted, or modified with regard to new religious diversities.

Reversing the argument, different notions of religion also inform which concrete empirical phenomena are recognized as religion in the first place, or at least that which is the focus of nonreligious organizations. Some nonreligious organizations extend their agenda beyond what is commonly considered to be at the heart of a religious field (such as institutionalized religious traditions and their respective experts). Phenomena such as spirituality, New Age, esotericism, relativism, and pseudo-science constitute respective others in many cases. In that sense, nonreligious actors might not only have quite diverging perceptions of what constitutes the most central and/or problematic (religious) phenomenon, but also at times disagree on what constitutes religion in the first place.

In other cases, actors focus on different aspects of religion and disagree on this basis on the evaluation of one religious group or tradition as well as on the adequate nonreligious response to that group or tradition. To give an example: against the backdrop of the disestablishment and liberalization of the Church of Sweden, some Swedish secular humanists, who focus on illiberal and value conservative characteristics of religious and other phenomena as well as the social influence of religion when it comes to ontological and epistemological questions, no longer consider the Church of Sweden as one of the most important opponents. Others, by contrast, focus on the integrative and ritualistic social functions of religion and on that basis regard the Church of Sweden as the most central competitor, especially in relation to their own efforts of providing social and ceremonial offers. These two positions resonate in different areas of humanist activism, as well as conflicts among members about the desired main focus of organized humanism. The example of Swedish Humanists thus shows how the focus on different aspects of religion resonates with different nonreligious identities as well as organizational foci (see Chapter 3).

In sum, nonreligious actors refer and relate to different religious others on the basis of different understandings and perspectives on religion. Any such positions, once generalized, can be challenged by changes in the religious field. Additionally, as the following two sections explain, nonreligious actors can stand in different kinds of relations with religious others, something that also echoes different objectives of social activism and is informed by different values.

Different foci of nonreligious activism: values, themes, and objectives

Nonreligious organizations can have different foci that orient their relations with different religious others. Under foci we understand, first, that the nonreligious position of actors is based on specific values and themes, which can conflict with certain religious positions. Second, we understand foci to refer to the different objectives that are central to the purpose of collective self-organization of nonreligious actors.

Different values and themes of nonreligious activism

Conflict lines between nonreligious and religious positions are influenced by different sets of *values* linked with certain themes or social debates such as those on gender definitions, relations, and equality, national identities, or perceptions of the world (and their teaching in schools), in which these values might clash with certain aspects of religion or religiously sanctioned symbolic orders. In that sense, the religion-relatedness of nonreligious actors is part of the broader values and themes they refer to.[9]

Values that seem to play a role in several contexts, including the ones of our case studies, are truth, social justice and equality, individual liberty, worldview pluralism, and community formation. (1) *Truth* often comes with reference to enlightenment, rationality, scientific and critical thinking, and an evidence-based life style. (2) The notions of *social justice and social equality* point to the privileges of some and the exploitation of others. Some organizations oppose religious, ethnic, gender, or other forms of discrimination and emphasize integration and equal access to social goods and services. (3) A third theme is *individual liberty*, which refers to other fundamental protections for what are considered natural or essential categories of human existence and action, and which also include positive and negative religious freedom.[10] (4) The last theme of *community formation* is based on an anthropological idea of man as a social and emotional being. Examples include when actors like humanist organizations argue about the question regarding whether all people are in need of (life-cycle) rituals or other expressions and forms of belonging.

In certain contexts, or among particular actors, certain values and themes may gain dominance over the others (compare Wohlrab-Sahr and Burchardt 2012). In other cases, different values and themes may be interrelated, as has been outlined by Quack (2012, 272) with respect to "epistemic-moral entanglements." Different values and themes can also remain co-present without being discursively entangled, which again differs from the possibility that e.g. different organizations explicitly or implicitly establish a division of labor so that each concentrates on one theme or value (Chapter 4), or when different values are placed centrally with respect to different themes or others.[11] The prominence of different values and themes might change over time due to certain events or dynamics in the religious field, respectively, the changing positioning of certain religious others or competing nonreligious others.

Different objectives of nonreligious self-organization

Nonreligious activists can further have different objectives they seek to realize through social activism and collective self-organization. We distinguish four such *objectives*:

(1) In the first case, the objective is to weaken the (religious) other. Previously, we indicated that this could take place by limiting the opponent's

influence on certain realms, or, as the case study on Sweden shows, by mirroring the other's religious offers to beat them on their own ground.
(2) A second objective is to strengthen one's identity through, e.g., explicating and consolidating an individual or collective actor's identity instead of putting the main emphasis on seeking external impact. This can take different forms, such as explicating a worldview, measures of creating a corporate identity, or simply more informal exchanges about shared experiences and views, which help to build trust and recognition among members (see Chapter 4).
(3) A third objective might be to encourage and gain (lay-)members. Some groups understand themselves as creating and offering goods for an existing or potential nonreligious constituency and membership. Such goods can range from beliefs or worldviews, to rituals, collective identities, and – often entangled with the aim of strengthening one's identity – with forms of belonging. The target group may not only include those who might enroll as activists but also passive supporters and, in the case of the Netherlands, voters.
(4) Finally, a central objective can be to influence society or one of its fields in a particular direction. The analysis of the internal debates between the Swedish humanists later shows how this can be contrasted to the first three concerns.

The objectives of nonreligious actors might differ from the actual impact of their activism. In some cases, the concern with the outside world, be it the religious other, a potential constituency, or the society at large, contrasts the de facto impact of the activities consisting in expressing, defining, and consolidating an activist identity and community (Quack 2012, 267–9).

Different kinds of relations

The different foci of nonreligious actors aid in understanding what is at stake in how they relate to (different) religious others and why they distance themselves from, reject, or approve certain aspects or manifestations of religion. This section centers on the *kinds of relations* actors can have with different religious others. We distinguish between four kinds of relations: *conflict, competition, cooperation*, and *dialogue*. With respect to conflict and dialogue, we deal with situations in which the relation between two parties is directly at stake (even if other goals can be co-present). Measures are taken to devalue and damage or to accept and value the other party, and therefore the principled legitimacy of the other is either challenged or acknowledged.[12] In competitive and cooperative relations, something beyond the parties' relation is at stake. Two or more parties become rivals or join forces to reach the same good (lay-members, money, social influence, interpretive predominance, etc.).[13]

Relations and foci can further be linked to each other through "elective affinities," e.g. the focus on truth and "the other" with a conflictual relationship or the discursive themes of social justice with the concern to change the larger society via cooperation with other groups. Certain relations and foci might be perceived as mutually reinforcing each other or as standing in tension or even in contradiction with each other. The match between certain relations and foci is neither exclusive nor absolute. In what follows, we rather point to common linkages between them that occurred in our case studies as well as those of other researchers.[14]

Conflict

In the case of conflicts, actors mutually aim to limit and contain the other's truth claims, social legitimacy, or scope of action. We follow Karstein (2012, 266–7) and Werron (2010) by taking conflict as a two-place relationship (in Werron's words, a "direct" form of struggle) where objection and re-objection follow each other directly. This can also be described as a concatenation of interrelated objections.[15]

Conflicts, like competitions, can involve third parties, but can in contrast to the latter also do without them (Karstein 2012 referring to Simmel [1908] 1992, 267). The notion of conflict relations being centered on the relation itself does not imply that there were no issues or interests at stake. Rather, conflict relations might be a consequence of, e.g., perceiving certain religious others as an obstacle to a certain goal. Situations of conflict can have stages of acceleration or moderation, and they can also lead to at least temporary victories for either side. Schröder (2013) shows that a more durable conflictual setup can be essential for the perpetuation of some organizations. Indeed, conflict relations can work to the benefit of both religious and nonreligious actors in the sense of creating publicity and relevance. This shows how conflict relations can serve the identity formation of a group or its mobilization of supporters, and in this regard take on collaborative forms.

Competition

Competition in our case means that religious and nonreligious actors or organizations compete for the same goods. Analytically, it is possible to distinguish between "functionally close" and "functionally distant" forms of competition (Stolz 2010, 271–2); nonreligious offers can be both. Citing other work, Stolz provides examples for functionally distant competitive relations, such as secular ways of spending time that compete with religious practices, secular professions, which compete with religious ones, and the competition between the welfare state and churches. Along these lines, a central example of "functionally-close" competition is when nonreligious actors provide functional equivalents to offers important for the religious field, e.g., worldviews and secular life-cycle rituals.

Speaking of competitive relations implies similarity and equivalence between two objects. Entering into competition can thus also imply rhetorical strategies of creating such equivalences. Blechschmidt introduces actors in the Philippines (PATAS) that aim to disassociate religion from morality and truth to position themselves as offering equally good or better forms of morality and truth (see Chapter 4). The question regarding whether religious and nonreligious actors compete in the same market or to what degree their offers are comparable remains an empirical question, but is also likely to be a contested one.

The difference between competition and conflict or between competition and cooperation is not always easily determined, and one can transition into the other. Competition between religious and nonreligious actors can also function to uphold a certain market (for, e.g., immaterial goods) in the first place, and in that sense, their competition might be seen as a form of cooperation instead and as creating good business for both sides involved.

Cooperation

Cooperation means that different actors work together for the same goal. Nonreligious activism, e.g., for social justice, individual liberty, and self-empowerment, can conflict with certain religious positions – this is what construes it as nonreligious, but it might also share aims with other religious actors with which cooperation might seem beneficial. Issue-related commonalities and the strategic advantages of collaboration can push other tensions to the background and thus also crosscut the binary divide between religion and nonreligion our terminology suggests.

Cooperation can not only aim at very specific goals but also function to realize more general social reforms. When it comes to the institutionalization of religion, for example, nonreligious actors might find themselves in a similar situation as heterodox religious actors and collaborate with them for the sake of disestablishment. Also with regard to reproductive liberties, respective collaborations might be forged (compare Campbell 1971, 122; also Chapter 5). While the focus of our case studies was on nonreligious actors with value liberal ideas and somewhat liberal ideas of state secularity, nonreligious-religious collaborations are just as much possible on the base of, e.g., value conservative ideas on reproduction or communitarian ideals. In any case, such collaborations and liberal vs. conservative divides cut across religious-nonreligious binaries, an analytical thrust which resonates with earlier research on irreligious movements (Campbell 1971, 107–18).[16]

Cooperation then finds its limits in conflictual relations with religion or, of course, in generalized oppositions to religion. This also indicates that at times successful cooperation might make forms of dialogue necessary. If one focuses not only on explicit collaborations, but on more structural functions of certain relations, also competitive and dialogue-based relations can obviously be seen to either support or undermine established orders.

Dialogue

Dialogue means a relation based on mutual recognition and is motivated by the aim to exchange and share rather than to struggle or compete. Examples of dialogue-based relations are interfaith activities, e.g., the participation of a German Humanist Association in an inter-religious council (Schröder 2013), or the involvement of the Swedish Humanist Association in the recently established life stance forum for open dialogue in Stockholm, where Christians, Muslims, and Jews – "defined as religions" (Bjerkhagen et al. 2016) – and representatives of secular humanism engage in dialogue.

Such relationships and exchanges might benefit the identity-based interests of different actors, as well as increase public support for organizations and movements. Beyond that, dialogue initiatives might also be oriented towards further goods, such as social cohesion and peace. This indicates an overlap between dialogue-based and cooperative relations. Dialogue can transform into competitive or even conflict-based relations when, e.g., actors use it as a platform for advancing their societal position at the disadvantage of others, or suspect others to do so.

To sum up: so far, we have focused in a simplifying manner on the foci and relations between a specific nonreligious and a specific religious position, as if a certain field was made up of only two positions. Such a sketch is obviously oversimplified by ignoring the multitude of religious and nonreligious positions that together constitute a religious field, respective of its religion-related surrounding. In the subsequent two sections, we wish to add more complexity in two ways: first, we suggest understanding the complexity of different relations that nonreligious actors have with different others through the concept of assemblages. Second, we suggest that one way of understanding inter-relations between multiple religious and nonreligious positions is to focus on two particular themes with which nonreligious actors counter-distinguish themselves from competing nonreligious positions, "moving away from religion-likeness" and "moving away from religion-relatedness."

Assemblages of relations and foci

Given that both the religious field and the religion-related surrounding include a multitude of different interrelated positions, the focus on any particular of such nonreligious positions reveals a complex web of relationships with different religious others, as well as other nonreligious or areligious actors. We suggest understanding such webs of relations as *assemblages*. This is to emphasize that such a web of relations is structured in a certain way and that the different relations are thus interrelated. This does not mean that a nonreligious actor could not have different kinds of relations with different others. Rather, what we mean is that even where nonreligious actors stand in different relations with different (religious) others, these different relations are not random, but interrelated and structured in the sense of following a certain pattern which resonates with the foci central to this nonreligious actor. A classic example for this is that nonreligious actors committed to abolishing religion ("abolitionists") refrain from engaging in competitive relationships that mirror religious offers, whereas those who wish to substitute religion ("substitutionists") explicitly aim for them (Campbell 1971, 43, also Chapter 3).[17] The objectives of the respective nonreligious actors (abolition or substituting religion) thereby function in orienting assemblages.

We also speak of assemblages in order to understand how kinds of relations with certain (religious) others change and how they might affect each other. Kinds of relations can change over time (see the sections on conflict, competition, cooperation, and dialogue). Such changes can give expression to a more general shift of a group's nonreligious orientation at large (its focus and concerns), or initiate such a general shift. In both cases, a change in a particular relation with a specific (religious) other will also affect other relations in the respective web of relations. An example taken from Schröder (2013) is that the German Humanist Organization's participation in dialogue-based relations with religious others, and thus the acceptance to be framed as representing another confession, caused a profound programmatic-identitarian crisis within the organization.

Obviously, it is also possible that foci of groups remain ambivalent and that different relations with different others give expressions to competing concerns which remain in a situation of latent conflict with each other, without a stronger consistency being asserted. In other cases, different actors differ on what foci they want to place centrally as an organizational profile, and this leads to inner-group struggles, respectively, attempts to change existing foci and relations. This being said, different actors often also have competing perceptions of which particular focus or relation is at stake in a certain situation (Chapter 3); they, for example, have competing ideas on whether a certain good offered is equivalent to a religious one and thus a potential act of competition – an example being secular life-cycle rituals, which some might see as equivalent to religion and others not.[18] They also disagree on what is compatible with an established assemblage of relations.

As will be illustrated throughout the book, shifts in the focus and relations of nonreligious actors or groups can be a response to changes in the religious field, to inner-organizational changes, as well as to changes in the social context at large, such as, e.g., changes in state regulations towards religion, resources made available by the state (e.g., subsidies, offices, institutions, etc.) or other agents, changes in the economy or politics – the recent rise of populist and right-wing parties being a prominent example. Changes in the social context often necessitate or enable course changes and the adaption of new positions in the field, and motivate desires to change foci and relations. Shifts in foci or relations, however, can also be a response to internal developments within nonreligious organizations, or to external criticism and controversies between different nonreligious actors.

This last point, the possible critique of and controversies with other nonreligious actors, leads to the subsequent section, which introduces two narratives that nonreligious actors may use to reject a competing nonreligious position.

Tensions between different nonreligious positions

Nonreligious actors, as mentioned, shape and potentially wish to change their positions in relation to the religious field through engaging in, refraining from, or terminating certain forms of relationships. Reflections on and evaluations of existing relationships feed back into debates about the organizational profiles and collective identities within nonreligious groups. Processes of profile definition and identity formation in turn influence the kinds of relationships actors engage in or refrain from. An envisioned change of the kind of relation can be expressed as the wish to move away from a certain type of relation. We observed that two such aims are of particular importance here: moving away from religion-likeness and moving away from religion-relatedness. Both resonate with a central question that motivated this book, which is in what way nonreligious positions are shaped by or reproduce logics and rules of the religious field.

Moving away from religion-likeness

Being like religion is a crucial theme among many nonreligious actors, both in terms of their own self-positioning as well as the assessment of other nonreligious positions. In a structural sense, religion-likeness is a kind of equivalence. Competitive relations e.g. imply comparability and thus similarity on some points. Other relations can have an equating tendency as well by either stressing shared aspects of religious and nonreligious positions, or subsuming both under a superordinated frame. Religion-likeness can result from a close competition or conflict where nonreligious actors seek to beat religion on its own territory and offer subsidies or alternatives for religious offers – an example being the aforementioned humanist rituals or worldview offers (see Chapter 3).

Our intention with introducing the label of religion-likeness, however, is not to claim such religion-likeness, and surely not as an essentialist feature of certain actors or groups. Rather we wish to use it as a means to understand struggles about collective nonreligious identities.

Some nonreligious agents explicitly aspire to religion-likeness at least to a certain degree, for example as an attempt to fill a void apparently left by religion. Since the 19th century, the apparently diminishing role and authority of religion and the pluralization of competing religious and nonreligious worldviews raised the question of what might replace the shared religious frame of world perception and community. This question equally concerned the central founders of sociology (Terrier 2012) as well as liberal reformers

(Aerts 1997) and the emerging field of nonreligious and irreligious organizations (Campbell 1971). Still today, such questions resonate in competing notions of modernity and inform the differentiation between different modes of nonreligion.

Others, by contrast, aim to avoid any similarity with religion and seek to move away from perceived religion-likeness. An exemplary motive is a general hesitance or even a refusal towards creating functional substitutes for apparently outdated or otherwise rejected forms of religion. Substitutes might then be seen as reproducing the wrongs of religion in the sense of conflicting with whatever is at stake for the nonreligious position at hand (e.g., rationalization, individualization, or humanization) and are perceived to contradict an organization's on-going critiques of religion. Instead, these actors seek a position that is neither religious nor understood as a binary opposite to religion, i.e. they seek a position which we refer to as a *third space*. As Schuh shows, in the Netherlands the distinction between religious, irreligious, and third positions organizes positionings in the political field (see Chapter 5). Kind shows how contrasting positions regarding substitutes for religion mark the opposite poles in a conflict within organized humanism in Sweden (see Chapter 3).

All in all, thus, and following from what we said previously, religion-likeness can refer to a generalized notion of religion, or a specific religious institution, or certain aspects of a religious tradition, such as ideological beliefs, religiously endorsed normative orders and lifestyles, or modes of belonging. Reasons given for moving away from or towards religion-likeness can be embedded in discourses on truth, social justice, social equality, individual liberty, and social cohesion and community formation by declaring religious phenomena as irrational, pseudoscientific, dogmatic, exclusive, unjust, discriminatory, or as forms of communal belonging associated with group pressure, paternalism, social exclusion, and normative enforcements of postulated individual and social needs.

In line with what has been said previously, the respective foci of nonreligious organizations not only inform the relations with religion, but also nonreligious positions can be rejected on the same grounds as religious ones and thus for being religion-like from an emic perspective. We suggest a simplified sketch of relations that focuses on two respective competing modes of nonreligion (nonreligion 1 and nonreligion 2) and two competing modes of religion (religion 1 and religion 2).

Nonreligion 1 stands in a particular relation with religion 1, but the focus that orients this relation as well as the kind of relation itself is rejected by a nonreligious position (nonreligion 2) and labeled as too religion-like. To give an example: nonreligion 2 actors might accuse nonreligion 1 actors of propagating a dogmatic and therefore quasi-religious worldview or ideology. A structurally similar accusation would be that certain nonreligious actors would be too ritualistic or community focused. Such assessment of nonreligion 1 as religion-like is prone to conflict with the self-positioning of nonreligion 1 as being distinct from religion. Important for our conceptualization, however, is that from the perspective of nonreligion 2, the distinction between nonreligion 1 and religion 1 is less important if compared to what they seem to have in common.

Potentially the critique of nonreligious 2 actors will be supported from a second religious position (religion 2), which shares the same conflict line with religion 1. To take up the first example, both religion 2 and nonreligion 2 criticize both religion 1 and nonreligion 1 as dogmatic and wish to self-construe as undogmatic.

Again, and in order to avoid any essentialist tendency, relational dynamics are based on mutual co-constitution. This also means that from the perspective of the nonreligious 1 position, it might be nonreligion 2 that shares problematic features with religious positions and might be equally seen as religion-like. To give an example, we might briefly look at a particular conflict line within skeptic circles. Michael Sofka (2000) criticizes his fellow skeptics as being religion-like by pointing out how they have many myths about science as well as themselves. In this perspective, Sofka claims a nonreligion 2 perspective towards nonreligion 1 positions of fellow skeptics. These accused skeptics, however, reproach Sofka of subverting scientific truth claims and therefore of being as irrational as religious attacks on science. From that perspective, the nonreligion 2 perspective of Sofka is criticized by a nonreligion 1 position as religion-like. The case study by Kind further exemplifies that what is at stake are contested foci and relations as well as mutual accusations between actors (see Chapter 3).

Moving away from religion-relatedness

A second important narrative, contrasting the different relations outlined previously, is that of moving away from religion-relatedness in the sense of cutting relations. It is an attempt to establish an identity independent of religion and to move towards an areligious position. An ideal of indifference might express the idea of religion being of the past, or at least irrelevant for whatever is seen as important to actors. It might further be a consequence of the fact that whatever relations actors have with religion, this might make them vulnerable to critiques of being religion-like.

Whatever the motive, such an aim for an unrelated position can face different degrees of resistance, and actors might still be drawn into genuine relations with the religious field. In an edited volume, we discuss this in terms of religiously indifferent populations (Quack and Schuh 2017). We argue how both religious and avowedly nonreligious actors often consider the indifferent a potential constituency and seek to draw them into more engaged relations with religion. Several contributions to that volume showed that from the perspective of secular activists, indifference constitutes both an appreciated distance from religion as well as bears the risk of re-mobilization into religion (Burchardt 2017; Remmel 2017). As shown by

Blankholm in the same volume, relations that are cut and genuine indifference remain unobservable, while observation can threaten to undermine and undo indifference by setting actors in relation to religion (Blankholm 2017).

Diverse modes of nonreligion in relational perspective

In the previous sections, we have discussed several concepts with which to analyze nonreligious positions: different religious others, different foci of nonreligious activism, as well as different kinds of relations between nonreligious and religious others. We have further introduced the concept of assemblages in order to grasp the web of complex relations with different (religious) others that comes into sight when one focuses on a specific nonreligious (collective) actor. All of these concepts help to capture aspects of what constitutes different modes of nonreligion.

The notion of modes of nonreligion is here understood as a particular assemblage of kinds of relations (conflict, competition, cooperation, and dialogue) with specific religious and nonreligious others, based on certain values and themes (truth, social justice and equality, individual liberty, worldview pluralism, and community formation) and objectives (weakening the other, strengthening one's identity, encouraging and gaining members or support, and influencing the larger society). The empirical case studies of this book show how such debates take place in different organizations against the background of very diverse contexts when it comes to religion and secularity.

With regard to concrete historical cases, further aspects need to be taken into consideration – examples being factors such as milieu, organizational structures, the broader social constellations, and the religious and secular normative orders in a given context – but these are so specific to particular cases that we refrained from a general discussion here. A comprehensive description of a distinct, historically and culturally concrete mode of nonreligion not only takes all mentioned factors into account, but also understands their individual form and combination in a specific empirical context (Quack 2014, 444, 451–2). It comprises a comprehensive analysis of various characteristics, relations, and positions. The challenge therefore, describe and analyze how the relevant characteristics, relations, and positions are interrelated, e.g. – as argued by Blechschmidt, how specific relations to a specific religious other, the organizational structure of the organization, and the milieu of its members feed into each other (see Chapter 4).[19]

In other words, the level of concepts is obviously distinct from that of historical and culturally specific cases, and concepts will never be found in empirical reality at a one-to-one level. But they aid in understanding concrete cases, if only because they reflect the difficulties in discerning what foci and relations are at stake in a particular case, e.g., given that different actors involved often have different ideas on the stakes. Our aim is not to condense our findings into different ideal types of modes of nonreligion. What we do instead aim for is to analyze concrete cases on the basis of the concepts introduced previously. At a rudimentary level, the individual case studies still prepare the grounds for such further conceptual condensation.

Modes of nonreligion in relational perspective

The purpose of this second chapter of the book was to introduce our understanding and operationalization of the notion nonreligion. We conceptualized nonreligion as a position outside a religious field, which nevertheless stands in relevant and determinable relations with positions therein. In taking the concept of nonreligion as central, we aimed to place great importance on understanding it in a non-essentialist way. As a concept, nonreligion is not an intrinsic characteristic of people, but denotes a position that actors or phenomena can be in relation to certain others, denoted as religious. As a concept, nonreligion is not identical with people's self-description, but it still builds in important ways on self-positionings of agents in relation to religion. And the other way around, while the actors' perspective is often crucial, it still is possible to speak of nonreligion even where this is not an explicit label of self-positioning as long as actors do not understand themselves as religious. Obviously, determining within specific empirical cases, it might still be difficult and debatable to discern what can be considered nonreligion and what can't – a point which inevitably comes with conceptualizations.

A second point that has been central for our understanding of nonreligion is that we have extended the concept's scope beyond the focus on self-declared public critics of religion or organized atheists, humanists, and freethinkers – all groups that are most obviously treated as nonreligious. Even if such groups are important also to this book, we consciously include e.g. political or scientific positions that self-understand as nonreligious. Against this background, we introduced several conceptual tools for differentiating diverse modes of nonreligion.

In what follows, we wish to demonstrate the usefulness of these analytical tools for analyzing empirical cases. Our case studies thereby illustrate how the position of nonreligious actors, their room to maneuver, and – on a different but often related analytical level – their identity constructions are in important ways constituted by the respective social contexts and the varying social positions of nonreligious people. Individuals who consider themselves not (very) religious constitute a small minority in the Philippines but a majority in Sweden and the Netherlands. Irrespective of these social settings, we also find that all groups are engaged in ongoing struggles for further disestablishment and equality vis-à-vis religion.

Notes

1 The Introduction, Chapter 2, and Chapter 6 of this book were jointly written by Kind, Quack, and Schuh, and all three authors have made more or less similar

contributions to the different chapters. Rather than listing the authors always in alphabetical order, we decided, however, to mix the order of authors.

2 Areligious phenomena are not related to religion: "The important (not clear-cut but gradual) difference between nonreligious and areligious phenomena, [. . .] is that analyses of nonreligious phenomena require a relation to 'religion,' while areligious phenomena are generally described and analyzed without any reference to religious phenomena" (Quack 2014, 446).

3 Other authors have contributed new conceptualizations regarding the outside of fields: Fligstein and McAdam, for example, dedicate more attention to the *embeddedness* of specific fields in broader environments of "countless proximate and distant fields" (2012b, 3) as well as their dependence and interdependence on each other. Uta Karstein (2012) focuses on struggles between and the transformation of fields. Martin (2003, 33) observes, in general, that action outside a field was seen as less analytically interesting and criticizes this limitation since "field theory, by never making explanation reach outside the field, must forswear any legitimating arguments that there is a reason why the field must be as it is."

4 Indeed, the very idea to distinguish the "religious field" from other "fields" implies an acceptance of prior judgments about a specific understanding of religion as well as of social differentiation. To the degree that Bourdieu's notion of field presupposes a functionally different society, it stands in tension with societies differentiated in other ways.

5 Beyond that, Bourdieu conceptualizes a *field* as being complementary to the notion of "habitus." Striving in the fields is coordinated neither by *ideology* nor by conscious strategy but by the habitus, a cultural unconscious, a matrix of dispositions that serves to affectively organize perceptions (see Martin 2003: 23). A habitus is linked to a respective field position (or at least a position in social space, in turn related to a field position). This leads to an *ontological complicity* between the world and our faculties for making sense of it. We do not aim to thoroughly follow a Bourdieusian approach. While we are inspired by his work and see our approach as fully consistent with his basic social theory, we primarily utilize the implications of his field metaphor with a particular focus on the co-constitutive outsides of the religious field.

6 The relative weight or power of a field depends on the generalization of its capital and its influence on other fields (Mangez and Liénard 2014, 182).

7 As a distributor of resources, the state can influence religious-nonreligious relations by, e.g., granting privileges for *things religious* and thus setting incentives for nonreligious actors to seek parity status and to establish a notion of nonreligious equivalents to religion (see Chapter 3). Control over the state might be an object of religious-nonreligious struggles.

8 Not all interactions in, at the borders of, or in between fields necessarily lead to durable re-configurations of field borders. Rather, they might also be of a situational nature (see also Fligstein and McAdam 2012a, 10).

9 The argument that secularities are linked with different value positions and value struggles has been emphasized by Wohlrab-Sahr and Burchardt (2012) (see also Chapter 5).

10 In the sense that liberty leads to diversity, religious and worldview pluralisms can be seen as a collectivist model of organizing freedoms.

11 In Sweden, SHA members emphasized the importance of themes related to moral questions throughout the last years (next to scientific themes), whereas Vetenskap och Folkbildning (VoF), described as *the Skeptics*, and an organization collaboratively associated with the SHA, particularly focuses on questions about truth and scientific methods.

12 An example where the differences between competition and conflict are fruitfully applied is Karstein's study (2013) on the former GDR. Karstein concludes

that we are not dealing with developments internal to the religious field due to (market-like) competition, and instead proposes that we speak of a conflict between the religious and the political field, with which the SED was trying to delegitimize the religious authorities and institutions to fully replace them in all activities and functions (2013, 229). Indeed, what is at stake here is the existence of an independent religious field as such (Karstein 2013, 67).
13 The choice of labels does not imply avocations of an economical or market-theory or a conflict-theory approach. See Karstein (2013), who refers to Swartz (1996) for further reading on struggles, and to Simmel ([1908] 1992, 284–382), and Werron (2010) for the distinction between competition and conflict.
14 Unmentioned for now remains the fact that the respective foci also inform various relations with other actors which are not the focus here.
15 Critiques of religion have been a central genre of 18th century philosophy that emerged in the wake of the Enlightenment, and they constitute one predecessor of the scholarly engagement with religion (Rudolph 1985). In current debates, in particular with regard to Islam, the genre has found renewed attention (Brown 2009).
16 Campbell (1971, 123) argues that irreligion might be a transient stage on the way to more specific radicalism, but it might also "divert attention from pressing social and economic problems to the 'sterile' field of theological controversy."
17 While the distinction between abolishment and replacement is also important for us, we think that it does not give full justice to the debates and contestations about foci and relations we observed. This is because it does not grasp the relativity of what is considered religion and what is not (see also Quack 2014, 452). Here, *religion* is a placeholder for a range of different associations, interrelated with the different foci and relations.
18 Evaluations in the field again might further differ from the evaluation of the researcher.
19 See e.g. the discussion of the relation of liberal and socialist modes of nonreligion in Chapter 5 and Campbell (1971, 109).

3 Contested humanist identities in Sweden

Susanne Kind

Introduction

In literature and reporting, Sweden is known for several, apparently contradictory, phenomena: on the one hand, there is Sweden's reputation for being one of the most secularized countries in the world (Inglehart and Baker 2000; Jänterä-Jareborg 2010; Therborn 1995; Therborn 2012; Tomasson 2002).[1] This narrative is mainly based on traditional religious sociological parameters, such as low attendance in church services and a majority population that does not adhere to traditional evangelical beliefs, e.g. the existence of a personal god, as well as references to the separation of state and church in 2000. The World Value Survey reveals that the Swedish population occupies an extreme position compared to others: Swedes value both "secular rational values" and "self-expression values" very highly (Inglehart and Welzel 2015). In this regard, they lead those societies which "place less emphasis on religion, traditional family values and authority"[2] and are more likely to consider divorce, abortion, euthanasia, and suicide to be acceptable. On the other hand, it is being emphasized that the Evangelical Lutheran majority church, despite its separation from the state, continues to play a "semi-official role" in numerous areas and that the majority of the population enjoys a "life long relationship" with the Church, which is described as being part of an "invisible religious normality" (Bäckström, Beckman, and Pettersson 2004, 244).

What has barely been addressed in the literature so far is how this normality is perceived and discussed from the point of view of secular humanists, namely members of the *Swedish Humanist Association* (SHA). In the following, I will argue against the backdrop of an analysis of negotiations among secular humanists in Sweden that the perception and the experience of a *religious normativity* strongly depends on the understanding of religion that lies at the basis of such experiences.

The material which the following arguments are based on was primarily gathered throughout an eleven-month-long field study in the urban region of Stockholm and Uppsala. The analyzed material comprises interviews with SHA members,[3] mainly with members of the local organizations of these two cities, but also with members who are part of other local departments such as Humanisterna Syd, based in southern Sweden, or Humanisterna Umeå in the North. Additionally, insights are based on participant observation at membership events, such as regular meetings, congresses, and thematic events as well as publications, e.g. in member magazines, their blog Humanistbloggen, their homepage, as well as their publications in the form of books and articles in Swedish newspapers.

The interviews and publications provide insight into different understandings of humanism and religion, as well as diverging perceptions of members when it comes to their activism and problem-diagnosis in relation to religion. In the following, I argue that on the basis of the empirical material, two ideal-typical meanings of humanism can be identified: *life stance humanism* (LSH), which especially refers to the establishment of a humanist community and related social activities, and *opinion-making humanism* (OMH), which particularly focuses on socio-political and educational activism, and the importance of rational arguments and critical thinking.[4] In the organization's recent past, these two understandings and the related foci of activism led to heated debates among members. At the heart of these discussions are questions about their organizational identity, the question of how they as a humanist organization want to relate to religious actors. Understanding what these negotiations regarding the organizational identity and relation to religion were about sheds light on what secular humanism in Sweden means to its representatives and how religious influences on moral norms are viewed from nonreligious positions of actors who are more and more successful in getting their voices heard.

The chapter starts by depicting Sweden's religious landscape as well as some aspects of on-going secularization processes and religious change. Special emphasis will be placed on the position of the Church of Sweden, which is by far the biggest faith community in Sweden and has decisively shaped secular humanist activism since the establishment of the organization in 1979. Following these contextual remarks, section two will briefly introduce the SHA's organizational work, foci, and history. Against this backdrop, the conflict between members and their negotiation about the character of their organizational identity will be analyzed in sections three and four of this chapter. One example, which will be further elaborated in the last section of the chapter, is the discussion about the organization and character of humanist ceremonies as a central part of their organizational activities, a prime example for the overarching disagreements. Linked to the respective self-understanding and focus of members, this discussion will demonstrate that SHA members consider different opponents or others to be the most central and define the varying kinds of relationships that are suitable and legitimate vis-à-vis those antagonists.

Religious context: Sweden

Sweden, one of the "Nordic" countries, is similar to other Scandinavian nations when it comes to religion. It is known for both being quite secular as well as its Evangelical Lutheran majority church. David Martin (2005, 69) speaks in this regard of a "centralized ethos of Scandinavia where a monopoly church found itself mirrored in a dominant Social Democracy."[5] Recent statistics from the Church of Sweden show that its membership numbers have decreased since the beginning of the seventies. Whereas back in 1972, 95.2 percent of the Swedish population were members of the Church, by 2016, the Church listed 6,116,480 members, accounting for only 61.2 percent of the Swedish population (Svenska Kyrkan 2015, 2016a). The records display a particularly sharp decline of church members since the separation of church and state in 2000.[6] Furthermore, the numbers of church visits and all of the different ritual categories conducted by the Church, including baptisms, confirmations, weddings, and funerals, are steadily declining (Svenska Kyrkan 2016c, 2016d).[7] This points to the fact that some Swedes break with the tradition of a "lifelong relationship" with the Church.

This decline is not due to a controversial position of the Church of Sweden, given its quite liberal positions on many issues that apparently make people turn away from institutionalized religions elsewhere: since June 2014 and for the first time in the Church's history, the archbishop of Sweden is a woman, Antje Jackelén. Other examples include that the Church weds same-sex couples and that it is a supporter of and participant in different pride parades all over Sweden, where it displays banners with the slogan, "The church at Pride – The greatest of all is love!" ("Kyrkan på Pride – Störst av allt är kärleken!," Kyrkan på Pride 2016).

Since its disestablishment in 2000, the Church of Sweden is no longer a state but a "folk church" and, despite its dropping membership number, hitherto continues to be the biggest faith community in Sweden (Bäckström, Beckman, and Pettersson 2004). Apart from this, a special law on the Church of Sweden (SFS 1998:1591) remains in place, which characterizes the Church as an open folk church, a faith community with an Evangelical Lutheran profile that is democratically organized and manifests itself through parishes and dioceses responsible for nationwide activities. Despite the fact that since 2000 other faith communities have an officially equal standing with the Church of Sweden, the latter still occupies monopoly positions in certain areas: it plays a role in official events, like end of school year celebrations, which in most cases take place in the premises of the Church of Sweden, and the yearly ceremony and mass for the opening of the Swedish parliament, which takes place in Storkyrkan, the cathedral church of Stockholm. Additionally, the legal primary responsibility for cemeteries and the management of funeral services lies with the Church, independent of the respective religious or nonreligious identity of the deceased (SFS 1990:1144).[8] The Church of Sweden also possesses a large part of the national cultural heritage in the form of medieval churches and other historical buildings, which are of special cultural and historical significance, and was entrusted by the state with the management and maintenance of the same (SFS 1988:950). Several researchers speak, with regard to the remaining areas of activity and statutory characteristics, of a "semi-official role" of the Church of Sweden, as a state-regulated institution on the one hand and a religious organization on the other (Bäckström, Beckman, and Pettersson 2004, 20; Cavallin 2011, 45; Pettersson 2011, 123–4). Another regulation that has remained intact despite the separation of church and state is the legal requirement that the monarch, king or queen, as the head of the state, must belong to the Evangelical Lutheran faith and has to raise his or her children according to this faith. Any member of the royal family who is not professing the same faith is by law excluded from the right of succession (cf. Sveriges grundlagar. Successionsordningen 1810, §4). Furthermore, the state collects membership fees for the Church, commonly called "church taxes" (cf. SFS 1998:1591). Since 2000, however, other officially recognized faith communities have the opportunity to use this service and to apply for public funding as well.

In order to become an officially recognized faith community (*trossamfund*), and a legal personality, faith communities have to possess a statute, which provides information about the objectives, structure, and activities of their association. Registration is a prerequisite for public support, financial or otherwise (SFS 1998:1593). The state decides which faith communities get public funding. Funding is supposed to enable faith communities to "pursue active and long-term oriented religious activities in the form of worship, pastoral care, education, and care" (SFS 1999:932). Only a faith community that "helps to maintain and strengthen the fundamental values which society rests upon, and is stable and has its own vitality" (SFS 1999:932) will receive financing. Nilsson and Enkvist point out that the law for the Church of Sweden and especially the law for faith communities exemplify the "techniques of religion-making" and the "performative role" of the Swedish state with regard to the recognition of faith communities (Nilsson and Enkvist 2016). Through these laws, the state exercises power by regulating and thereby decisively shaping institutionalized forms of religion. Importantly, the state's "performative role" in this respect also effects the construction of nonreligious collective identities as well as the activism of those actors, whose declared aims include equal treatment with established faith communities.

Interestingly, in addition to being known for the Church of Sweden's monopoly position, Sweden has a reputation for being one of the most secularized countries in the world (Inglehart and Baker 2000; Jänterä-Jareborg 2010; Norris and Inglehart 2004; Therborn 1995, 2012; Tomasson 2002). Researchers described it as part of a "Nordic paradox" (Bäckström, Beckman, and Pettersson 2004, 30) that the majority of Swedes seem to distance themselves from traditional Evangelical teachings (only 15 percent of Swedes state that they believe in "a personal god"),[9] and barely visit or participate in worship services, while the number of people who continue to be members of the Church of Sweden and make use of its life-cycle rituals remained high for a relatively long time. Grace Davie points out that at first glance, the seemingly paradoxical situation of church membership remaining high for a long time, despite low church attendance and the fact that most Swedes do not seem to believe in the traditional Lutheran theology, appears to be a phenomenon of people who "belong without believing" (Davie 2000, 3). Quoting a Swedish observer, she explains that despite this impression, it is rather the case that: "what the Scandinavians believe in is, in fact, belonging. Membership of their respective national churches forms an important part of Nordic identity" (Davie 2000, 3). In an interview, Davie further emphasizes this point:

> . . . I certainly think there is in a sense that the Nordic churches, including the Church of Sweden, expose national identity as opposed to religious identity. . . . "I'm a member of the Church of Sweden, cause I'm Swedish." . . . But that of course is all falling apart now.
> (Davie, interview 2012, 450–6)

In this regard, the majority of Swedes are or were members of the Church of Sweden not because of their religious beliefs but because church membership was considered part of Swedish citizenship, or as others frame it, part of Swedish "tradition," Swedish "culture."[10] Furthermore, Martin stresses that in countries with long traditions of church establishment, a "welfare-view of religion" (Martin 2005, 68) is a widespread perception of religion. Davie conceptualizes this prevailing view with the concept of "vicarious religion," defined as a "religion performed by an active minority but on behalf of a much larger number, who (implicitly at least) not only understand, but, quite clearly, approve of what the minority is doing" (Davie 2007, 22). But this vicarious role of the Church of Sweden is, as Davie points out in the end of her previous quote, vanishing in relation with its disestablishment and decrease in membership, as mentioned previously.

Willander points out that the description of Sweden as one of the most secularized countries in the world is only a suitable expression with regard to certain aspects and depends on which secularization theory one has in mind. Religious practice in terms of church visits in Sweden has not changed as drastically as the narrative of a "secularized Sweden" may suggest, but has instead remained rather constant. Despite the decreasing numbers of church visits in the Church of Sweden (Svenska Kyrkan 2016c), for at least the last 100 years only a small proportion of the Swedish population (never more than 10 percent) regularly visited the Church of Sweden's Sunday services or those of other churches (Willander 2015, 60). Besides the increasing number of people leaving the Church since its separation from the state, being a member in the Church of Sweden without participating in worship services partly was and continues to be regarded as "a form of normality in Sweden" (Willander 2015, 63). The description of the Swedish population as a highly secularized one might, according to Willander, be appropriate, if one understands secularization, like Luckmann (1967), in terms of individual-oriented forms of religion that lack a formal organization and are relegated to the private sphere (Willander 2015, 67). Often the narrative of "secular(ized)

Sweden" is based on church-oriented tendencies but does not account for the interest of people in spiritual milieus or for the fact that nearly half of the Swedish population states that they "believe in some sort of spirit or life force" (46 percent[11]). Willander describes the latter expression as a common form of how Swedes express their beliefs. The answer option in this respect can be regarded as a "cultural norm" (Willander 2015, 65).[12] Other studies furthermore show how various new arenas with religious alignment or elements are being established, e.g. in the form of study and health centers as well as religious fairs outside the institutional context of the Church of Sweden (Frisk and Åkerbäck 2013).

Swedish culture was very much shaped through uniform welfare provision and a prevailing understanding of religion being a "private matter." These features fed into an ethos of social equality, egalitarianism, and centralization. Throughout the last decades, this ethos and the concept of privatized religion have been challenged through neoliberal restructurings of the welfare system as well as a growing, migration-driven religious diversity (Bäckström 2014; Schenk, Burchardt, and Wohlrab-Sahr 2015). Sweden has been a country of immigration for several centuries, but it has only been the immigration of migrant workers and asylum seekers since the Second World War, particularly over the course of the last two decades, that has lastingly changed the ethnic and religious population structure. Of the 9.9 million people living in Sweden, about 22.2 percent have a foreign background (SCB 2015).[13] There are no nationwide surveys on people's religious affiliation in Sweden. It is therefore difficult to gather exact figures in this regard. Among the few available data is the statistic of the Swedish Commission for Government Support to Faith Communities, SST Statistik, which lists the "contribution-based" members ("bidragsgrundande personer (betjänade)") of only the officially recognized faith communities.[14] According to the SST statistic, the Uniting Church in Sweden (Equmeniakyrkan)[15] has 127,378 members, the Swedish Evangelical Mission (Evangeliska Fosterlandsstiftelsen) 42,423 members, the Evangelical Free Church in Sweden (Evangeliska Frikyrkan) 49,447 members, the Pentecostal movement (Pingströrelsen) 110,762 members, and the Roman Catholic Church 109,967 members (naming only the five largest religious associations in this statistic – which doesn't include the Church of Sweden) (SST Statistik 2014). The ("contribution-based") members of all officially registered faith communities (not including the Church of Sweden) taken together, 761,584 people, amount to around 7.8 percent of the Swedish population.[16] This overall number also includes 110,000 members of the Islamiska sammarbetsrådets riksorganisationer (ISR), an umbrella organization for several Islamic organizations. Aside from the number of "official members" of Muslim communities, recent estimates assume that the Muslim population in Sweden comprises between 350,000 and 500,000 people, about 5 percent of the population (Larsson 2016, 559). With respect to ethnic and linguistic backgrounds, Muslim communities are very diverse, and there is no group that clearly dominates the picture: ". . . today Muslim communities are made up of Arabs, Iranians, Africans, and South Asians, as well as a growing number of individuals of a Muslim background who were born and brought up in Sweden, and Swedish converts to Islam" (Larsson 2016, 549). Particularly Shi'i and Sunni Muslim communities but also several other faith communities – be they Christian-based or part of a religious minority – have grown in numbers in the last couple of years (Larsson 2016, 550). Islam is a constant part of news coverage. International events like the war against ISIS and the role of Swedish Muslims who join this war as foreign fighters, but also more generally the public visibility of Islam, for example, wearing a hijab, and demands of Muslim communities for institutionalization, inter alia, in the form of building mosques or opening schools with a Muslim profile, similar to cases in other European countries, have increasingly led to debates. Beyond these discussions about the role of Islam, ". . . mosques and Islamic institutions have become the targets of hate crimes and Islamophobia . . ." (Larsson 2016, 553).

While most of the remains of the Church of Sweden's monopoly position, e.g., with regard to burial services and the maintenance of architectural heritage as well as the provision of services by religious representatives of different faiths in public institutions, such as the military, prisons, and hospitals, do not seem to cause upheavals within the Swedish population, public debates arose in relation to the dominant position of the Church of Sweden when it comes to the end of school year celebrations in the premises of the Church (Pettersson and Leis-Peters 2015, 50f.). More generally, public debates about the differentiation of and boundaries between religious and secular spheres, e.g., about secular education and religious schools, show that secularity is prevailingly negotiated in relation to cultural notions of social equality and national unity (Schenk, Burchardt, and Wohlrab-Sahr 2015).

Humanisterna – the Swedish Humanist Association

The Swedish Humanist Association has a history that reaches back four decades, beginning at a time when the Church of Sweden held a central position in Swedish society as the state church, far beyond its remaining monopoly position of today. The organization was established under the name Human-Etiska Förbundet in 1979 and was renamed Humanisterna in 1999. Today, it consists of twelve local organizations nationwide and has around 5,300 members (SHA kongresshandlingar 2016, 1). Humanisterna is the biggest and most active organization of secular humanists in Sweden. The SHA's demographic composition resembles many nonreligious organizations in other countries. An internal membership survey from 2013 shows that the majority of members, 64 percent, is 50 years or older, and that 78 percent of all members are men. Additionally, 81 percent have a university education.[17] The vast majority of secular humanists consider themselves atheists (83 percent) (Jansson 2013).[18]

The SHA's aims encompass working towards a completely secular state, in the sense of a total separation of religion and politics. Religion is understood to be a private matter and a secular society the prerequisite and basis for a well-functioning democracy.[19] On its homepage, the SHA states that they represent a naturalistic worldview as well as an immanent secular morality centered on individual freedom, integrity, universal human rights, and democratic values. The former includes the view that most phenomena in the world can be explained by science, despite the fact that mankind has yet to find answers to all questions. They perceive science to be the key for providing solutions for social and worldwide problems, like "poverty, environmental and climate threats, global conflicts, and discrimination of various kinds" (SHA program of ideas 2016, 4). In relation to the role of science, members emphasize the importance of critical thinking and the use of proper scientific methods for gaining knowledge. In this context, fighting "pseudo-science" as well as postmodernist ideas is a central objective.

The organization's fields of activity include opinion-making work with a special focus on human rights topics and religious criticism as well as educational and ceremonial work. Beginning in the 1990s, members of the SHA established a comprehensive offer of humanist ceremonies, including welcoming ceremonies for newborns, humanist confirmation camps, weddings, and funerals (Gunnarson 2016). At the end of this chapter, it will become obvious that ceremonial work is a quite contested part of activism among members. Alternative offers to religious ones further include the publication of *Den Svenska Högtidsboken*, a nonreligious alternative to the Church of Sweden hymnbook, published in 2000, as well as a nonreligious alternative to the inauguration of the Swedish parliament by the Church of Sweden.[20]

SHA's opinion-making activities aim at the promotion of a naturalistic, scientific, and humanist worldview and proving the falsity of religious and superstitious beliefs. These activities include organizing lectures and seminars about scientific topics, human rights issues, the relationship between religion and politics, and the irrationality and danger of phenomena like pseudo-science or New Age practices, to name only some areas of interest. They also organize panel debates about issues where they would like to see change occur. Educational issues as well as questions related to schools and teaching gained special importance in membership discussions. Several thematic events and working groups that focused on education were organized throughout the last couple of years, and "school" was the organizational "topic of the year" in 2014 and 2015.

The SHA has a rather international orientation, visible in the coverage of and exchanges about events in countries worldwide. Member activities, however, primarily take place in Sweden. On its homepage, the SHA recommends several internationally active organizations, including HumanistHjälpen (Humanist Aid Sweden), a charity foundation that funds projects that work against the infringement of human rights and to help people, "who for religious and traditional reasons are subjected to oppression, persecution, honor violence and exclusion,"[21] and Oum el Banine, a project against the religious oppression of women. Members' wish and efforts to expand their activities beyond the Swedish context have so far been very limited by the availability of resources, money as well as workforce. All members work on a voluntary basis in their leisure time.

The SHA has become a visible actor in public debates and has gained political influence throughout the last years due to the chairmanship of public figure Christer Sturmark[22] (2005–2018),[23] the increased media-intensive activities that he initiated, as well as the prominence and visibility of "New Atheist" representatives in Swedish media and social media channels. These factors contributed to the sharp increase in membership, up fivefold since 2005 (Thurfjell 2015, 98).[24]

Member of the SHA also participate in panel discussions with representatives of different faiths and life stances, they advise the government with respect to certain law proposals, and they are continually present in media, particularly in the daily Swedish newspapers, where they discuss certain societal and political issues (Gran 2013, 9).[25] The SHA supports the LGBTQ movement in Sweden. One activity in this context, along with thematic publications, is their participation in the yearly Stockholm Pride Festival, where they organize discussion rounds and take part in the Pride Parade.

Several members perceive the most urgent problem worldwide to be the spread of religious fundamentalism and dogmatism throughout many countries. Examples given by members often refer to incidents and phenomena in countries like India, Bangladesh, or the United States, as well as the war against the so-called Islamic State. Interviewees stated that with respect to Sweden, religious fundamentalism is not a major problem; they are, however, worried about new age tendencies, nihilism, and postmodernist, especially relativist, ideas. Its members consider postmodernism and relativism as one of the most harmful schools of thought in academic circles and harmful influences in public debates. According to them, they open the back door for dangerous phenomena, like irrationality, racism, and those grouped under the label "religious fundamentalism," that in comparison with other countries like the US or India are not highly influential in the Swedish context so far. The Church of Sweden, on the other hand, is often described as a very liberal church, even among humanists, as it is considered to represent values that overlap with those of secular humanists in Sweden to a great extent.[26] With regard to the Church, humanists mainly fight its remaining semi-official, partial monopoly position. They criticize the remains of the former position of the Church as state church together with the state regulations for all faith communities for the inequalities and forms of exclusion they represent and solidify, particularly in relation to nonreligious life stances such as secular humanism.

The following sections, four and five, analyze the understandings of humanism and religion that SHA members expressed in interviews as well as their views of the purpose and role of the SHA as a humanist organization.

The meaning that secular humanism and the SHA as an organization have for members vary, of course. The positions and views that are compared in the following analysis overlap in praxis. The concepts of life stance humanism and opinion-making humanism, which will be introduced, are ideal-typical descriptions of understandings that have been expressed repeatedly in similar forms during interviews as well as in publications of members. These two ideal types of humanism differ from each other with regard to the following aspects:

(1) Activism, including (a) the goals of collective activism, (b) the focus with regard to certain themes and values, (c) the postulated scope of activism (e.g. society at large, individual life styles);
(2) Different kinds of relationships with religious actors;
(3) Organization, including (a) the pursued organizational form, (b) the self-image, perception of the organization as well as its function; and
(4) The orientation towards different social fields regarding the type of action, the mobilization of resources, and the institutionalization of secular humanism.

Shift of focus – how secular humanists discuss their focus of activism

It has been more than twenty years since SHA members began to organize humanist ceremonies, a central part of humanist activism in many countries worldwide. Despite the passage of time, members who are engaged in this work only recently succeeded in raising awareness and demand for secular offers in Swedish society (Nosti 2016). What distinguishes the SHA from other humanist associations is that social work only accounts for a small proportion of SHA activism compared to that of other countries. In interviews, members mentioned different reasons for why this field of activism has not expanded as it had in other countries, such as the Netherlands or Norway. One is that some SHA members refuse or oppose expanding into this area, which will be discussed in detail in the context of the internal conflict that arose in 2012 in the following sections. Another rather long-term reason points to the specific national historical trajectories of Swedish humanism. Whereas in Norway humanism was publicly recognized as a nonreligious life stance vis-à-vis religious ones already in the beginning of the 1980s (Alberts 2010, 222), humanists in Sweden are still fighting against the Church of Sweden's remaining monopolies in this area and for the public recognition of humanist ceremonies on equal terms with religious ones. As mentioned previously, public recognition, which in this form so far only applies to faith communities, entitles the respective organizations to state funding. SHA members identified missing monetary resources and – linked to this – the lack of a paid labor force as important obstacles to social work. The financial problem has partly been solved thanks to the

Norwegian Humanist Association's commitment to financially supporting the expansion of humanist ceremonies in Sweden (Timmerby 2018). With this and other smaller successes in mind, some members have been calling for humanism to be taken to the next level: towards a more comprehensive, full-scale life stance community (Gunnarson 2016, 11f).

Humanism as a holistic life stance

> It is sometimes said that humanism stands on three pillars: the freethinking pillar, the ceremony pillar, and the life stance pillar. In Sweden, Humanisterna stands firmly on the first, is limping with the second, and is dragging the third behind.
>
> (Palmstierna 2012, 19)[27]

Proponents of a more comprehensive humanist social community and social activism state that religious groups, particularly the Church of Sweden in Sweden, are quite successful in meeting people's need for togetherness. Accordingly, they, at least partly, positively evaluate the functions and strategies of Christian practice and emphasize that in this regard they can learn from religion and the success of religious communities (Gunnarson 2009, 26f., 2012; Damaschke and Ericsson Qvist 2013, 17).[28] Some of these proponents expressed their opinion that they, as humanists, should not allow faith communities to be "the only game in town" (Damaschke and Ericsson Qvist 2013, 17). In their view, the Church of Sweden requires a secular alternative community that is based on reason and places the human being at its center (Damaschke and Ericsson Qvist 2013; Palmstierna 2012). Advocates of life stance humanism (LSH) emphasize social aspects of secular humanism by pointing out the importance of social work within society, like ceremonies, as well as the role of a social community for nonbelievers and social activities within their organizational framework, e.g., a humanist (boat) cruise or the desire to establish a humanist choir like the Humanists UK, formerly known as the British Humanist Association.[29] The SHA could function as a place for like-minded people to meet, a safe harbor, where activities exceed the operations of working for common goals. Accordingly, some members aim for a holistic life stance (livsåskådning) that encompasses the whole lives of humans in the sense that it has importance for and guides people in their everyday lives as well as in life-cycle events and times of tragedy. This holistic perception includes a moral compass based on humanist values and ethics as well as critical and scientific thinking and methods.[30]

Members in favor of such a view argue that people search for some sort of community, and that it is therefore important to build communities that are not harmful. Humans have an emotional need to belong to a larger social community, a basic human need that has survived as an instinct until modern times. Although the internal social community and the social work within society are different areas of activity, the latter could play, according to some members, an essential role for the overall success of the organization, e.g., in terms of state funding, the mobilization of potential members to join the organization, and becoming part of the humanist community. The former, on the other hand, is, according to some voices, important for keeping members interested and engaged. Damaschke and Ericsson Qvist (2013) argue in this regard that every movement needs some sort of social community to be successful and to remain alive. Group dynamics can include, for example, inspiration and motivation (Damaschke and Ericsson Qvist 2013). The positive aspects and the advantages of a social community and engagement are expressed in statements like this:

> We have much to gain by creating a community and ceremonies around the humanistic life stance. We can help each other become more aware of cognitive biases and logical pitfalls. We can establish a social climate where open and objective dialogue is highly valued. We can prevent negative group dynamics and dogmatism by encouraging and praising constructive questioning. We can inspire each other to seek knowledge and develop our thoughts. We can create ceremonies that recall the importance of reflection and reconsideration. By offering an appealing and engaging community Humanisterna has greater opportunities to spread the good memes of reason and humanity.
> (Damaschke and Ericsson Qvist 2013, 17[31])

Damaschke and Ericsson Qvist argue that this exchange within an organization can be used to strengthen the group and spread humanist thinking. In publications and interviews, representatives of such an understanding of humanism and this focus of activism often describe LSH as being "positive," "practical," and "constructive" in character, referring to all activities besides pinpointing and discussing problems in society and beyond (Blom et al. 2013, 49; Gunnarson 2009, 26; Gunnarson 2016, 12). The stress of a "positive" side of humanism is, among other reasons, a reaction to external criticism, which accuses secular humanists of focusing only on the negative and of having overemphasized religious criticism in the past. In the view of LSH proponents, the latter contributed to the SHA's partly one-sided and negative public image in Swedish society and the negative reception of the international humanist movement more generally (Gunnarson 2016, 12).[32] Life stance humanists try to distance themselves from a sole focus on the criticism of religious actors, working instead towards more "productive" relationships of competition. They want to show people that the SHA is not just about "being against" different things. For the future, they want to communicate a "clear" and "positive message" and "what they stand for," like their human rights focus and humanist values as a moral compass, guiding people in how to live a good life as well as what they as humanists have actually put into practice like humanist ceremonies (Yanis 2013,

103–4; Erik 2014, 242–7; Gunnarson 2009, 2013; Damaschke and Ericsson Qvist 2013).

Numerous references to the social needs of people, especially in relation to the practices and role of the Church of Sweden in Swedish society, show that LSH focus on functional aspects in relation to religion as well as humanism. If one looks at the number of people who choose the Church of Sweden's ceremonial offers, the folk church remains the most influential player in the field, despite a significant decline since the 70s and especially since the separation of church and state in 2000. Ceremonial occasions still constitute one of the main areas where Swedes come into contact with Christianity. Regarding the Church of Sweden's functional role, SHA members have, alongside the ceremonial function, highlighted that priests offer people individual and family counseling in times of crisis or tragedy, as well as counseling services for moral guidance in hospitals, military settings, and prisons (Erik 2014, 263–4; SHA kongresshandlingar 2013, 49, §13 Motion 1). In addition, the Church more generally provides people with opportunities and spaces to meet other persons with whom they can share everyday experiences or talk about existential questions in life, not the least through formats like sewing clubs or choirs. However, such a functional perspective on religion must be distinguished from a basic functionalist definition of religion. While LSH representatives emphasize that meeting social needs using, e.g., ceremonies is the Church's social role, for them, it is not the ceremonies themselves but the Christian content and procedures that make them "religious." In this respect, they rather tend to have a substantial understanding of religion. The social role, on the other hand, can potentially be met with secular offers. This is the field in which they want to be a more active and serious competitor. In other countries like the Netherlands or Belgium, similar alternative offers are already a constitutive part of humanist activism. There is even an international initiative to connect "European Humanist Professionals" in order to "cultivate and stimulate dialogue, exchange and cooperation between humanist professionals working in Europe" (European Humanist Professionals 2016, webpage). The SHA wants to establish an exchange with members of this forum to learn from their experiences (SHA kongresshandlingar 2014, 50).

Staffan Gunnarson, a long-standing SHA member and former vice president of the European Humanist Federation (2009–2016), argues that humanism must replace religion in every social respect in order to become a "holistic life stance" (Gran 2013, 1, quoting Gunnarson). Otherwise, people who are still church members will not leave the Church. Irene Rune, a humanist celebrant of the SHA, agrees with Gunnarson that establishing secular humanism as a life stance community, which "embrace[s] the whole person" (Gran 2013, 7, quoting Irene Rune) and includes ceremonial work, is the key for attracting new, especially female, members. These views emphasize a functional understanding of humanism, not least due to this competitive logic which permeates humanist activism. With their alternative offerings,

LSH advocates have strategically established a competitive relationship that is more comprehensive and, in the sense of Stolz (2010), functionally as close as possible to offerings of the Church of Sweden. Narratives like the one mentioned previously, saying that they should not let religious communities be "the only game in town," underscore this competitive logic. Representatives of LSH hope to substitute religion and to become a more influential social movement. In this regard, they hope that progress in either of both aims will reinforce success in the other; the more they are successful in offering an alternative to religion, the more their movement will grow in size and influence. They also contend that the more humanism grows and gains resources, the easier it will be to replace religious offerings. Moreover, proponents of this view emphasize the interdependence of social work and institutionalization in society: the more social work they do, the higher their prospects of gaining access to established structures for institutionalization and desperately needed resources that depend on the related official recognition, and the more institutionalized they are, the more they will be able to extend their range of social activities. To expand their offerings, e.g., for the establishment of humanist counseling in state institutions, such as hospitals, military institutions, or prisons in Sweden, those resources, as well as an institutionalized cooperation with the state, are essential. Aiming for a further institutionalization, LSH point to humanist counseling activities and the social impact of humanists in Norway, Belgium, and the Netherlands as role models for future development (Erik 2014, 256–98; Finn 2013, 2340–7). Such references show that the concept of life stance humanism is not only shaped by its respective local context, but that it is also strongly influenced by common elements of how humanist organizations in several countries position and present themselves in relation to religious life stances and communities, e.g., in competitive logics within particularistic organized systems for religious and nonreligious life stances.

Nevertheless, alongside this external inspiration, LSH representatives tend to display an *inward-oriented* focus on the development and further emancipation of the humanist community. They also have an outward-oriented focus in the way they want to change certain aspects of – or solve problems in – society, but the focus on their own humanist identity and community seems to prevail.[33] This could partly be the case because they consider such a further development to be a necessary step that would grant them the position to dominate the "playing field." While some humanists regard the stabilization and expansion of the humanist community as preliminary goals, or as a means to another end, others value this community in itself.

In particular, the endeavor of LSH representatives is to promote humanism as a moral compass for organizing and shaping everyday life. Thus, developing offerings to help people manage personal crises, similar to humanists in the Netherlands and Belgium, or for celebrating personal occasions shows that their postulated scope of humanism also extends to individual lifestyles in addition to their own community and the Swedish society.

In summary, life stance humanism as an ideal type is characterized by:

(1) (a) The main goals of empowerment, emancipation, and growth to strengthen the humanist community, and to fulfill the social and emotional needs of people through humanistic offerings, (b) an orientation towards and dealing with values and issues that are related to the relationship between religious and secular beliefs, and in particular their equality, and (c) the postulated scope for humanism covering individual everyday life, the humanistic community, and society;
(2) Functionally close competitive relationships with religious actors, with the objective of replacing them in their commonly known functions;
(3) Proponents working to (a) establish humanism in the form of a life stance organization/community, and (b) regard the humanist community as having a value in itself; and
(4) Representatives orienting themselves towards the religious field, including related legal regulations and the activities, status, and role of faith communities.

Humanism as an opinion-making force

Representatives of opinion-making humanism (OMH) aim for a categorically quite different humanist activism. They characterize humanism as being goal- and problem-oriented and aim for changes in society when it comes to specific issues. When these SHA members talk about humanism as a worldview, they refer to taking positions on "a whole range of questions" (Jana 2013, 538–48).[34] These members point out that, in terms of their humanist activism, they reject both the movement towards a strong social community and towards offering a comprehensive range of nonreligious alternatives to religious activities. In the fourth edition of the member magazine, HumanistInfo, in 2012, the then-vice-chairman of the organization, Per Dannefjord, wrote an article about the "downside of community" (2012, 16). As the title suggests, he fears that the establishment of a strong community could have disadvantages for the organization. He fears that a focus on the social collective could change the emphasis from rational thinking and having as well as being accessible for good arguments on special issues to focusing on the life stance-based community as an end in itself. For him, this is the essential difference between communities and political or lobbying groups. Whereas both include shared ideas, the focus of the former lies on the social collective, in contrast to political or lobby groups, who are focused on their common interests, aims, and problems to address. If a social community becomes an end in itself, if the feeling of belonging and consistency get stronger, rational thinking and arguments, in his opinion, will fade into the background. Instead, OMH want to be an interest organization with an NGO character, which is politically active and working with and promoting a value basis that is not fixed but a matter of negotiation based on rationality and reason.

This set of values includes human rights, and, more specifically, children's rights and freedom of expression.[35] Jana describes the role that she perceives the SHA to play like this:

> [. . .] that's where I see that Humanisterna can make the most impact. That's where I feel like we really can fill a void. We take on issues that other children's rights organizations for example are too "afraid to handle," for example the circumcision of boys was one of those issues that was part of a debate about a couple of years ago.
> (Jana 2013, 80–4)

According to her, there is no similar organization like the SHA in Swedish society and, therefore, it is urgently needed:

> We're brave, like we take on issues and you know in the media debates and political debates that people are uncomfortable about discussing. And we stick with it and we take on those debates and we start new ones that people maybe perhaps haven't thought about, or dared to talk about. With that follows of course that people find it annoying.
> (Jana 2013, 141–6)

In this regard, she purports that the SHA can add to public discussions when it comes to specific questions or problems. In interviews and publications, members compared the international humanist movement and themselves to Amnesty International several times, with the explicit difference being that they deal with religion-related questions, e.g., negative religious practices and beliefs and religious oppression, whereas Amnesty International does not (Andersson et al. 2009; Gran 2013, quoting Bergström and Sturmark; Leon 2014, 243–57). In addition to the aforementioned activities, they would like to extend public education offerings. They concentrate on arranging lectures, seminars, thematic projects, study groups, and philosophy cafés. The declared objective is to "try to . . . apply critical thinking, philosophical thinking and scientific thinking to a lot of subjects, and make people interested in thinking this way, about a lot of things" (Malte 2013, 641–3). Proponents of such an understanding of humanism and the SHA point in addition to the importance of political activism, like advising the government and political parties regarding law proposals.

In contrast to some other humanists from their own organization as well as internationally, opinion-making humanists within the SHA want to create an organizational identity that does not primarily fight for their own emancipation,[36] but focuses instead on changing society as a whole. OMH expressed their wish that the priorities within the organization would be further rearranged towards raising human rights issues alongside scientific matters, instead of aiming for the equal treatment of humanism with faith communities (Jana 2013, 337, 427–30; Leon 2014, 297; Malte 2013,

630–2). In this respect, they want to spark public debates concerning various issues, regulations, and the influence of special actors and phenomena, which they perceive to be more problematic than those related to the regulation of faith communities in Sweden e.g. the remaining church monopolies. Instead of an inward-oriented focus, they primarily want to have an *outward orientation* that does not aim to become a social community as a value in itself but forms an organization as a means to an end, a platform and organizational frame to reach goals.[37] This does not contradict an interest in meeting like-minded people and having inspiring talks, but instead marks that the community does not play a decisive role in their choice of becoming, or staying, a member of the organization. Jana describes the difference between members like this:

> There are certain people within Humanisterna, as I said before, that I really enjoy hanging out with and having discussions with, but I don't have to do that organized, we do it, whenever we want. We have a beer or we, you know, I don't need to have that organized. That's not why I'm part of Humanisterna and it is the reason why some are, to have that social thing, with the people that are like-minded.
>
> (Jana 2013, 632–7)[38]

Jana does not go to or take part in local "social events." She has never gone to one of the pub evenings. She problematizes that being part of a group can become "too uniform" (Jana 2013, 109). However, the criticism is directed less towards internal forms of social meetings within the organization like pub evenings, journeys (cruises, etc.). They seem to be perceived as rather trivial for those critics and of a voluntary status for those who want to take part in them. It seems as if they are unproblematic as long as they have the position of a side product for the SHA instead of being one of the main activities.

Nevertheless, Dannefjord (2012) states that a life stance does not necessarily require a social-collective form. Representatives of OMH argue that social groups can develop rather negative group dynamics (e.g., peer pressure, exclusion) that could undermine their norm-critical work and negotiations about the best arguments. They emphasize that agreements should not be based on what they perceive as partly irrational arguments relating to social bonds. In this regard, Dannefjord (2012) distinguished between those aspects of their activism that are based on rational arguments and others that are based on emotions and matters of identity. He further points out that a social community manifests itself and finds expression in rituals and joint action, which have, according to him, a more or less fixed form and, therefore, cannot be neutral. According to the critics of humanist ceremonies, rituals solidify social norms within a community. The danger for organizations or other social associations with political goals, therefore, is that the attempt to establish a social community on the basis of a shared life stance will lead to higher degrees of closure and exclusiveness of the organization. When a philosophy of life is increasingly solidified in the form of a social community over time, it becomes more difficult for members of this community to be open to new ideas, and "it is becoming increasingly impossible to change, which is necessary for any political, reason- or idea-based organization. This is especially necessary for an organization like Humanisterna, whose entire ideology is all about intellectual flexibility and changing itself in light of new arguments" (Dannefjord 2012, 17).

The analysis of the interviews showed that the criticism of social work goes beyond the debate about ceremonies alone: one of the main points that characterizes this understanding of humanism is the rejection of a social institutionalization of humanism in more general terms. The proponents of this view in Sweden are not in favor of concepts like humanist kindergartens, universities, or humanist counseling services. In connection with his rejection of a social institutionalization of secular humanism, Malte explains that he would, for example not support the establishment of "humanist schools" because the teaching of "all schools, on all levels" should be based on humanist values and science:

> I would not like to describe that by saying that they're humanist schools because no, they're not, they're just good schools, and many, I mean most, schools today are like that . . . in Sweden. So, it's no big problem also, so I think it would send the wrong signals to have a separate humanist school. Instead, we should try to . . . if we see something in the curriculum for the schools that is not based on science and reason, then we should try to discuss that, publicly, but we should not say now we have our own school here.
>
> (Malte 2013, 325–42)

Malte (2013, 382–4) emphasizes the universal value that he grants humanist principles. He argues against concepts of institutions that are part of a particularistic logic, like humanist kindergartens as an alternative to Christian ones or humanist universities to other ones: "Okay let me say it like this: I don't understand how a humanist university would be better than another university which is good enough, . . . where the activities are based on scientific principles and research." OMH think that holistic life stances cannot be universal and that the institutionalization of a humanist life stance in a particularistic logic impairs the universalism of human rights and secular ethics by granting competing ideologies and values legitimacy. Such acts thereby contradict their principles.

OMH's points of criticism mentioned so far were predominantly of a more general nature. Beyond that, the resentment of different aspects of the LSH concept also refers to certain forms of relationships with religion, which are perceived as being explicitly or implicitly linked to the understandings of LSH. Concerning the understanding of secular humanism as a substitute and functional alternative to religious stances, Malte explains that:

There are many people who want it to be more like a replacement for a religion and they tend to say things that like, we should . . . learn from the religion, how they teach their message . . . , so we should also have ceremonies and we should have, well confirmation, and we should have maybe some churchlike place, and we should, and it's very important how we, that we sort of, marknad för oss [advertise for us], that we sell our organization . . . with a clear message and . . . I do not like this at all because then I think the whole point is sort of spoiled, because for me the whole point is to be skeptical, . . . and to make people more . . . aware and . . . thinking for themselves and not just accepting things that come to them, not just accept things that we or any other people say to them, but try to instead help them think for themselves //I: critical thinking // yes, critical thinking and scientific thinking and all that, yes, and that is not really consistent with a view where you should try to manipulate people into thinking your own way; that is exactly what we should not do, and for me ceremonies and such things are part of such a manipulation actually.

(Malte 2013, 245–61)

In this quote, Malte emphasizes that he rejects the whole strategy of replacing religious actors by mirroring or copying their characteristics and concepts. Malte opposes producing and establishing norms and ceremonies as manifestations of norms, as part of such a replacement strategy and a type of manipulation. In this regard, OMH accuse LSH not only of producing norms by aiming for a stronger social community and a holistic life stance, but also of re-producing Christian norms by trying to copy church offerings. Both forms are regarded as incompatible with their aim of being those critical of norms. They are, on one hand, calling attention to injustices and mechanisms of exclusion related to existing norms, and criticizing religious forms of norm-producing practices on the other hand. As such, OMH's criticism reproduces parts of the external criticism of the organization as a whole for being religion- or church-like internally and realigns it to a special group within the organization, the proponents of life stance humanism. Malte's quote already indicates that the criticism of LSH focuses on the negative aspects of how religions are involved in social-community work as they describe it as a mistake for religions to "get into all aspects of people's lives" (Malte 2013, 316). They also emphasized that they always want to be "careful" (Malte 2013, 319–20) with their own values and norms. Highlighting the perceived difference between their own view and the LSH concept, OMH emphasize that they do not regard humanist values as a basis for the production of norms that communicate a special sort of lifestyle as the good or even the right one. In opposition to those members who call for communicating a "clear message" as secular humanists, they explain that the advantage of a rather political organization is that, compared to a community, you do not feel obligated to affirm to a whole package that belongs to a specific life stance, theoretically, normatively, and emotionally

(Dannefjord 2012, 17). In relation to this negative evaluation of the holistic influence of religion, proponents of opinion-making humanism work to distance themselves from efforts and desires that seek to mirror a religion's scope of impact:

> People who want to have ceremonies for example they would agree with me in this thinking [critical and scientific thinking], but they would add that, we also have to give people some alternative to religion, so wherever people turn to religion we should be there with something else and say "no, choose this instead," and I don't think we should do that.
>
> (Malte 2013, 634–45)

Advocates of OMH would like to exclude, or at least minimize, activities aiming for a comprehensive humanist community and social work, like the provision of humanist ceremonies, from organizational activities. Instead, they want to focus their activism solely on opinion-making in public debate. Malte furthermore calls for being "another type of organization," different from religious types:

> For me the most important issue is to try to disconnect religion from morality, but in order to do that of course we cannot make ourselves be seen as one kind of religion, we must be more sort of another type of organization which argues more for scientific reasoning, critical thinking, without getting religious about it, I mean you should be skeptical also towards critical thinking of course.
>
> (Malte 2013, 271–6)

The metaphors the actors used in interviews, including "another type of organization," "without getting religious about it," "fields that shouldn't be mixed," or "the whole point is sort of spoiled," point to the fact that these members see a fundamental difference between the underlying logic of their activism in contrast to the one that structures the work of religious organizations. For some, such logics not only compete with each other but are also mutually exclusive. OMH are trying to *move away from a religion-likeness* they associate with the popular and partly established logic of a holistic life stance that guides certain parts of humanist activism. They want to form the SHA into an organization that is independent of the logic developed in relation to religious associations, especially Christianity. In connection with their desire to exclude the remaining activities based on such logic from organizational work, members in favor of OMH regard state structures, like the one for funding of faith communities, as unsuitable and inappropriate points of orientation for their activism. They are not aiming at the SHA's emancipation as a nonreligious organization in comparison to faith communities. In relation to this perception, another member rejects entering into the existing life stance or worldview logics and structures, as she does not want to be compared to faith communities:

> If you look at who gets money from the state as a worldview organization, it'll be like, "oh, it's the Christian, it's the Muslim; it's the dedede [indicating further examples] and it's the humanists." And like well, . . . it just feels wrong to be included in that group, to me.
> (Jana 2013, 691–4)

While LSH advocates encourage that "positive humanism" should be more clearly promoted to other people, sympathizers of opinion-making work express their doubts about a humanism that concentrates its work primarily on "positive" aspects:

> Some people [referring to fellow members] think that we should be more telling other people what we're for, what we like, whereas some people say that you know we should be out, and take debates about what we don't like, things we would like to see changed. . . . Maybe they just wanna talk about positive things. Me, personally, I don't see how only talking about positive things will change the bad things.
> (Jana 2013, 570–6)

It is hard to trace when and where this debate between LSH and OMH started, but it gained momentum and has explicitly been expressed in 2012, 2013, and 2014. Some members perceive the debate about these different understandings and visions of secular humanism and the SHA as an organization as a factor that more or less "splits the organization in half" (Jana 2013, 423, see also Mats 2013, 348–51). OMH agree with other members that humanism as a life stance has two dimensions: first, a descriptive dimension, in the form of a perception of reality, an epistemological and ontological stance, and, second, a normative dimension, in the form of a set of basic values (Lindenfors and Sturmark 2015, 17–18). But apart from this basic definition of a life stance, OMH do not agree with LSH when it comes to whether such a life stance should form a communal basis for the organization. In the interviews and publications, it becomes obvious that the question is, what kind of collective identity should they strive for? OMH proponents are concerned with the questions about the degree to which their organizational identity and social relations as members of the humanist organization are based on basic principles relating to critical thinking, rationality, arguments, and agreements on common goals, or a shared life stance (community), a group that shares views about the world, e.g., with regard to naturalism or the existence of god (atheism). They also look at whether such views, explicitly or implicitly, function as conditions for joining the organization. For Dannefjord, the SHA is currently both "a political association with a clear agenda, but at the same time a life stance organization (livsåskådningsorganisation), where people share understandings about the world that they consider to be a part of their identity" (Dannefjord 2012, 17), which is where the SHA encounters problems, as community activities could bring people to drop their political objectives.

In summary, the ideal type of opinion-making humanism is marked by:

(1) (a) The main goals of promoting and defending the differentiation of politics and religion as well as secular values, (b) a primary focus on values and themes associated with universal, individual human rights, and (c) a postulated scope for humanism, which extends to the humanist organization and society, but excludes individual life styles;
(2) Advocates engaging in relationships of conflict and criticism with religious actors, while rejecting functional-close competitions (cooperative relationships and functional distant competitions are unproblematic as long as they do not require a common religion-like logic);
(3) An organizational form that is (a) similar to a political interest organization working for secularism and human rights, and (b) regarded as a means, a platform to achieve shared objectives; and
(4) An orientation towards public discourse, the wider political field, and alternative funding possibilities that are not associated with the status of faith communities, e.g., for youth-related activities.

Responding to internal criticism

In the course of such heated discussions, LSH advocated for their understanding of humanism and responded to several of OMH's points of criticism. For LSH, central parts of secular humanism include both strands of activism, establishing a humanist community and an alternative nonreligious life stance to religious offerings on the one hand, and opinion-making work, and the promotion of critical thinking and science, on the other hand. The question which predominantly guides both forms of humanist activism is, according to Gunnarson, a question of prioritization:

> We humanists are primarily carriers of a life-affirming philosophy of modern, critical thinking and secularized people. Then, secondly – and as a result of this – we form a political resistance movement, which among other things wants to protect freedom of religion and life stances, free research, a science-based and non-confessional school education etc. One must distinguish between the main issue and the side issue.
> (Gunnarson 2013)[39]

Advocates of LSH criticize that opponents of activities like ceremonies often have a one-sided and too simplified focus on rationality. In their opinion, the criticism of ceremonial work does not properly reflect people's social needs. Ignoring such needs, according to members who would like to expand social work, only leads to a strengthening of the irrational forces in society, as good alternatives to religious offerings would then be missing (Damaschke and Ericsson Qvist 2013, 17). One LSH advocate said that he refuses the vision of some other members who want the SHA to become an organization like Amnesty International, just with a special focus on working against religious oppression. For him, the SHA requires a social dimension in order to gain further support in the wider public, earn credibility, and attract more female members (Gunnarson 2013, 4). In response to the criticism regarding the desire for a stronger humanist community, other members emphasize the advantages and the necessity of social relationships for humans: "[...] community is an important prerequisite for our personal well-being," "even though there is a risk of peer pressure and groupthink it does not outweigh the potential for greater personal fulfillment" (Damaschke and Ericsson Qvist 2013, 16f.). They state that those communities are based on free will and voluntarism and therefore have a smaller risk of catalyzing peer pressure than others. As groups and communities can be very diverse, it is important for them to look at the purpose of why a community is created and what internal culture it comprises. Group dynamics not only occur in a negative form but can also take on positive forms like inspiration, good challenges, motivation, or joined forces for positive purposes.

In relation to the accusation that they produce religious-like offers, they emphasize that they are not importing Christian values but rather do what Christians have also done: they create cultural expressions that are similar to those that people in today's society are familiar with and fill them with a different content – the content people desire (Damaschke and Ericsson Qvist 2013, 17).[40] A frequently used example is humanist confirmations, with which teenagers celebrate their coming of age. Instead of indoctrinating them, teenagers are being encouraged to think for themselves and to reflect, e.g., through group discussions.[41]

The debate about humanist ceremonies

Humanist ceremonies "are on the rise" (Engelke 2015, 216) in several countries, such as England and Norway. There are early signs of an increased demand for "civil" ("borgerliga") and humanist ceremonies in Sweden as well (Nosti 2016). Despite the growing popularity, the existence and arrangement of humanist ceremonies were the most controversial topics among SHA members between 2012 and 2015.[42] While humanist ceremonies have reached a well-established status in countries such as Norway, the Netherlands, and England, some SHA members still fight for state recognition and for humanist ceremonies to be officially accepted on an equal footing with religious offerings in Sweden. Alberts nevertheless shows that even in countries where humanist ceremonies enjoy an established position, as in Norway, they can be a matter of heated disputes among humanists (Alberts 2010).

Humanists in Sweden consider ceremonies one of the most central and popular components of the remaining influence of the Church of Sweden. While LSH want to copy these offerings because they aim for a complete replacement, OMH reject this strategy for exactly the same reason. One member described this debate as "the discussion about what sort of organization we actually should be" (Malte 2013, 244–5), which already shows that the meaning of this debate, and the arguments from LSH and OMH related to the endorsement or the rejection of humanist ceremonies, reach beyond the provision of such offerings themselves.

Since 2012, several members have questioned – more concretely than before – whether the SHA should organize humanist ceremonies as an alternative to religious offers. Additionally, some members do not question whether ceremonies should be organized but focus instead on how it should be done. These matters have been a continuous and lively discussion at member meetings, congresses, and conferences, as well as in the member magazine. The question as to whether the SHA should organize and arrange humanist ceremonies splits – as some members define it – the organization between two main camps, while various subgroups have emerged from them as well (Jana 2013; Mats 2013, 348–51). The two main camps are perceived as: (1) those in favor of humanist ceremonies being a part of the SHA's activities; and (2) those who oppose the same. At the autumn conference in 2013, it became obvious that there are positions within those camps that differ from each other: some proponents of humanist ceremonies consider them to be crucial in terms of their goal to promote humanism as a life stance within Swedish society, and, therefore, have the desire to include explicit references to human rights, humanist songs, and poems in the ceremonies. Other proponents emphasize that humanist ceremonies are based on a flexible, open, and personalized concept, without any fixed content. It is expected that people express their wishes and perspective with which they want the ceremony to align (Rune 2013).

Within the group of those members who speak out against the organization of humanist ceremonies, there is a subset of members that is not per se against humanist ceremonies as a concept. They take the position that if people want nonreligious ceremonies as an alternative to religious ones, if, in other words, a respective demand exists, people should have the opportunity to choose them. They are, however, against the fact that the SHA should plan and organize these activities, as they feel that other institutions, independent of the SHA, should be in charge of them. The fourth potential position comprises opponents of the concept of humanist ceremonies as such, no matter who organizes them or how they are held. This, however, exists as a mere potential position, as there does not appear to be any actual proponents for it among the active members of the organization who participate in the internal discussions at membership congresses and conferences. For members, the most important questions associated with the debate are: should ceremonies be a part of the SHA or not, and if so, what should they look like and how should they be conducted? The members involved in this debate are aware that questioning humanist ceremonies means to question a central part of the SHA. Abandoning these ceremonies would mark a decisive change for the organization, as they have been part of humanist activism for a relatively long time.

Towards a future expansion of ceremonial work?

For LSH, humanist ceremonies are the future of the SHA.[43] They assume that there will always be a demand for ceremonies, since celebrating the most important events in life is an expression of the social needs of people and those ceremonies mean something to people. Therefore, there will always be a demand for an organization like the SHA to provide nonreligious ceremonies. Some LSH, in this regard, seek to establish and provide such humanist offers beyond the abolition of religious competitors.[44] Proponents of ceremonies emphasize that exactly in times like this, when the demand for religious offerings is decreasing, it is important that the SHA offers appealing secular alternatives to those people who want them. Ceremonies not only respond to people's needs but also help them to live a good and full life without religion (Gran 2013, 4, quoting Gunnarson). Proponents of LSH emphasize that the SHA could play a greater role in the everyday lives of a multitude of people by means of these and other offerings, e.g., humanist counseling services, and could, thus, develop into a "popular movement" (Blom et al. 2013, 49–52).

Proponents of humanist ceremonies argue that rituals are as old as mankind itself and that most of the respective events were celebrated even before Christian churches declared them important life events. As religious actors just filled them with religious content at some point in history, it would not be reprehensible to do the same and fill them with their own, nonreligious content. Some members think that religious communities like the Church of Sweden are no longer successfully providing ceremonies because their references to religious content deter people in Swedish society. They do think that the logic of how community building worked within the Church might be useful and will be successful again, if the religious content is removed and filled with personal desires and humanist thinking and values, while also being based on the principles of critical thinking and rationality.

As a central part of humanist social activism, sympathizers of an understanding of humanism as a life stance would like to extend ceremonial work considerably. Humanist ceremonies are an example of the envisaged "constructive solutions" (Gran 2013, 4, quoting Gunnarson), besides being critical towards norms and being skeptical. In this regard, its advocates argue, as described above, that secular humanism must be as comprehensive and as all-encompassing as religions are. According to Gunnarson, ceremonies also play an important role in being officially recognized as a life stance by the Swedish state. If they abandon this part of their activism, they have fewer chances to be accepted, as ceremonial work is the main occupation of a life stance (Gran 2013, 4, quoting Gunnarson). Some proponents of humanist ceremonies fear that without social, and particularly ceremonial work, the SHA would become an elitist club, "a small clique of men who write incomprehensible articles" (Gran 2013, quoting Rune; see also Gunnarson 2009). Rune describes the requests to abolish ceremonial work as based on an unrealistic perception of what people expect of the SHA. People would turn to them with their needs for ceremonies. From this point of view, the vision of humanism without organizing ceremonies resembles a "desktop theory" (Gran 2013, quoting Rune) that is out of touch with reality. Ceremonies, on the other hand, give humanism a "humane face" (Gunnarson 2009, 26).

LSH defend the concept of humanist ceremonies against what Dannefjord describes as their negative characteristics and related dynamics, namely, that they are relatively fixed in their form and are unable to be neutral, and that as manifestations of social communities, they contribute to dynamics of exclusion and closure. In contrast, LSH argue that humanist ceremonies always were and will remain voluntary and that no humanists are forced to use these ceremonies. As such, LSH see no risk of ceremonies infringing on the voluntarism of the organization. In response to the argument that ceremonies, including humanist ceremonies, are not and cannot be open or free of content, they state that they of course express humanistic values and that they follow a specific framework, but that they are "[. . .] open and free in the sense that they adapt to the individual needs and desires to a much greater extent than, say, most religious ceremonies" (Damaschke and Ericsson Qvist 2013, 17). Additionally, they emphasize that they are open to new celebration types and forms, that ceremonies can have a personalized nature, and that people simply have to suggest them: "If a couple wants to get married on the beach with all the guests naked, that's also fine" (Rune 2013, 5). For Damaschke and Ericsson Qvist (2013), the function and form of ceremonies do not necessarily lead to dynamics that humanists perceive as being characteristic of religion, e.g., mechanisms of exclusion or conformism. They argue that the only way to influence the development of ceremonies in a positive way and to minimize the risks that ceremonies might become firmer or dogmatic in character is to be aware of negative risks and apply critical thinking for the further development of ceremonial work. In this regard, aims for the future entail communicating the openness and flexibility of the concept of humanist ceremonies for other ideas, e.g., the celebration of other events in life, like the relationship between more than two persons, being single, divorced, or overcoming an illness or addiction (Erik 2014, 394–407).

Outsourcing ceremonial work from SHA activities?

In one of the interviews, an outspoken critic of humanist ceremonies explained his position in more detail. Considering the argument of proponents of humanist ceremonies, that the latter have no fixed content and are highly personalized in their character, he says:

> Yeah, that is what they say, they claim that, "but there is no message in our ceremonies" and so on, "our ceremonies are not like the religious ones." But, I think that may be true in some cases. But I think, and I also get support from people I know, who work in sociology, that . . . the step between having ceremonies and a religion is not so big as you might think because once you have ceremonies you decide what is worthy of a ceremony and then it is a short step from there to actually worshipping something . . . now I mean not worshipping a god, but "worshipping" in a broader sense . . . for example if you have a ceremony for . . . marriage . . . then in some sense you will not question marriage. There are several ways to live your life and marriage is just one and why should the humanist movement have any opinion about that. And as soon as we have an opinion about it, we will, we may also begin to say other things about how people should live their lives and so on. And I don't think that is our task, that is what religion does, right, I mean they try to tell you this is a good life, it should contain that and that and that and that and I think we should say no, you can live your life in a lot of different ways.
>
> (Malte 2013, 286–303)

Malte criticizes religion as a bearer of conservative normativity, which, with the help of institutions such as marriage and confirmations, establishes normative rules for individual lifestyles. He explains further that one of the reasons why fellow members, in his view, are not critical enough of the far-reaching meanings and functions of ceremonies is that they are blind to the norms they grew up with. The main point of criticism that OMH express regarding the concept of humanist ceremonies is, as mentioned in relation to Dannefjord's criticism previously, that ceremonies, organized in the name of a life stance community, are understood as being manifestations of prescribed values and norms. They are also perceived to be tools for further solidifying norms and an existing, sometimes latent, religio-normativity is reproduced. They argue that rituals necessarily must be filled with some kind of content, which is why they cannot be neutral or completely open. This is one of the main reasons why sympathizers of the OMH concept would like to exclude ceremonial work from organizational activities. That organizing ceremonies and being critical towards norms are perceived as contradictory and as counteracting the work that OMH think the SHA should do is also visible in Jana's perception of the internal debate about ceremonies:

> Those that are pro ceremonies wanna see us developing that part and make it "get bigger and more and we should really be proud," and to me I wanna like scale back on it. . . . It's not that we don't think it's

important that there is an alternative in a secular society. People that don't believe in God should have alternatives when it comes to celebrating certain moments of their lives. I'm totally for that, but we should not provide that. We should argue that it should be provided in a country, but we should not be the ones providing it. Because then you mix fields, that shouldn't be mixed. And also we're an organization that tried to be critical of norms, not just accept norms but like for example, it should be a man and a woman, the view of family and we're like no, people should be able to choose and we think with ceremonies, typically ceremonies celebrate birth and having children and marriage, that kind of partnership and that's just two people, we celebrate two people getting together, not four or five, we don't celebrate being single. So ceremonies are very conformative when it comes to norms and we try not to accept that, and we try to think beyond that. And, I think, having ceremonies contradicts that work.

(Jana 2013, 452–68)

Some proponents of opinion-making humanism argue that the purpose of nonreligious ceremonies, to make people aware of secular options as alternatives to religious ones, has lost importance in comparison to the earlier days of activism in the 1980s and up to the 1990s. Malte, speaking about another member who is a proponent of organizing alternative offerings, and ceremonies in particular, and has been a member for approximately thirty years, describes a historical shift within the organization:

His description of the movement and his ideals and visions, I think reflect the older movement, because of course he wants it to be as it was then, because then it was a lot about having alternative ceremonies. And there may have been good arguments for that then. Because remember then, we had still a state church in Sweden and no one or almost no one was aware that you could marry someone without doing it in a church. And no one was aware that you could bury someone or have their funeral, that you could have a nonreligious funeral and so on. People were not aware about these things, they just did it by habit and then of course in such a climate in such an environment there is a reason to actually show people, "now look, you don't have to involve religion in this." Of course, well he is still there and today most Swedes I think are aware that, you actually can do this without a church. So, I think that is not a good argument today, but it may have been then.

(Malte 2013, 496–509)

In this regard, defining secular humanism in relation to the Church as the central opponent is perceived as being outdated and obsolete due to recent social developments. What becomes obvious here is that, from his perspective, the legitimate relevance that the activism around ceremonies had back then was making people aware of alternatives. Now that people are aware, he considers their duty done, and perceives the role of the SHA obviously as not being a provider of such alternatives.[45] In connection with this shift, Malte describes the differences between the "old movement" and the "new movement" as lying in a thematic shift towards human rights issues and a global perspective:

> I think they were more interested in just forming this secular alternative, because they were tired of the Swedish Church being involved everywhere. But I think that today the focus is more about human rights internationally. I think that the most important questions . . . , or problems are not in Sweden but in other parts of the world of course, because in Sweden religion is not that important to most people anyway. So, I think that the perspective has become more global and . . . more oriented towards human rights.
>
> (Malte 2013, 524–9)

Whereas both OMH and LSH welcome this shift towards human rights issues, some advocates of opinion-making humanism, like Malte, refer to this shift in order to point out that linked to religion-related problems, they perceive a focus on humanist ceremonies as outdated. In addition, humanist ceremonies are, in their view, a central topic where they decide as members how religious- or church-like they want to become. For Jana as well as Malte, ceremonies are an essential part of this resemblance, which has a much broader scope, beyond ceremonies themselves, and might, according to her, in the end only exclude the belief in God:

> [. . .] no, we shouldn't have the ceremonies, we shouldn't be a substitute for the Church, we shouldn't be you know another version of religion without, just without a god, like we shouldn't, I'm really not comfortable with the idea of us becoming just like a secular church. That's not why I joined.
>
> (Jana 2013, 421–30)

According to some critics, humanist ceremonies inevitably reproduce the values of other life stances, if they orient themselves towards established (religious) ceremonial offers. In the SHA's case, the criticism of humanist ceremonies and the reproduction of norms in this regard connects a general criticism of the role and function of the same to an explicitly religion-related criticism of the reproduction of not any, but Evangelical Lutheran norms and forms of practice (Dannefjord 2012, 16–17). In this regard, Malte points to the fact that humanist ceremonies have been constructed as nonreligious alternatives to the Church's offerings and celebrate the exact same events in people's lives, birth, coming of age, marriage, and death: ". . . I try to say to them, 'but look, this is just what religion says are milestones but do we have to say that also? . . . that may not be a milestone for everyone'" (Malte 2013, 554–6). In this regard, in addition to questions of which events should be celebrated, the criticism also addresses how ceremonies are arranged in a "Christian-like" form. For example, interviewees mentioned a welcoming ceremony for a child that was performed at a member conference for people who never took part in one before.[46] While this demonstration was intended to reconcile the different positions within the organization, it seems instead to have reaffirmed critics of the similarity between humanist and Protestant ceremonies. Jana says that, for her, this performance "was very much like a baptism, which I didn't like" (2013, 511–12). She elaborates her impression of the similarities between the event and its Christian equivalent as follows:

> It's the water thing on the head and it's lifting up the kid, it was just very much like that. I don't know how you could do it differently, but I just felt like it was mimicking how Christians would do it. With the huge difference of course that it doesn't end with "and now you're a humanist," which is very important, it does not end like that.
> (Jana 2013, 516–20)

In her evaluation, she mentions similarities as well as differences with a christening. An evident similarity with the latter is the use of water, which is a central element of baptisms. The water, which is poured on the child's head, reminded Jana of Christian effusion, reminiscent of the death and resurrection of Christ. She emphasizes that despite resemblances with the Christian ceremony, an important difference is that there is no wording that stands for the initiation into a community, like the initiation into the Christian church. Humanist ceremonies are in this regard not connected to an official membership in the SHA as an organization or the affiliation to a humanist community in a narrower Christian sense of an organizational frame. Proponents of humanist ceremonies, who emphasize their strategic importance in order, e.g., to attract more female members, according to Anna Bergström, an outspoken critic of the concept of life stance humanism, "sacrifice principles" (Gran 2013, quoting Bergström) only in order for the organization to grow.

Recent developments

At different points during the interviews, people referred to other members who share their views to point out that their positions are not isolated within the organization. With regard to the distribution of members within the organization who are in favor of and those who are against an extension of the social and especially ceremonial dimension, Malte assumes that among the active members, more members are in favor of a life stance concept including a community than those who are not.[47] He points to the fact that even though the majority of all members might share his view, the organization will most likely develop in another direction if active members predominantly have other interests, as they are the ones who influence decisions through their votes. The SHA's own membership statistics seem to support Malte's assumption in terms of members' interests. The majority of members are interested in secularism and the promotion of critical thinking, but less interested in social activities and activism. Of all members, 77 percent want the SHA to work towards a secular society,[48] while 70 percent want to promote critical thinking and a scientific approach to knowledge. Only 18 percent stated that they want the SHA to work on extending secular ceremonies, while 15 percent want the organization to conduct humanistic aid work, and only 8 percent are interested in social activities within their respective local association (Jansson 2013, 11). It is important to note that a lack of interest in social work and activities does not necessarily mean that they oppose this part of humanist activism. These numbers only give insight into the distribution of interests among SHA members.

At the spring conference in 2013, SHA members voted on the question of expanding humanist ceremonial work in the near future. The majority of elected members (ombudsman) voted to maintain and extend ceremonial work as a part of their organizational activities (SHA Kongressprotokoll 2013, §11d). Only a minority of active members seemed to support the idea that the organization should transform into a solely opinion-making association. After ongoing heated debates within the association, the board initiated and prepared a thorough debate about ceremonial work within the organization at the autumn conference of 2013. Considering this discussion as well as "the international and historical background" (SHA Kongresshandlingar 2014, 15), the board thereafter decided to continue ceremonial work. This was further strengthened in 2014, when the Norwegian Humanist Association decided to fund the expansion of humanist ceremonies in Sweden (Timmerby 2018).

The SHA and the interplay of social and organizational changes

The internal conflicts are to a great extent the result of the interplay between social and organizational changes. Social variations that have had and continue to have major impact on the SHA are processes of secularization and religious change in Sweden (as described in first section of this chapter). In addition, the internal situation within the SHA changed, with a high influx of members since 2005. The following section argues that it was these changes that came together to urge SHA members to move towards a re-orientation of humanist activism.

Social changes

In interviews, members state that the social changes that have decisively shaped the SHA include the separation of church and state in 2000 as well as the liberalization of the Church itself. To a large extent, this led to an alteration of the organization's objectives, since the separation of church and state and the fight against dogmatic and conservative Christianity have been among the SHA's main aims since its establishment. However, it is difficult to assess the actual role played by the SHA's continuous criticism of the church-state relationship with regard to its separation.[49] Around the year 2000, the SHA's influence on the formation of public opinion and political decisions was much smaller than today. Additionally, the liberalization of the Church made it partly obsolete in terms of being the SHA's dominant ideological opponent. Regarding some theological and moral questions, the Church of Sweden is perceived as being vague or nearly identical to the SHA's values. Thereby, an important part of the SHA's identity construction ceased to exist in its prior form, and this created a vacuum in the form of a gap that according to some members needs to be filled. At the same time, the separation of church and state opened up new possibilities for the Swedish Humanists in redefining parts of their identity. As the state church before 2000, the Church of Sweden occupied a dominant position that was unattainable for others. The law for faith communities, which is part of the legislation that replaced the former laws on the state church, placed the Church of Sweden on a legally equal level with other faith communities,[50] a change that opened up new possibilities for the SHA. Against the backdrop that all religious communities since 2000 have the right to be treated completely equally, they argue that only nonreligious life stances like secular humanism are still being discriminated against. This change might grant their demands for legal equality between religious and nonreligious life stances greater legitimacy and could open up new room in which the organization is able to maneuver. Additionally, this change provided the SHA a wider scope for action. A central part of SHA activism since the beginning has included emancipation work for nonreligious people and institutionalization as a secular life stance. Now, however, new and more realistic possibilities for being included in established structures, like those for faith communities, have emerged. The state decisively influences the structure of the religious field by granting privileges to officially recognized faith communities, while also exerting power over the constellation of the field. Proponents of the life stance understanding of humanism aim at becoming part of existing structures and changing them from within. In this regard, they seek to extend and transform the present religious field into a life stance field. Despite the fact that their numerous applications for getting accepted as a faith community (trossamfund) and receiving state funding were declined, they were successful with regard to other aims. Examples of their successes include a change in school curricula as well as changes to textbooks, as secular humanism is now explicitly included. Humanists have also been active as advisors (remiss instans) for law proposals that deal with topics related to religious and moral questions. Rather than arguing for life stance regulations and structures, proponents of a more political agenda want to realign the SHA towards new objectives, which, under these new circumstances, are more important in their view than those that focus on the Church. Some of their efforts aim at distancing themselves from their quite pivotal church opposition.

Organizational changes

Organizational changes also play a central role in explaining why the debates discussed in this chapter developed into decisive conflicts. Different SHA members' perceptions were visible as early as the 1990s: already back then, members had begun to split themselves between those who deemed criticism of religion to be central to their activism and those who placed a nonreligious social community and social activism, like secular ceremonies, at the center of the organization (Mattsson 1995). The perception that both strands of activism are incompatible with each other seems to have come about, or at least gotten stronger, among the active members with the membership influx since 2005 resulting from, as identified previously, the high visibility of Christer Sturmark, chairman of the SHA from 2005 until 2018, and the rising popularity of representatives of the so-called New Atheism (Thurfjell 2015, 98). During Sturmark's chairmanship, the number of members in the organization increased about fivefold. One interviewee described the organizational change connected to a change of chairmanship like this:

> And then also the movement was, as I have understood it, very, rather small. But the increase came with Christer Sturmark because he, as I said, was so active in the media, he's that kind of person, and that also, yeah changed then of course the, the membership became different, the opinions of the members became different.
> (Malte 2013, 509–13)

According to several interviewees, Sturmark's activist agenda, from the time he began his chairmanship in 2005 and the first years after it, focused in particular on religious criticism, fighting the bad consequences and influences of religion. Quite a few of those members gained interest in the organization when they took notice of Christer Sturmark's engagement in public debates and his display of secular humanism.

Malte is one of those members who became aware of the SHA because of Sturmark's presence in Swedish media "debating with priests and all kinds of people" (Malte 2013, 218–19):

> I thought that, okay, this organization sort of, also thinks like this about religion, that you should be actually skeptical towards it and that it's not so good for human rights as many people may believe, and it's important to discuss those issues, yeah so that I think was the reason I joined.
> (Malte 2013, 228–31)

Jana joined the organization around 2010 after listening to one of Sturmark's regular presentations about what secular humanism stands for. Specifically, with regard to the universality of human rights for which humanists advocate, Jana realized that they have "the same ground to stand on," adding that "they talked about human rights the way I see human rights" (Jana 2013, 46–7). Fighting cultural relativism by promoting human rights as universal is her driving motivation for activism. In the internal membership survey of 2013, 70 percent stated that they joined the organization in or after 2007. The reinforced efforts of other members to get secular humanism officially accepted as a life stance in existing structures developed for faith communities encouraged members of opinion-making humanism who joined the organization over the course of the last ten years like, Jana and Malte,[51] to question and challenge this approach more explicitly than ever before.

Some interviewees who belong to the group of those members who joined the association before Sturmark became chairman said that they, of course, also welcomed the membership increase that he brought about and value him as their chairman. At the same time, however, some disapprove of what they perceive as a primacy of rational thinking and a one-sidedness based on rationalism. The social side of humanism, on the other hand, has in their view been neglected in public debate and humanist activism. This communicated an oblique and one-sided image of humanism to the outside and in turn led to an increase in members who were mostly interested in the promotion of rationalism, secularism, and religious criticism (Gunnarson 2016, 12). The primacy of opinion-making work is discursively linked to Sturmark's display of humanism since 2005, not only by opponents of such an emphasis, but also by proponents of the same.[52]

The variations in membership at least partly explain why conflicts between those different understandings and positions have emerged. In this regard, Sturmark's influence and focus brought about a major change for the SHA. The internal membership change can already be regarded as a manifestation of changing times and activism. The perception of members of the secularized context they operate in coincides to a great extent, but the places they envision for themselves in this context differ. The two "camps" of members respond quite differently to the challenge of re-orientation. The previous analysis showed that not all members consider the diversity among members to be a strength, but that they see it as a weakness due to the fact that multiple understandings of humanism and foci might lead to multiple views, which, in turn, lead to multiple diverging forms of activism.[53] Different strands of activism may, accordingly, be perceived as being incompatible with each other under certain circumstances within the same organizational framework. Decisions on the topics in question will guide future development, and the lack of a settlement or decision might lead more members to resign from the organization.[54]

Summary and concluding remarks

The Swedish case study on secular humanism exemplifies how different groups of members of the same nonreligious organization can consider certain organizational foci as incompatible with each other or of central importance for activism, particularly in their combination.

In interviews, it becomes clear that SHA members share a general conception of the human being. They depict humans as having sides that respond primarily to rationality as well as those that respond primarily to feelings and social relations. Members agree that these sides are linked to each other, but the difference between *life stance humanists* and *opinion-making humanists* lies in their perceptions of how these sides interrelate, and which side of humans they should address as a humanist organization. LSH see the social side of human beings as something that in principle falls within the reach of humanists, as an area where they can perform valuable work in the form of ceremonies and counselling activities, for example. OMH, by contrast, do not regard this side as something that they should address or primarily focus on with regard to their organizational work as secular humanists.

In addition, questions of how secular humanists should relate to religion, and which relationship they should have with religious actors, lie at the heart of the described disagreements. The negotiation between proponents of the concept of humanism as a holistic life stance and those who advocate for humanism as a form of politically engaged opinion-making show that from the perspectives of their representatives, certain self-images and identity-related foci suggest that the organization should engage in certain kinds of relationships while they seem to rule others out. While LSH aim for a full-scale competition with religious actors like the Church of Sweden, OMH refrain from engaging in such competitive relationships. For OMH, the primacy of (religious) criticism and the conflicting relationships seem to be a natural consequence of their problem-oriented focus and the fact that they engage in issues that others, according to them, do not dare to speak about. In this regard, SHA's religion-relatedness, as well as the kinds of relations and their interplay in a certain assemblage, are contested among members.

Proponents of OMH are trying to move away from the religion-likeness they associate with the content and function of the internationally popular, and in Sweden, partly established logic of a holistic life stance that guides certain parts of humanist activism (LSH). They want to see the SHA transform into an organization that is independent of this logic, which developed in relation to religious associations, especially Christian churches. In connection with their desire to exclude the remaining activities that are based on such logic from organizational work, members in favor of OMH regard state structures, such as the one for faith communities, as unsuitable and inappropriate as an orientation point for their activism. They do not seek SHA's emancipation as a nonreligious organization in comparison to faith communities. The internal conflict within the SHA, in this regard, highlights the fact that members construe being religious, or religion-like, differently to some degree. OMH define religion and religion-likeness in relation to what they perceive to be functions and mechanisms of religion, its holistic character, and especially, the production of norms that deal with personal ways of living while also defining how a good life ought to look and what is worth being celebrated. In this regard, they criticize LSH for already being religion-like and for aiming to become even more so through an extension of, e.g., ceremonial work or applying for state funding on the same terms as faith communities. OMH instead only aim to promote and negotiate humanist values on a social level, instead of "get[ting] into all aspects of people's lives" (Malte 2013, 316).

From a field-theoretical perspective, LSH try to engage in competitive relationships with and play the same game according to the same rules as faith communities, while OMH emphasize that they are part of a different game. Therefore, OMH refrain from playing according to rules that apply to religious groups; adopting an established religious logic that would undermine their work. LSH and OMH strive for participation in different fields and established certain parts of their activism accordingly. LSH seek to transform and extend the religious field into a life stance field, which includes the religious and nonreligious on an officially equal basis.[55] Advocates of OMH, on the other hand, increasingly try to position themselves differently, as, e.g., experts in and promoters of science and critical thinking in the educational field, instead of visiting schools to promote humanist ceremonies or humanism as a nonreligious life stance alternative to religious ones. As an interest organization with an NGO-character, they aim to take a position differentiated from any religion-related or life stance-related logic, which implies a basic conceptional and/or functional similarity between secular humanism and religious life stances. However, they remain religion-related, e.g., through religious criticism.

OMH proponents are concerned that adapting to an established religious life stance logic they perceive to be in contradiction to their own self-understanding could undermine their work as well as their credibility when it comes to religious criticism. LSH advocates, on the other hand, regard an expansion of humanist activism towards a full-scale life stance and a comprehensive offering as the necessary next step in order to grow as a humanist community and movement. They not only perceive this approach to be the best strategy, but also as an essential part of all life stances.[56] For them, the competition linked to ceremonial offerings is a natural battle arena, but the participation in the same is neither what characterizes the religious field nor religion-likeness. Religion-likeness, in their view, is not so much based on the functions of life stances, e.g., that they fulfill certain needs of people, but that the content, the substance, of the same renders them religion-like.[57]

The examples presented in this chapter provide insight into the ways in which a shifting organizational focus as well as changing "(religious) others" are intertwined with organizational changes, such as a changing membership composition as well as social changes which, more generally, render certain foci "outdated" in the eyes of some members and urgent in the view of others. The religious criticism has to a large degree been shaped through processes of secularization and religious change. Throughout the 1980s and

1990s, religious criticism was for the most part directed at the Church of Sweden as the "religious other." Advocates of both understandings today regard the Church of Sweden as mostly liberal, unproblematic (measured in how dogmatic or illiberal religion, according to them, could be), and representing values that, to a great extent, overlap with those of humanists. The difference is, that based on their own understanding as a holistic life stance, LSH focus on the biggest and most influential remaining player in the field, which despite processes of secularization and religious change, remains the Church of Sweden. In this sense, today's mirroring activities, such as humanist ceremonies, understood as being a pivotal part of an effective competitive relationship, still address the Church, whereas (religious) criticism, which OMH focus on, addresses actors regarded as being far more religiously fundamentalist/dogmatic and/or dangerous than the Church, including actors who are perceived to represent, for example, New Age practices or postmodernist and relativist ideas.[58]

Notes

1 This chapter is an excerpt of my doctoral thesis "Secular Humanism in Sweden: Non-Religious Activism in 'One of the Most Secularized Countries in the World'" (in preparation).
2 World Value Survey, www.worldvaluessurvey.org/WVSContents.jsp?CMSID= Findings [20.07.2017].
3 Interviews were coded and interpreted using the grounded theory approach (Glaser and Strauss 2009).
4 SHA members often use the terms life stance and worldview synonymously. In relation to humanism, life stance (*livsåskådning*) seems, however, to be the more commonly used expression.
5 The longest uninterrupted Social Democratic rule lasted from 1932 to 1976, decades in which, besides other things, the Swedish welfare state was established.
6 In the thirty years from 1970 to 1999, an average of 14,418 members left the Church of Sweden every year, while in the seventeen years from 2000 up to and including 2016, the annual average of members leaving the Church of Sweden rose to 58,100 (Svenska Kyrkan 2016b). The separation of church and state in this regard is not only a decisive event in the organizational history of the Church, regarding its relation to the state and vice versa, but also shows in the number of people who are leaving the Church. The Church itself interprets the decline partly as a reaction of many people to their tax return and tax assessment ("Från och med 2001 utträder många i samband med deklaration och skattebesked." [Svenska Kyrkan 2016b, 2]).
7 In 2016, 33.7 percent of all marriages and 74.3 percent of all funerals were conducted by the Church of Sweden; 44.1 percent of all newborn children were baptized and 26.8 percent of all 15-years-olds were confirmed by priests of the Church of Sweden (Svenska Kyrkan 2016d).
8 Roman and Greek Orthodox Catholics, Jews, and Muslims have access to their own cemeteries (Jänterä-Jareborg 2010, 20).
9 Willander (2013, 124), referencing the European Value Study, conducted in Sweden in 2010.
10 Based on interviews from 2012 A. U., 1197–205, F. R., 799–800, L. E., 320–1, Berglund, 221–4, Pettersson, 825–6.

11 This answer was chosen by a relatively constant percent of the population throughout the thirty years and four executions of the European Value Study. The percentage of people who do not believe that there is some sort of spirit, god, or life force amount to 20 percent, and this might be considered relatively low for a "secularized country" such as Sweden (Willander 2015, 63, based on the data of the EVS of 2010).
12 Interestingly, based on the EVS data, Willander showed that this answer option is a widely chosen one, irrespective of whether the respondents are members of the Church of Sweden or not members of any religious organization (Willander 2015, 65).
13 People with a foreign background are defined in these statistics as persons who were either born in another country or whose parents were both born in other countries.
14 The SST statistic does not give insight into those faith communities who never applied to be officially recognized or those whose applications were rejected.
15 In 2011, the Mission Covenant Church of Sweden, the Baptist Union of Sweden, and the United Methodist Church of Sweden merged and formed the Uniting Church in Sweden (Equmeniakyrkan) (Equmeniakyrkan's webpage 2016).
16 This percentage is based on the SST statistic of 2014 in relation to the total Swedish population in 2014, 9,747,355 million people (SCB 2014).
17 Asked about their political preferences, 19.1 percent stated that they sympathize with the Liberal Party (Folkpartiet), 17.5 percent with the Social Democratic Party (Socialdemokraterna), 17.2 percent with the Moderate Party (Moderaterna), 13.4 percent with the Green Party (Miljöpartiet), 12.1 percent with the Left Party (Vänsterpartiet), naming only the ones that were chosen the most (Jansson 2013).
18 Other options to the question, "What do you consider yourself to be today?" next to "atheist" included "secularist," "agnostic," "other," "don't know," "religious seeker," and "religious believer." In addition to the 83 percent who stated that they consider themselves to be "atheists," 28 percent of SHA members ticked "secularists," 17 percent "agnostics," 3 percent "other," 1 percent "don't know," 0.4 percent "religious seeker," and 0.2 percent "religious believer" (Jansson 2013, 28, multiple responses were possible).
19 A secular society is, according to them, a "society in which all citizens have the right to exercise their life stance, alone or in group, provided that this does not conflict with the rights of others. No citizen is forced to adhere to or belong to a certain cultural custom or belief. A secular, open and democratic society is a prerequisite for life stance freedom for all" (SHA program of ideas 2016, 2).
20 Since 2012, the Swedish Humanist Association organizes a simultaneous alternative, secular opening ceremony taking place in Konstakademien in Stockholm. In 2016, the Riksdag, the Swedish parliament, officially recognized this secular offering as an equivalent opening ceremony to the religious one of the Church of Sweden, and included both on the invitations for the members of parliament (SHA webpage 2016a, 2016b).
21 SHA webpage (2017). Humanitär hjälpverksamhet.
22 Sturmark is a well-known figure in Sweden and a regular participant in public debates about the role of religion in society. He is known for his former occupation as an IT entrepreneur and his present work as an author and publisher. He is chief editor and head of the publishing house Fri Tanke. Among other things, they publish Swedish translations of books by so-called "New Atheists" such as Richard Dawkins, Sam Harris, Christopher Hitchens, and Lawrence Krauss.
23 In April 2018, Anna Bergström, a long-standing SHA member and researcher in the field of global health, took over the chairmanship of the SHA.

24 One SHA member pointed out that despite the benefits arising from "New Atheism," it also produced some kind of a negative "backlash" for the international humanist movement: the attention given to "New Atheism," according to him, together with the lack of a thorough discussion about the humanistic outlook and activism, created a "skewed picture" of those nonreligious alternatives that are available, which since then plagues humanist organizations (Gunnarson 2016, 12).

25 Media presence plays a key role in the visibility of the SHA in Swedish society. Next to presenting secular humanism in social media channels and online portals like Facebook, Twitter, and YouTube, members engage in discussions on their humanist blog (humanistbloggen.blogspot.com). Despite the decisive relevance of online activism, it is obvious that traditional media channels like the debate section in newspapers have not lose importance so far. Members of the SHA regularly spark or participate in discussions in some of the most renowned newspapers in Sweden, like *Dagens Nyheter*, *Svenska Dagbladet*, *Aftonbladet*, and *Expressen*.

26 Borg and Sturmark (2011).

27 While Palmstierna differentiates between a ceremony pillar and a life stance pillar, the former will be described as a central part of the latter, life stance pillar, in the following sections, based on the analysis of interviews with SHA members.

28 The narratives regarding "learning from religion" and what religion can "teach" humanists are part of recurring debates about how similar to religious organizations, in Sweden, especially the Church of Sweden, humanist organizations in general and in particular the SHA should be (Malte 2013, 245–61; Fragell 2002, 116).

29 Members of course are not necessarily interested in both the social work within society and social activities for SHA members: there are, for example, members who consider the social work within society as central to their activism but are personally only to a limited extent interested in a lively organizational or collective identity in the form of an internal humanist community. For the London Humanist choir, which is a part of Humanists UK, see: https://london.humanistchoir.org [11.12.2018].

30 In terms of a general moral compass based on human rights and the importance of critical thinking, life stance proponents principally agree with members who are rather in favor of a focus on opinion-making work, instead of social community activities.

31 All Swedish quotations from SHA members' publications and public statements have been translated into English by the author, if not noted otherwise.

32 "The humanist movement also wanted to move on with the positive view of life [livssynen] and its consequences in constructive, practical and social activities, as seen and widely appreciated as a more responsible role" (Gunnarson 2016, 12). The narrative of a "positive" worldview can also be found in relation to the New Atheists, who emphasize atheism as such and atheists as moral and good (LeDrew 2016, 119).

33 Such an inward-oriented focus can also be associated with the wider humanist movement, not necessarily registered members but people who engage in humanist activities more generally, as well as the exchange within the international humanist movement.

34 The personal data of interview partners were anonymized. Interviewees are quoted using newly given names.

35 Regarding human rights, SHA members especially refer to the UN Charter of Human Rights and the UN Convention on the Rights of the Child.

36 See Cimino and Smith (2007, 2014) about the minority discourse within the secular movement in the USA.

37 Ironically, the internal debate about the future development of the SHA partly led to the fact that matters of identity have been at the very heart of some OMH advocates' activism for some time, a fact that some of them self-critically noted in interviews.
38 The narrative of finding people, who "think the same way," "like-minded people," has been mentioned in interviews several times with reference to different aspects: members in this respect referred to, e.g., the same way to understand human rights as universal and individual rights as superordinate to any group rights, the same way to think about potentially harmful religious influences in society, and/or a "safe haven" for outspoken atheists and religious criticism (Jana 2013, 25–50, 636–7; Malte 2013, 227–31; David 2013).
39 In the previous section, we could nevertheless see that for some members it is not a question of prioritization, but a matter of contradiction to work towards both of these objectives simultaneously.
40 ". . . vi skapar kulturella uttryck som på ytan liknar de som människor i dagens samhälle känner igen, men fyller de med ett alldeles eget innehåll" (Damaschke and Ericsson Qvist 2013, 17).
41 The criticism of ceremonies is less directed against humanist confirmations/humanist youth camps, but rather against humanist welcoming ceremonies for children, weddings, and funerals, since they are perceived to be more religion-like. Humanist camps, where children spend one week together and discuss certain topics, including human rights issues, are considered less of a copy of Christian offerings, in this case confirmation rituals, than the life ceremonies such as weddings. Additionally, they are organized by a certain group of members, who are seldom humanist celebrants, whereas the other ceremonies are organized by celebrants.
42 Other topics of debate include questions about whether the SHA should receive state funding on the same terms as faith communities, and how they should represent themselves in public more generally, and in publications, at school visits and in textbooks more specifically.
43 It is not surprising that interviewees who are involved in the organization of humanist ceremonies themselves, e.g., as celebrants, are sympathizers and promoters of a humanism that dedicates its forces towards establishing humanist social work and a humanist community within society. There are, however, proponents of humanist ceremonies beyond that, for example, the people who made use of humanist ceremonies themselves or took part in one, as well as those members who are personally not interested in this offering but consider it a central and strategically important part of humanism.
44 Others might not even aim for abolition, but regard the humanist offering of ceremonies as a value in itself without further purpose. Some scattered voices, on the other hand, expressed assumptions and hope that in the future the demand for ceremonies will decrease altogether. For them, this strategy is only a temporary strategy, appropriate for present times.
45 Celebrants, on the other hand, argue that many people who participate in humanist ceremonies as visitors are surprised that such offerings even exist; a clear sign that humanist ceremonial offerings need further promotion (Rune 2013, 6).
46 This presentation took place at the member conference in autumn 2013.
47 "The representatives are only the persons that are . . . mostly active locally. And many of those people do not share my view. I think that I don't know but, I think that I have more support among the people that are just, ah, not active members, they joined the organization because they think it's important to be aware of those questions, like me. But they are not so interested in the life stance and so on, and therefore they are not so active I mean it's not, it's easy to believe that or reasonable that if you really want to have a gemenskap [community], that is in a life stance organization, if that is what you want, then you may be more

active in the organization than if you do not want that. So I think that my view is underrepresented among the active people in the organization. And that of course makes it more difficult to vote on it" (Malte 2013, 1024–51).
48 In their internal questionnaire, SHA members do not further specify what exactly is meant by a secular society.
49 Despite the fact that the Church maintained a semi-official role and monopoly positions in specialized areas.
50 See the section "Religious context Sweden."
51 Despite the fact that many members were motivated to join the SHA during that period by their interest in religious criticism and a focus on public debate, the motivations and interests of members can of course shift. Some members, who had been attracted to the SHA by activism regarding religious criticism, were and will presumably never be fond of social work, whereas others became interested in this part of activism over time and perceive it as an important part of humanism (Erik 2014, 253–61).
52 In contrast to those SHA members who focus mainly on opinion making humanism or life stance humanism, the SHA chairman positions himself in a way that allows supporters of both sides to identify with certain of his positions and activities while critically evaluating others.
53 Such diversity, and the difficulty of dealing with it, seems to be a common characteristic for nonreligious groups like the SHA. Members as well as people close to humanist and atheist organizations described the effort of bringing together members of such organizations, who value individuality very highly, as "herding cats" (Kirmer 2002, 138; Dawkins 2006, 5).
54 Several SHA members told me in interviews that they would leave the organization if the decision was made to extend ceremonial and social work more generally, or if the SHA would be funded on the same terms as faith communities (Leon 2014, 477–82). I also interviewed one former member who left due to tendencies in this direction (Ida 2013, 129–44). Others, on the other hand, stressed that they do not see the point of continuing with their humanist activism if ceremonial work would be abolished (Gran 2013, quoting Rune).
55 In, e.g., applications for official recognition and funding on the same basis as faith communities, SHA members argue that they fulfill the same functions as faith communities, besides others' care of souls ("själavard"), in the sense of "existential reflection and support, based on a life stance" (Sturmark et al. 2012, see also Sturmark 2014). Competition, however, can also seek the complete replacement and eradication of the other, which blurs the boundary and difference from a conflictual relationship (see Chapter 2, "Concept," section "Different kinds of relations").
56 Linked to the phrase "beating religion on 'its own territory,'" used in the conceptual chapter ("Concept," section "Tensions between different nonreligious positions"), this territory, if defined in functional terms and in relation to ceremonial work, might not be regarded as the legitimate territory of solely religion, in the LSH view, but also the territory of nonreligious life stances as well.
57 The central difference between religion and nonreligion for them is that most religions represent value conservative norms, that they establish rituals as a condition for participating in community life, that these offerings are potentially harmful due to their link to beliefs in transcendent phenomena, their often dogmatic and illiberal character, and their stiffness due to a lack of flexibility and openness for change. That is what in their view characterizes many religions, their offerings, and the religious field more generally. In their opinion, humanist ceremonies, on the other hand, reference only universal, liberal values, which are not harmful. Those references do not even need to be part of the rituals, if people would like to fill them with a different content (Rune 2013).

58 In all the relationships with religious actors like the Church of Sweden that emerged in the internal discussions, only a segment of the complex assemblage of relationships with multiple other actors were evident. The criticism in relation to/of the Church in practice can, but does not necessarily, resemble the criticism of other phenomena, such as the role and treatment of women in Muslim communities or the influence of postmodernist thought. Kinds of relations, like criticism or competition, with different others might be similar or vary with regards to certain aspects as well as in the intensity in which they are pursued in a certain context and time.

4 Collective nonreligiosities in the Philippines

*Alexander Blechschmidt**

Introduction

On December 7, 2013, I attended my very first LGBT Pride March, which took place in Metro Manila, the crowded and vibrant capital city of the Philippines. Two organizations, the "Filipino Freethinkers" or "FF" and the "Philippine Atheists and Agnostics Society" or "PATAS,"[1] on which I conducted my research, had been actively participating in the Pride March for several years. FF, PATAS, and all the other participating groups were arranged in alphabetical order according to their official names. During the march, I was thus constantly running back and forth to take photos of both FF and PATAS and talk to their respective members. This allowed me to observe something very interesting and telling. Several times, both FF and PATAS passed some of the religious protesters standing at the side of the street holding up their signs: "It's not ok to be gay, it's a sin!" "Gay marriage is NO marriage at all in the eyes of GOD," etc. At one point, when FF was walking by, one of the group's core members called upon the others: "Let's open their hearts!" and everyone in the group started to sing. In sharp contrast, some members of the other group, PATAS, started to shout loudly Nietzsche's famous proclamation: "God is dead!"

This ethnographic vignette from my fieldwork in Manila indicates that FF and PATAS share certain things, e.g. their strong support and activism for LGBT rights, as well as differ in important ways, such as in their particular approach towards their religious opponents. In this case study, I illustrate how the concept of local modes of nonreligion helps to approach these commonalities and differences between the two groups, which are located in the same cultural and urban context. As an adaptation of the

---

* **Alexander Blechschmidt** studied Cultural Anthropology, Biological Anthropology, and History of Science at the Georg-August-University Goettingen. From 2013 to 2016, he was part of the DFG Emmy Noether research group, "The Diversity of Nonreligion," and finished his PhD project on "The Secular Movement in the Philippines" at the Department of Social & Cultural Anthropology at the University of Zurich, Switzerland, in 2018. During his ethnographic fieldwork in Manila, Philippines, from August 2013 to May 2014, he was affiliated as a guest researcher at the Anthropology Department of the University of the Philippines (U.P. Diliman).

concept of "modes of religiosity" by the historian of religion Ulrich Berner, Quack introduced the term "modes of unbelief" in his study of the atheist organization *Andhashraddha Nirmulan Samiti* (ANiS) in Northern India. His description of an "ideal-typical" ANiS activist is based on ethnographic fieldwork among members of the group and has "to be understood in its Weberian meaning of assembling the most characteristic elements of a phenomenon (the activists of ANiS) which might not correspond fully to any given singular case (one specific rationalist)" (Quack 2012, 272–3). The concept was later refined – and redefined – as local modes of nonreligion as part of a larger conceptual approach (Quack 2014) that was again revised in this book (Chapter 2).

At the core of reconstructing the particular mode of groups like FF and PATAS lies an analysis of "a range of specific relationships to the respective religious field" (Quack 2014, 452). In the case of the Philippines, the latter is characterized by a strong dominance of the Catholic Church. Based on an empirical exploration of their diverse relations with religion, which become manifest in their members' discourses and practices in various concrete situations and contexts, the groups' general position in this regard can be described. I refer to this generalized religion-relatedness as their particular *collective nonreligiosities*. However, what the term modes of nonreligion in reference to a distinct empirical case emphasizes is the need to approach organized nonreligion as an embedded phenomenon, i.e. to see these groups' respective stance vis-à-vis religion – their *collective nonreligiosity* – as strongly integrated into their overall profile and agenda, and therefore interrelated to other constitutive elements like, for example, their organizational structure and membership composition, their foundational history, the social milieu of their members, and their socio-political activism, and further as shaped by their situatedness in a larger socio-cultural and historical context (cf. Quack 2012, 2014).

In the following, I will thus first provide a very brief overview of the country's Christian-dominated religious landscape and then introduce and situate FF and PATAS – as the main representatives of the local diversity of organized nonreligion – within this broader context. Following this, I will illustrate the multi-dimensionality of FF's and PATAS' *collective nonreligiosities* in more detail by looking at three different but interconnected dimensions in an exemplary manner: (1) the dynamics between their public discourse and their more internal positions and practices; (2) their "active" and "passive" relatedness with the religious field; and (3) their transnational connections and exchanges with like-minded groups and movements around the world, on an institutional as well as on an ideological level. On this basis, it will become clear that both FF's and PATAS' *collective nonreligiosity* is characterized by being continuously contested and negotiated among their members and is thus subject to potential change. I will describe such broader changes of both organizations and point out some of the factors that might have played an important role in this regard. Lastly, I will illustrate the relational embeddedness of FF's and PATAS' *collective nonreligiosity* in their respective overall profile and agenda by pointing out how it might be interrelated to its other aspects, in particular the (ascribed) social milieu of their members and the focus of their social activism. As mentioned previously, these other dimensions, which go beyond the groups' immediate relation towards religion, likewise form constitutive parts of their specific modes of nonreligion.

Being "nonreligious" in a "religious" country: a short contextual overview

When arriving in the archipelago's capital, Manila, for the first time as a foreign visitor, one might be astonished not only by the city's infamous traffic situation, which is "widely recognized as among the very worst around" (Lahiri and De La Cruz 2014, 19), but also by the omnipresence of religious symbols among the latter's very cause: one rarely finds a cab without wooden crosses or a crucifix hanging from the rearview mirror or little statues of the Virgin Mary on the dashboard, sometimes combined with Chinese religious ornaments; on "jeepneys," the Philippine's typical public transport vehicle, there are often colorful paintings of Jesus and other religiously themed images, while the interior is often decorated with banners like "God bless us"; during the ride, passengers frequently cross themselves when bypassing a church; on the bus, it is also possible to observe someone will suddenly stand and begin preaching in the aisle, firmly holding the Bible in his hands while the vehicle tries to find its way through Manila's congested streets – to name just a few examples.

"Religion" is not less visible in the metropolis's general architectural landscape (cf. Gomez and Gilles 2014): big churches and small chapels are spread throughout the whole city, be it the monumental *Basilica Minore de San Sebastian* in Quiapo, or the *Manila Cathedral* in Intramuros, the impressive, voluminous architecture of the *Iglesia Ni Cristo* headquarters in Quezon City – the northern part of the metropolitan area – or the so-called "Golden Mosque." Even at rather unexpected places, religious spaces can be encountered: the capital's famous meeting places for entertainment, consumption, and leisure activities – the huge shopping mall complexes spread all over Manila – are now vested with small built-in chapels providing people sacred air-conditioned sites for their spiritual needs.

But even without traveling to the Philippines, it is possible to come across the country's ascribed "vibrant religiosity" (Sapitula and Cornelio 2014, 3) via (social) media channels such as newspapers, YouTube, or Facebook. Images and videos of the well-known self-flagellations and crucifixions performed during Holy Week in Kapitangan or San Pedro Cutud, Pampanga, are now circulating globally. These ritual practices draw thousands of spectators – including both foreign and domestic tourists as well as journalists – annually to these small villages in the metropolis's surrounding provinces, and have thereby become large media events (Bräunlein 2012). When Pope Francis visited the archipelago in January 2015, his mass in Manila was extensively covered by local and foreign news stations, declaring it a "record for a papal gathering" (AFP 2015) because of its estimated 6 million attendees.[2] Held in the nation's capital region, too, but on a more regular basis, the famous Black Nazarene procession is not less impressive in terms of numbers: every year the religious event, certainly one of the biggest of its kind worldwide, attracts several millions of devotees to the ritualized carrying of the statue of Christ from Luneta to Quiapo Church – a procession that, despite the short distance, can last up to twenty-two hours, thereby, unfortunately, often causing injuries and even deaths among participants and spectators (cf. Paterno 2012).[3]

Given such impressive (public) displays – and further examples could easily be mentioned – of a seemingly impassionate "religiosity" in the local context, it is not surprising that the Philippines is commonly regarded, or referred to, as an overwhelmingly "religious" country. At least, when one looks at the official statistics on religious affiliation, this image of Philippine society seems to be more than confirmed: around 92.6 percent of the population subscribes to Christianity, which makes the Philippines – besides East-Timor – the only Christian-dominated country within the entire Southeast Asian region.[4] The vast majority, around 81 percent, of these Christian Filipinos, professes Roman Catholicism, which first was brought to the archipelago by European missionaries accompanying the Spanish colonization from the 16th century onwards. Protestantism, to which around 7.3 percent of the total population subscribe, entered the country mainly through American missionaries in the first half of the 20th century, in the wake of United States' colonial overtaking of the Philippines. Two churches, the *Iglesia Filipina Independiente* (IFI) and the *Iglesia Ni Cristo* (INC), which were both founded in the Philippines during the first half of the 20th century, count for 2.0 percent and 2.3 percent of Protestants, respectively. While Islam had arrived in the Philippines prior to the evangelization of most parts of the country via Spain and the US, Muslims today only account for 5.1 percent of the population with a majority of Sunnites, most of whom live in the Southern islands, Mindanao, and Sulu.

Leaving aside their obvious limitations, such official statistics substantiate further some of the aforementioned examples of the strong dominance of Catholicism. Catholicism in general and the Catholic Church in particular have, indeed, always played important roles in Philippine society and the nation's history. As social scientists and historians alike argue, this influence – which even extends into the political sphere – has to be seen in the context of a historically shaped, discursive "co-construction between Catholic identity and national identity," a process that Philippine scholar Natividad (2012) called "religio-nationalism."

Catholic Church hegemony? Religion, politics, and national identity

> Under a post-dictatorship political environment, the Church has become a virtual policy maker.
>
> (Leviste 2011, 9)

While other religious organizations are similarly seen to be politically influential to some extent, e.g. through the practice of bloc voting or the endorsement of certain political candidates (cf. Quilop 2011), what Leviste (2011) calls the "Catholic Church hegemony" has been at the heart of past and current debates on the relationship between religion and politics in the Philippine context (cf. Cornelio 2013). Despite the firm anchoring of the principle of a separation between church and state in the current Constitution of 1987,[5] the *de facto* impact of this Catholic Church hegemony has been underscored by various contemporary socio-political issues, e.g. constitutional amendments, environmental policies (Quilop 2011), or public health programs regarding HIV/AIDS (Apilado 2009). Furthermore, its imprint on the country's legal system is reflected, for example, by the nonexistence of a divorce law (Quilop 2011, 161, 166).

As indicated by the above quote from Leviste's study, the Catholic Church's prominent role and its particular relation towards the public and political sphere has to be seen in the light of the country's recent history. While Catholicism had already been intimately tied to Spaniards' political endeavors from the 16th century onwards, it also later became, somehow ironically, the "idiom" through which resistance against these very efforts were articulated (cf. Bräunlein 2008). Particularly, the Church's role in the popular uprising of 1986 and its interpretations are important in this regard. This crucial historical event, which became known as the "EDSA People Power Revolution," eventually led to the ousting of president/dictator Ferdinand Marcos. Millions of Filipinos followed the call of then archbishop of Manila, Cardinal Jaime Sin, to join a peaceful protest against Marcos' authoritarian regime and its "Martial Law" policy on one of the city's main streets, the *Epifanio De Los Santos Avenue* (EDSA). Thus, in this important incident, the Catholic Church and the "Catholic Bishops' Conference of the Philippines" (CBCP) appeared as actors for the "Filipino people" or, in other words, as actors for the re-installment and fostering of "democracy" (cf. Moreno 2006). This association shapes the public perception of the Church and its role in civil society to a considerable extent until this day: "Indeed," as Bautista puts it, "the contours of Church-state relations in the Philippines can be seen in the very idea of a 'People Power Church'" (Bautista 2010, 33–4). The active and constant reproduction of the "symbiosis of religion and the post-EDSA state" as incorporated in this Catholic People Power narrative are manifested in concrete ways, for example, in the EDSA shrine, which was built along the street in the aftermath of the historical event (Claudio 2013, 27ff.). It has been nurtured by the CBCP and its predecessor, the *Catholic Welfare Organization* (CWO), for several decades in pastoral letters and official statements, as Francisco (2014) shows in his genealogy of this "Catholic nation imaginary." This specific discursive context enables and legitimizes the Church as it presents itself as "the moral compass of the nation" in contemporary socio-political issues like the aforementioned decade-long controversial debate on reproductive health (RH) policies (cf. Bautista 2010; Claudio 2013; Natividad 2012; Racelis 2012).

"You are not alone!" Organized nonreligion in the Philippines

> With a strong Roman Catholic background
> brought about by 300 plus years of Spanish rule,
> professing atheism may well be social suicide.
>
> (*Sanchez 2008*)

It is this specific context, that is, the visibility and prominence of religion and its various symbols and manifestations in Metro Manila and the daily life of its inhabitants, the (statistical) vast majority of people with religious affiliation, the strong political influence of the Catholic Church, and the aforementioned discursively constructed "religio-nationalism," in which *non*religious groups are situated. As self-declared atheists, agnostics, secular humanists, etc., members of both FF and PATAS thus often report – on their organizations' websites as well as during the numerous conversations we had during my fieldwork – about the (negative) social consequences of their publicly professed unbelief. Offended friends and family members, associations and accusations of being "evil" or influenced by "Satan," discriminatory experiences in the workplace, etc., are frequently mentioned as common reactions in this regard. Similar to the section epigraph, which quotes a journalist, but in an even more drastic and provocative tone, one PATAS member under the pseudonym "Antonio ~" put it like this in his online article: "I am an atheist but I am unhappy because I am where I am. It is like being the only Jew in the Nazi party" (2012).

Statistically, self-declared *non*religious people, indeed, constitute a minority in the Philippines: recent estimations speak of 1 percent or less of the population (cf. Wilfred 2014). In fact, it is a common narrative of those FF and PATAS members who regard themselves explicitly as nonbelievers that before joining these groups they thought, "I was the only one." This strong feeling of being lonely or marginalized in a social environment perceived as dominated by "religion" led many of them to look actively for "like-minded" people, whom they eventually found in FF and PATAS. This underlines and points to the great importance of the "community" building dimension of such groups. The official website of FF, for example, emphasizes:

> Community is the lifeblood of Filipino Freethinkers. One of the most common things new members say to us is that they never knew there were others like them. It is undeniable that in the Philippines, non-believers are marginalized and experience disproportionate representation in the public sphere. However, even in their private circles, freethinkers experience discrimination and familial strife because of their beliefs or lack thereof. We aim to provide a venue where freethinkers have a voice and

have the opportunity to have fellowship with other freethinkers and to know that they are not alone.

(FF n.d.-b)

The last part of this quote resembles the slogan of a website called "SEA-Atheists.org" (site discontinued), which aims to provide "information about communities of non-believers in South-East Asia." Its front page declares, "You are not alone!," and some examples are given of what is meant by the term "non-believers": "Yes, non-believers: Atheists, Agnostics, Secular Humanists, Freethinkers, and with whatever name we choose [. . .]." For the Philippines, FF is listed on the website alongside PATAS. The latter group, similar to FF, also stresses the importance of providing Filipino nonbelievers a platform. The organization's official vision and mission statement, where the organization's purpose and aims are listed, establishes that PATAS is supposed to "set up a community" and "encourage camaraderie" as well as "fellow atheists and agnostics to be more visible, to speak against discrimination, and to provide support for the atheists and agnostics community" (PATAS n.d.).

These organized forms of nonreligion, supposed to provide marginalized nonbelievers a community and a platform to enter the public sphere on the ground of their identity as such – to give them "a voice" – must be considered, however, a recent phenomenon in the country. In contrast to other national contexts with long traditions of free thought, secular, and atheist movements, like, for example, India, the UK, or the US, the first groups in the Philippines with a similar outlook were to my knowledge established only in the 1990s. Since then, however, a plethora of groups and organizations has emerged,[6] especially after local access to the Internet became easier and the use of social media increased.

As indicated by their official websites, Facebook presence, forums, and YouTube videos, for FF and PATAS – as mentioned, the biggest and most active nonreligious organizations in Metro Manila at the time of my fieldwork – such digital channels have always been of great importance. It is mostly through web 2.0 that activities are coordinated and announced, and that current events are shared, discussed, or commented on. Both groups also, however, organize so-called "meetups," where members regularly meet face-to-face in order to discuss philosophical, ethical, and political topics, scientific discoveries, and current events in a more or less formalized way, as well as to have casual conversations afterwards over food and drinks.

In fact, it was this kind of meetup that brought FF into its very existence: the group was officially founded on February 1st in 2009 when twenty-six individuals came together at Starbucks in Shangri-La mall in Ortigas, a famous business district in the eastern part of Metro Manila, to meet and talk with like-minded people they had only become acquainted with from online discussions on several atheist mailing lists. Red, who initiated this very first meetup in order to encourage more such "offline" interactions among members of these digital platforms, is still the president and uncontested leader of what now has become, in their own words, "the largest and most active organization for freethought in the Philippines" (FF n.d.-a). While the meetups have always formed the basis, "the bread and butter," as Red put it in one of our conversations in order to emphasize their function as the group's irremovable foundation, FF later also became engaged more and more in socio-political activism, promoting, for example, LGBT rights. The public debate on the implementation of certain reproductive health (RH) policies in the country became one of the most important issues for FF in this regard, as I will outline in more detail later. Further, the group's members organize various other events based on FF's official slogan "Reason, Science, and Secularism" or "RSS" (see FF n.d.-a).

About two years after FF's foundation, the *Philippine Atheists and Agnostics Society* (PATAS) was established in February 2011. Some local activists regard it as an "offshoot" organization of FF. Both groups organize regular meetups, fight for common goals, and actively collaborate with each other on some occasions, and several of the activists I met during my fieldwork were or are members of both groups, i.e. they visit each group's gatherings and/or follow their respective activities, at least online. As indicated by my introductory remarks on the Manila Pride March, PATAS, too, strongly supports the LGBT rights movement. Aside from the regular participation at the march, the group's LGBT wing even formed its own subgroup called "Bahaghari Atheists and Agnostics Society" (BATAS) and organized several events under that name. Like FF, PATAS was also engaged in the aforementioned debate on reproductive health (RH) policies, fighting for the passing of the so-called "RH Bill," which proposed certain public measures in this regard. More recently, the group had decided to focus increasingly on humanitarian activities under the motto of "Good without God" in order to counter perceived public stereotypes about the "immorality" of nonbelievers. Its most ambitious project related to that was certainly the "Free Medical Clinic," which the group had organized several times in 2014 in poor neighborhoods around Metro Manila. Similar to FF, the promotion of "reason," "science," and "secularism" constitutes another building block of PATAS' agenda.

Against the "People Power Church?"

Researcher: "*Generally speaking, when I say 'religion in the Philippines,' what comes to your mind?*"
FF member: "*Uhm, the Catholic Church is the easiest one . . .*"
PATAS member: "*Well, the first religion that comes to my mind is Catholicism because it's the one that's very active politically in the Philippines . . .*"

These were some of the answers I got from my interviewees when I asked them about "religion in the Philippines." Considering the particular shape of the local religious field as sketched out previously and as the quotes underscore, it might not be overly surprising that it is the dominance and prominence of the Catholic Church – or, the "People Power Church" – that represents the main target of the criticism articulated by both FF and PATAS.

However, their criticism is based on slightly different grounds, at least in their official discourse. FF – composed not only of "non-believers" but also of "progressive believers," as stated on their website – criticizes the Church mainly as a hierarchical institution deemed as "dogmatic" and as constantly violating "secularism," the constitutionally anchored separation of religion and state. This becomes clear, for example, in an interview with Red Tani, the founder and president of FF, and Kenneth Keng, an Episcopalian and long-time member of FF, in which the journalist Katrin S. Santiago (2012), who had just attended a public forum organized by FF in 2012, told them: "You guys are labeled radical anti-Catholic Church activists." Red replied: "I want to make it clear: anti-Catholic Church hierarchy." When Santiago further told her interviewees about the "discomfort" she had felt while listening to FF for the first time at the forum, because – as she put it – "it sounded like at its core was just anti-Catholicism," Kenneth countered: "We say that FF is anti-any-ideology that puts at its forefront the systematic oppression of women and of minorities and of their rights. And in that sense the largest most obvious institution that does this with the most degree of non-accountability would be the Catholic Church in this country." What Kenneth specifically refers to in this passage is the aforementioned controversy over reproductive health (RH) measures as proposed by the so-called RH Bill, which later became the RH Law. That the bill could not be turned into law and implemented for more than a decade is ascribed largely to the Catholic Church's resistance to it. Its official public organ, the "Catholic Bishops' Conference of the Philippines" (CBCP), "represented the most vocal and consistent opposition from any institution to every government legislation and program on reproductive health matters" (Francisco 2015, 225). To many observers, scholarly and otherwise, the debate about RH policies thus exemplifies the particular and very complex relationship of church and state in the country, as outlined before. As Red Tani told me, when I asked him in our interview about how FF became engaged in this debate as a group, "after several discussions and debates internally, we decided that supporting the RH Law, or the RH Bill back then, was something that would be in line with our reason-science-secularism thrust. You know, it has all the rational arguments for it, scientific and statistical evidence for it . . . and most of the arguments against the RH Bill were just very theocratic in nature. So, like a win for RH would be a win for secularism, and, of course, reason and science" (Interview with Red Tani, FF 2014).

In contrast to FF, PATAS is more explicitly focused on promoting atheism among society and more exclusive with regard to its membership. As the organization's "membership qualifications" underscore, to become a member an individual must identify "as either an atheist or an agnostic" and support the group's vision and mission in order to qualify. As a self-declared group of nonbelievers, PATAS can and does attack the Catholic Church more fundamentally than does the FF. To them the Church is only the main institutional representation of what they see as the root cause of many of the country's problems: religion as such.

This distinction of FF being more focused on the issues of "secularism," while the focus of PATAS lies more explicitly on "atheism," is actively drawn by members of both groups themselves. When I asked, for example, FF's president Red Tani during our interview about the distinguishing factors between the two groups, he told me:

> Well, when it comes to PATAS, it's, of course, primarily their exclusive, ehm, being exclusive to atheists and agnostics. And also they have a more antireligious, anti-theist trajectory, or purpose, you know. They need to talk about religion more than we do. So, we don't necessarily promote atheism, they do. And the topics that they discuss are more atheist-taken, anti-theistic than ours.
> (Interview with Red Tani, FF 2014)

Almost complimentary to Red's answer is the characterization I received from the then-president of PATAS, Tess Termulo:

> Well, Filipino Freethinkers, they're more of, they're central [. . .], if I should say, is secularism. So, they're more after the political issues connected to secularism and they do not really advertise themselves as atheists, although a lot of them are atheists [. . .].
> (Interview with Tess Termulo, PATAS 2014)

In other words, while it is possible to claim that both groups – FF and PATAS – certainly represent recent manifestations of a long tradition of "church criticism" specifically targeting the local Catholic Church, FF largely remains – "publicly" at least, as I will discuss in more detail later – within this tradition, while PATAS, in contrast, articulates its focus and emphasis on "atheism" as a more explicit form of "criticism of religion."

While this initial characterization and distinction – "secularism" vs. "atheism," "church criticism" vs. "criticism of religion" – provides a helpful general picture of FF's and PATAS' stance on, and approach towards religion, and in particular towards the Catholic Church, in the following I want to complicate this picture. In fact, as I will illustrate, all of these dynamics and tensions manifest in both groups' discourses and practices.

The multi-dimensionality of "collective nonreligiosities"

> *If one of FF's goals was the active promotion of atheism,*
> *then I most probably wouldn't be part of it,*
> *because I'm not an atheist.*
> (Kenneth Keng, member and Reproductive Health Advocacy Director of FF, in Santiago 2012)

In the second half of the introduction round at a regular FF meetup, two guys – both apparently first-time attendees – introduced themselves as "Muslim" and "Catholic" respectively. They added, with a mixture of amusement and insecurity, that they somehow felt "out of place." Red and some other FF members were quick to try and convince them that there was no reason for such a feeling, since "religious" people are, indeed, very welcome at the meetups. In consideration of the group's particular composition, however, their reaction is understandable. During all of FF's regular meetups I was able to attend during my stay in Manila, *most* people introduced themselves with terms like "atheist," "agnostic," "agnostic atheist," "secular humanist," etc. The first half of the introduction round at the meetup mentioned here was no exception in this regard – hence, the two "religious" attendees' impression of being "out of place."

"Yeah, it can seem a little off-putting, just because the majority of the membership is nonreligious," Kenneth Keng told me when we talked about this incident. Despite being an Episcopalian, and thus one of the few "religious" members himself, Kenneth identifies strongly with the group and its aims – precisely because the explicit or "active" promotion of atheism is not part of its agenda, as he made clear in another interview with the local news station GMA, from which the section epigraph is taken. "It used to be that I was the only religious person in the group," he continued, "but now we have a number of them, and they *do* come, and we have another couple in the core group for consultation and stuff – so yeah, it's slowly starting. . . . But I will admit that it could be somewhat off-putting" (Interview with Kenneth Keng, FF 2014).

That FF is first and foremost a group both for and of self-declared *nonbelievers* of various kinds – and is widely perceived as such – is, of course, not entirely surprising. As described, FF evolved from online "atheist" mailing lists. At the same time, however, the organization also attempted *not* to be an exclusive atheists' or nonbelievers' organization from its earliest days. As the official website declares, FF is a "group of non-believers and progressive believers in the Philippines," although the latter label specifically refers only to a certain group of "believers," i.e. those with rather liberal or progressive views on particular issues. That FF, in fact, has been able to attract such "progressive believers" is illustrated, for example, by Kenneth's long-term membership. He has been FF's official "Reproductive Health Advocacy Director" for a long time now – an internal position it is hard to imagine a more conservative believer would be willing to hold.

These short glimpses into some of the discussions and dynamics to be considered when approaching FF's general stance on "religion" illustrate that there is not only a certain heterogeneity of individual opinions and views among members, external observers, or opponents, but that there are also various dimensions, where such positions are manifested in different ways. In the following sections, I will point out some of these dimensions in an exemplary manner, first by presenting further empirical data and ethnographic observations on FF's ambivalent relation with religion, before turning to PATAS and its particular position in this regard.

On "public talk" and "internal discursive realities on the ground"

In this section, I will explore the multi-dimensionality of FF's *collective nonreligiosity* by discussing what Dominik Müller, in his study on the youth wing of the Islamic political party PAS in Malaysia, has described as "the dynamic relationship between the two different levels of official public talk and internal discursive contestations on the micro-level" (Müller 2014, 113). Approaching the latter through ethnographic fieldwork, e.g. by attending the regular so-called *usrah* meetings of PAS, during which religious education is combined with discussions about the party's political and public strategies, Müller recognized the "significance of such informal processes of deliberative will-formation behind closed doors, which take place in *usrahs* and elsewhere, where the strict norms of public behavior do not apply" (Müller 2014, 113; italics in original). His "access to PAS' internal discursive realities on the ground" thus proved to be crucial for a more adequate understanding of "community creation and interactive deliberation of normative orders" among the party's members (Müller 2014, 113). Similarly, as I have illustrated and will show in more detail in the following section, what I observed during the regular FF meetups I attended during my fieldwork in Manila indeed allows for a more complex picture of the group's general positioning vis-à-vis religion. Like PAS' *usrah* meetings, FF meetups provide its participants both an important venue for articulating their mostly *non*believer identities and thus for creating and confirming a corresponding "like-mindedness," while, at the same time, contesting this "atheist" character of the group, thus underlining the ambivalence of FF's relationship with religion.

In fact, this ambivalence is already manifested in the group's very name: "freethinkers." In her famous history of the freethinking movement in the United States, scholar and activist Susan Jacoby states that while "[o]ften defined as a total absence of faith in God, freethought can better be understood as a phenomenon running the gamut from the truly antireligious [. . .] to those who adhered to a private, unconventional faith revering some form of God or Providence but at odds with orthodox religious authority" (Jacoby 2004, 4). What she calls the "inclusiveness" of freethinking groups regarding their membership is also what made Red Tani choose the name "Freethinkers" when he founded FF back in 2009. In our interview, he said that "there were agnostics, there were deists, pantheists, some religious people there, so we couldn't use the word 'atheist' fairly to represent everyone in the group" (Interview with Red Tani, FF 2014). In another interview – the one with the local news station GMA, in which Kenneth made clear that he supports FF as a "believer" – Red Tani, the founder and president of FF, likewise emphasized that this is "a common misconception that we are focused on atheism. [. . .] But it's not that we have as a goal the promotion that there is no God" (in Santiago 2012). In these concrete contexts, FF members clearly stressed the inclusive character of FF – according to whom the group should *not* be considered as an exclusive atheist or nonbeliever organization.

However, as mentioned previously, FF's "internal discursive realities on the ground," e.g., its regular discussion meetups and the informal post-meetup gatherings, make it difficult to uphold and implement this claim to inclusiveness as it appears in such public comments. Here, it is exactly the explicit atheist or nonbeliever character of the group that becomes particularly apparent, bringing the aforementioned ambivalence in this regard to the fore. These formal get-togethers seemingly provide members a kind of "safe space" for the articulation of their identities as nonbelievers – a space they lack in other contexts, as I was often told. In the introduction rounds at every meetup, this articulation takes a formalized, or an almost ritualized form. When I asked Red why meetup participants – especially, when it is their first time attending – are prompted to mention their "belief system" and their journey towards it, he told me:

> We do that because we know that a lot of people don't do that. Like, you rarely get to share how your beliefs changed, or like for some people, they rarely come out, you know, you rarely say: 'I'm an atheist now and this is how it happened . . .'; or 'I'm a progressive Christian now and not a fundamentalist or very conservative Christian now and this is how it happened.' You don't get to do that, like you know that yourself, but we assume that a lot of people haven't articulated it. So, now you get to articulate it in public and it feels good to do it, I mean for you it feels good to come out, to own your beliefs. And it's also good to hear these stories, I mean it's kind of a topic in itself, like hearing people, the journey that people have, because doing that makes people reflect on their own, they hear some stories and then they remember theirs, and they're kind of reminded that they weren't always maybe atheist or whatever [. . .].
>
> (Interview with Red Tani, FF 2016)

As illustrated by the aforementioned two religious attendees' feeling "out of place," most FF members' current "belief system" consists of an explicit form of unbelief. Being able to relate to each other's stories and experiences as nonbelievers in a country generally regarded as overwhelmingly religious by the group's members certainly contributes to the community building and strengthening of such a collective nonbelievers' identity. The great importance that is commonly attached to the act of "coming out" – thereby, not coincidentally, resembling the gay and lesbian rights movement (cf. LeDrew 2016, 130) – and the possibility to do so in a "safe" environment point to the fact that such an identity is based on a rather marginalized worldview in Philippine society, as it is in other contexts like the United States (cf. Cimino and Smith 2014). Furthermore, this institutionalized form of talking about one's "belief system" during the introduction round is complemented by numerous conversations in the more informal context of the post-meetup gatherings. Here, in a relaxed atmosphere over food and drinks, people often share – with amusement, curiosity, or outright anger – their experiences on an even more personal and intimate level and express their thoughts and views on related issues like the involvement of the Catholic Church in Philippine politics.

In fact, it is humor in particular that seemingly constitutes an important venue for FF members to express religious criticism and reaffirm each other's "like-mindedness." Jokes about religion and the Church are quite common. At one of the meetups of the southern chapter, FF Metro Manila South (MMS), for example, members were asked in the introduction round to mention their favorite *fiction* book from their high-school days. One of the attendees shouted: "The Bible!" thereby provoking laughter among the others. A bit later during the same meetup, the topic "Special treatment for religious organizations in/by the government" was discussed. One member pointed to the case of child abuse by the Catholic clergy to illustrate his statement that religious people, who commit such crimes, could get away with it too easily. Another member then added sarcastically that a nice way for revenge would be "to infiltrate the Church with HIV-positive altar boys."

While self-declared religious people are, indeed, welcome at the meetups, it is not only a rare occasion; it also sometimes seems to function as a reinforcement of the *non*believer's identity of the majority of the group's members. At another meetup of the MMS chapter, for example, *Ben,[7] who had attended a few meetups before, shrugged his shoulders when it was his turn to introduce himself to the other meetup attendees and to mention his "belief system." "Still Catholic . . ." he apologized tongue-in-cheek, provoking laughter among the others. "We don't mind!" *Tony assured, and gave an amused grin. At a previous FF MMS meetup, Ben had mentioned that he would like to invite some of his "religious" friends, so that they would have the chance to understand what type of persons "freethinkers" really were. "To understand," he emphasized, before adding in an ironic tone, "Not to fight!" Ben also admitted that he himself had certain prejudices about "freethinkers" before he actually attended any FF meetups, imagining that they were "influenced by evil." This led the other attendees – visibly amused about his confession – to mention and make fun of what they regarded as some of the most common misconceptions about atheists and nonbelievers in Philippine society.

These examples from the internal contexts of FF show that, while on an official level the group might not be propagating "atheism" or "nonbelief," its actual composition and the internal discourses and practices still contribute to a reproduction and strengthening of a certain identity, which for the vast majority of FF members is based explicitly on various forms of *non*belief. The dynamic between FF's public positions and internal practices in terms of religion is, however, only one dimension of the group's *collective nonreligiosity*. Strongly intertwined with it is another dimension, which could be called the relationship between its "active" and "passive" religion-relatedness, to which I will now turn.

On relating and being related to religion

Despite its members' efforts to counter FF's image as an exclusive atheist organization – as illustrated, for example, by Red's and Kenneth's comments in the previously quoted interview with GMA – the group, indeed, seems to be perceived as such from "the outside." In a recent scholarly volume on "Atheist Identities," for instance, the editors provide an exemplary list of "atheist organizations" from around the world in their introduction (Beaman and Tomlins 2015). Interestingly, it is FF and not PATAS that is listed there. In addition to this, some members themselves mentioned that they considered FF a group of atheists before they actually joined the organization. During one post-meetup dinner, for example, I was talking to *Jannice, a first-time attendee on that day. She admitted: "I was prepared to defend my faith." Still believing in a god or a godly creature herself, she had expected "to be tested" at the meetup by other members of the group. Another interesting case happened in the context of Pope Francis' visit to the archipelago in January 2015, which was extensively covered by local and foreign news stations. Red Tani published an article in one of the biggest English-speaking national newspapers, the *Philippine Daily Inquirer*, with the title: "Why I don't like Pope Francis" (Tani 2015). About one week later, the newspaper published a letter from "a faithful reader" with "a high regard for the Inquirer," who firmly expressed his dissatisfaction with the editors' decision to publish Red's article. In his letter he refers to FF as "a small group of atheists" whom – in his opinion – should not be given such space to voice a minority view (Gomez 2015).

Whether the group's atheist image is appropriate or not, what is crucial here is that FF reacts on the basis of how they think they are perceived by the wider public. Or, in other words: the way they *are* related to religion ("passively") in some contexts shapes the way they themselves ("actively") relate to it in other contexts. Consider, for example, the following quote from my interview with Kenneth Keng, in which I asked him about how he thinks FF was perceived as a group:

> Publicly perceived it seems to be, despite our efforts to the contrary [. . .] depends how hard working that public is, like if they seem to have studied the group, looked at it, then they'll, then they can see like, you know, the secular leanings [?], whatever. . . . But, like the easy, cursory examination would show it to be like 'angry atheists' – which we do acknowledge as a problem.
>
> (Interview with Kenneth Keng, FF 2014)

As quoted previously, it was in the interview with GMA that Red Tani similarly spoke about the atheist image of the group as a "common misconception."

It is, however, not only in such public contexts that FF's atheist identity is identified as "a problem" or a "misconception" and is as such contested or debated. While the meetups, as I have described before, mainly *reproduce* the nonbeliever identity of the majority of the group's members, they provide at the same time a platform for actively discussing FF's stance in this regard, for contesting and challenging its atheist image, and for deliberating the group's general positions and strategies. At one of the meetups I attended, Red asked the attendees, for example, about how they would like FF to evolve as a group. One regular participant, who identified as an atheist himself, complained about the fact that the group consisted mainly of *non-religious* people. Instead, he would prefer a greater diversity in this regard. Pointing towards Kenneth Keng, who was attending the meetup as well, Red replied tongue-in-cheek that FF was already practicing some "affirmative action." He then called upon the meetup participants, now in a more serious tongue, to point out to their friends and relatives that FF is *not* an exclusive atheist or agnostic club.

While so far I have drawn only on examples from FF in order to illustrate some of the dimensions and dynamics to be considered when reconstructing such an organization's *collective nonreligiosity*, I will now turn to the other group, PATAS, and its members, in whose discourse another important dimension becomes particularly apparent.

On transnational connections and dynamics

At one of my first PATAS meetups at the organization's headquarters located in Quezon City, the northern part of Metro Manila, I was proudly shown the collection of books by the evolutionary biologist and popular science writer Richard Dawkins, which form an important part of the group's own library. "Only two are missing," I was told while looking at the white-board shelves in front of me, all filled up densely with more than a hundred books. Right below the bunch of books by Dawkins I discovered a framed and personally signed picture of the neuroscientist and philosopher Daniel Dennett. "To PATAS . . ." is written on the photograph.

Dawkins and Dennett, whom the historian of science Peter J. Bowler calls "the champions of atheistic Darwinism" (Bowler 2007, 198–9) because of their naturalistic views on human evolution and social behavior, are – together with the publicist Christopher Hitchens and the neuroscientist and philosopher Sam Harris – commonly regarded as the main representatives of the so-called "new atheism." Sometimes ironically referred to as the "Four Horsemen," all four of these authors have published bestselling books in which they present a rather uncompromising critique of religion and its organized manifestations. The "new atheists" and their books had not only provoked almost immediately a large body of "apologetic" responses, but also aroused a growing interest among social scientists (cf. Amarasingam 2010). Some recent works have focused on specific aspects of the "new atheism," e.g., its role in self-proclaimed atheists' individual trajectories to nonbelief and its functioning in atheist groups' collective identity constructions (LeDrew 2013), its political dimensions (Kettel 2013; Plessentin 2012), or its manifestations in different national contexts (cf. Zenk 2012 for Germany). Cimino and Smith, who have studied the reception of the "new atheism" among members of secular and atheist organizations in the US, assert that the "new atheist books – and the enormous amount of secondary literature that interest in them has generated [...] – have succeeded in familiarizing much of the world with atheism" (Cimino and Smith 2010, 148).

An analysis of how the "new atheism" discourse is appropriated and articulated by members of PATAS, which I will provide in the following section at least in a rudimentary way, not only adds to these studies, but it also nicely illustrates the importance of the fact that many of these nonreligious groups, though located in sometimes rather different cultural contexts, are often very well integrated into such transnational networks and discourses. When reconstructing their relation towards religion, these dynamics thus have to be taken into account.

It was not only in the previously described materialized or symbolic form that I came across the "new atheists" during my fieldwork among members of FF and PATAS. Dawkins in particular is very prominent in the general PATAS discourse. In PATAS writings by co-founder and former chairwoman, Marissa Langseth (2011), who had met the British bestselling author and public intellectual personally, he is attached with great importance to the group's formation and motivation:

> I attended my first American Humanist Association conference in Cambridge, Massachusetts, USA, to see Richard Dawkins in person. He is the driving force of our group and our hero. I was successful in meeting him and have photos galore with him. These pictures were so valuable that our group in the Philippines tripled in no time. Must be Richard Dawkins.

Furthermore, on a more individual level, Dawkins (2006), as well as his controversial book, *The God Delusion*, often play a significant role in PATAS members' narratives on their personal nonbelief journeys. In his article, "My journey to godlessness" (Batista 2012), the author and PATAS member writes:

> Then I heard about this book called "The God Delusion" by Richard Dawkins. Got lucky to have bought a book then started reading it more than once and it awakened me further. I was not really that in depth in knowing what atheism really is before [I] read that book.

Apparently, for a young self-declared atheist, whom I met at the end-of-the-year celebration that PATAS had organized in December 2013, *The*

God Delusion has likewise been of great importance for his own unbelief. Dawkins was his personal "idol," and, as he further told me with a proud smile on his face, even one of his classmates had already begun "to doubt" after he gave her *The God Delusion* to read. Another PATAS member (under the pseudonym "Waking Nomad") reflects in an article on the group's website about how Dawkins' book, in which he "found a sample '10 Commandments' on how to live one's life," inspired him with regard to his own work as a science teacher: "The last commandment from the list is the one I always remind my students about; and that is to 'question everything'" (Waking Nomad 2012). In January 2014, long-time activist, co-founder, and former president of PATAS, John Paraiso, even hosted a public book discussion on *The God Delusion*. In his introductory speech, he explained why the organizers had chosen Dawkins' controversial book for the event. It was considered the "atheist bible" and was quite popular among nonbelievers here in the Philippines. Many had bought it, but not all of them have also actually read it, John added. What followed then was a lively discussion among the more than thirty attendees, sometimes drifting away from the book towards general assessments on the current situation of nonbelievers in the Philippines. While the views and thoughts on *The God Delusion*, not surprisingly, varied individually and thereby mirrored the ambivalent reception of the "new atheism" among like-minded groups in the US (cf. Cimino and Smith 2014), what became clear during the event was that these books, indeed, "provide nonbelievers a general canon with which to unify, dissent, and, most importantly, communicate with one another" (Cimino and Smith 2014, 83).

The formative potential of the "new atheists" on an ideological level further becomes visible in PATAS' enthusiasm and propagation of "science," "reason," and "rationalism" as the only reliable basis for the production of new and valid knowledge. These terms are thereby often mentioned in direct opposition to religion, which on the other hand is regarded as irrational, dogmatic, or backwards, relying solely on belief rather than evidence and reasoning. While many atheist, humanist, and freethinking groups around the world, past and present, frame and framed science and religion as strongly contradicting and irreconcilable phenomena, the "new atheists" might currently be considered as the most prominent proponents of such a view. In his historical contextualization of the contemporary atheist movement, LeDrew (2012) thus describes the discourse of the "new atheism" as representing a particular strand or tradition in the development of atheist thought: "scientific atheism." Looking at the PATAS discourse, one can find many instances where such a form of scientific atheism – "built on the premise that religion is the antithesis of science" (LeDrew 2012, 84) – is articulated. In one of the early documents published on the official PATAS website, the group's aforementioned former president, John Paraiso (2011), for example, wrote: "Let's face it, science will not compensate God but science is a threat to God. As science fills the gap with knowledge, the God of the Gaps is being kicked out. As more gaps are being filled, God is slowly left without a home." Similarly, another contributor to the website stated in his "Journey to godlessness" that "the more I appreciate[d] science the more I was convinced that there is really no god" (Batista 2012). Explicitly referring to Richard Dawkins, another PATAS member, Junn Dobit Paras (2011), clarifies in his "Story of my atheism:" "I believe what Richard Dawkins said, that evidence is only the reason to believe in something. No evidence? No talking snake or God."

While there is still a need for further and comparative reception studies on how the "new atheism" discourse actually manifests in local discourses of nonreligious groups around the world and potentially influences their positions and practices (cf. Lee 2015, 63), the case of the Philippines seems to underline what sociologists Cimino and Smith have emphasized in their aforementioned study on the atheist movement in the US: "Taken collectively, the books represent a vernacular in which a diverse and potentially global [. . .] population of secularists may invent and imagine their identities, narratives, and traditions" (Cimino and Smith 2014, 83). Thus, what the ethnographic observations and examples here have shown is that the general relation of groups like FF and PATAS to religion, their *collective nonreligiosity*, has to be seen in the context of their members' appropriation and articulation of such global discourses.

However, it is not only the ideologically formative potential of the group's integration into transnational networks that is of great importance, it is also the institutional dimension of such connections. From the beginning, PATAS was very successful in establishing cooperation with several likeminded groups around the world, e.g. *Atheist Alliance International* (AAI). Furthermore, PATAS became an official member of the umbrella organization *International Humanist and Ethical Union* (IHEU) and got connected to its youth wing, the *International Humanist Ethical Youth Organization* (IHEYO). These institutional connections proved to be very supportive on a financial level: PATAS was able to organize two large conferences in Manila in 2012 and 2015, and one in Cebu City in 2013, co-sponsored and attended by international guests from these and other nonreligious groups from Asia and beyond. That these international cooperative relations – on a personal, financial, and ideological level – may, indeed, shape these groups' religion-relatedness to a considerable extent and contribute to some broader changes in this regard, will be further discussed in the next section.

The contested and shifting nature of "collective nonreligiosities"

Dominik Müller, whose work on the Islamist party, PAS, in Malaysia I have quoted previously, has shown how PAS has undergone a recent cultural transformation, more specifically a "pop-Islamist reinvention" (Müller 2014). This change was, as he argues, influenced by some "internal factors" like generational changes and related conflicts within the party's leadership as well as by "wider societal tendencies," e.g. the "massive rise in the popularity of modern Islamic mass consumption" (Müller 2015, 339) and the competitive relationship with other political parties, especially the "United Malays National Organisation" (UMNO), with which PAS is engaged in a "pop-cultural competition" (Müller 2015, 337). Drawing on the work of political theorists Forst, and Günther on "normative orders," Müller conceptualizes these dynamics inside PAS accordingly as a "normative change." Sustained by so-called justification narratives, which can be disputed and questioned, such "normative orders" are thus themselves "by definition, negotiated and contestable. They can be challenged, changed or even abandoned by reconsidering their underlying justification narratives and establishing alternative counter-narratives" (Müller 2015, 320). The previously mentioned PAS *usrah* meetings are especially important in this regard. While, on the one hand, they function as "a ritualized practice which is particularly vital for the creation of community and like-mindedness" (Müller 2014, 110), these meetings, on the other hand, "can furthermore act as test sites for innovative and potentially transgressive ideas, or starting points for significant changes in the party's political behavior" (Müller 2014, 112).

As indicated by the previously described observations and examples of various concrete positions on religion articulated by members of FF and PATAS in different contexts, e.g. their regular meetups, the *collective nonreligiosity* of the two organizations, respectively, has likewise to be seen not only as constantly reproduced, but also as being continuously contested, negotiated, and debated among their members, and is, thus, potentially shifting. In the following sections, I want to argue that such a shift can, indeed, be identified and described for both groups when looking at them from a more long-term perspective.

Similar to political parties like PAS, nonreligious groups and their general stance on religion have to be seen as situated in and shaped by a whole web of relations to other actors and their respective positions, which includes not only those in the local religious field, e.g., in the case of FF and PATAS, mainly the Catholic Church and the CBCP, but also those in the religion-related field. The latter comprises, for example, other like-minded groups, both the ones situated in the same local context and – as nicely illustrated by the transnational connections of PATAS – also some organizations from other countries. Analogous to Müller's observations on PAS and its "normative changes," I want to point out how some of these complex relations might have contributed to the aforementioned broader shifts in the *collective nonreligiosity* of both FF and PATAS, briefly discussing some of the important "internal" as well as "external" factors in this regard.

As mentioned previously, the initial idea behind the foundation of FF in 2009 was to bring together members of several atheist mailing lists active at that time. The group thus was first and foremost a group for and of *non*believers to discuss and exchange ideas with each other in "real life." The core rationale behind FF – providing a community for such nonbelievers – is clear, for example, when looking at one of the group's earliest campaigns. As described in a post on the FF website (Tani 2009) about two and a half months after the very foundation of FF, a "Reach Out Campaign" was planned to gain (more) public attention and attract potential new members. The criterion for the campaign was that while it should be "aimed at freethinkers," it should likewise be "non-adversarial to non-freethinkers." One of the potential slogans for such a campaign, which the group seems to have agreed on in this regard, was the following:

> Don't believe in God?
> You are not alone.
>
> www.filipinofreethinkers.org

Similar to the previously mentioned "community" statement on the FF website, in which the terms "freethinkers" and "nonbelievers" are used almost interchangeably, the campaign's motto clearly shows that initially the group was formed quite explicitly around the "nonbelievers" identity of its members. Almost seven years later, in a follow-up interview I had with Red Tani during my short re-study in March 2016, we talked about what "kind of people" are attracted to FF. During this conversation, he mentioned:

> We do get people who have an idea of FF as a religion-bashing-group, and when they attend the meetup, they ask why aren't we bashing religion so much? You know . . . yah, we used to do that, maybe during the first year, and then it got old very quick, and you know, like, you can still, you know, like if it's the, in the context of the topic, you know, you can criticize religion as much as you want, but there's no "Let's criticize religion!" topic, you know, dedicated to that. . . .
>
> (Interview with Red Tani, FF 2016)

At one FF meetup, Red emphasized – similar to our interview – that in contrast to the online forum, there had been no discussion topic that was specifically focused on atheism or agnosticism at the regular FF meetups for three and a half years.

What such comments indicate – and also some of the observations I presented in previous sections – is that nonbelief or atheism as public or official identity markers for the group are not only contested by some members, but that apparently they also became less important as such. At the same time, FF became more involved in certain socio-political issues – mainly based on its support for a stricter separation of church and state. What factors might have played a role in FF's broader "normative change?" What moved the group's initial focus on building a community explicitly and mainly for *non*believers towards a more NGO-like organization fighting for political "secularism," thereby cooperating with religious supporters and groups as well?

FF's very successful activism regarding the issue of reproductive health (RH) policies in particular, I would argue, contributed to this shift. As stated briefly in the introduction, the issue of RH is one of the most important, if not the most important, topic FF had been officially engaged in as an organization. In an informal conversation with one of the core members of FF during my short re-study in 2016, he explained the group's immersion in matters of RH: "It made us!" In trying to influence this public debate, FF was involved in a large advocacy network called *RHAN* and thereby also collaborated with explicit religious groups like "Catholics 4RH."

Furthermore, I would argue that the involvement of aforementioned Episcopalian Kenneth Keng might have had a significant impact on the group's stance in this regard. As mentioned previously, at the beginning, FF members were organizing their meetups at a local Starbucks branch. However, after some time the number of participants grew too large and thus the group started to look for an alternative, noncommercial venue. Kenneth was able to arrange a meeting room at the Episcopalian Church, where he had been involved for quite some time. Although FF members – most of whom are self-declared nonbelievers – often joke about "going to Church on Sunday," this fact is quite telling with regard to the group's non-confrontational and more inclusive overall approach towards religion and religious people.

Moreover, I would say that the self-presentation and self-positioning of PATAS as exactly the exclusive "atheist club" that FF does not want to be seen as, enables the latter to actively distinguish itself from the former on that basis. Considering that both groups primarily cater to the same potential membership in Metro Manila, i.e. nonbelievers, its publicly declared focus on atheism, on the other hand, makes it possible for PATAS to legitimize its very own existence vis-à-vis FF. Thus, while it might be regarded as competitive in the first place, such a view neglects the symbiotic dimension of the relationship between FF and PATAS. To a certain extent, both groups also benefit from each other's existence, since it enables their members to emphasize their own distinctiveness.

On the other hand, PATAS itself seems to have undergone some broader changes in its approach towards religion. In fact, the group recently began to emphasize "humanism" instead of "atheism" as its core ideology, as manifest most visibly in the aforementioned "Free Medical Clinic," which the group had organized under the motto of "Good without God." Aside from some important organizational restructurings, e.g., a new chairman, an important factor for this "humanist turn" was certainly the attempt to establish a cooperation between PATAS and the *German Humanist Association* (HVD). With the prospect of receiving (financial) support from abroad for their social activism regarding the "Free Medical Clinic," PATAS officers were talking about the need to emphasize "humanism," since the term "atheism" was considered to have too negative a connotation. One member even questioned whether the group should change its name in this regard.

These shifts and changes of both FF and PATAS are, however, not entirely uncontested. Some members, for example, do not support FF's increasing focus on political issues, since to them the community aspect of the organization is more important. Similarly, PATAS' focus on "humanism" – in the form of the group's social engagement – was commented on rather critically by a former member, as he worried that the group might lose track of its original aim, which according to him consisted primarily in gathering Philippine nonbelievers and providing the general public with information about "atheism."

While so far I have focused mainly on the dynamics and dimensions of FF's and PATAS' relation to religion, or their *collective nonreligiosities*, as manifest in various concrete contexts, respectively, in the following section I want to describe some further differences and differentiations between both groups, which go beyond this *immediate* religion-relatedness, but which – as I mentioned in the introduction – nevertheless constitute important elements of their particular modes of nonreligion.

Activism, milieu, and "collective nonreligiosities"

On November 7th, 2013, "Yolanda" – internationally known as "Haiyan" – hit the Philippines at peak intensity with ten-minute sustained wind speeds up to 230 km/h. This so-called "super-typhoon" was globally one of the strongest typhoons ever recorded and became the deadliest calamity in the country's recent history, killing more than 6,000 people and leaving large parts of the Visayan Islands devastated. Soon after the catastrophe – with the death toll still rising almost daily – both groups, FF and PATAS, organized activities in Manila to help their fellow citizens affected by the typhoon. The particular forms that these activities took are quite important with regard to the argument that FF and PATAS represent different local modes of nonreligion.

Instead of holding its regular monthly meetup at its headquarter, PATAS decided to do volunteer work at a huge relief operation at "Villamor Airbase" located in the south of Manila. This operation was established to give immediate support to evacuees, who were flown in by the Philippine Air Force (PAF) from the typhoon-affected regions of the Visayan Islands. On arrival they were given food and water, received medical care if necessary, and were provided with temporary shelter. Beforehand, PATAS members prepared hundreds of food and hygiene kits and engaged in different activities at the airbase until late at night.

One week before PATAS' volunteerism at the airbase, FF also organized an event in support of the victims of "Yolanda." FF's activity, however, and the way I participated in it was quite different. Via live-stream I watched Red Tani, the president of FF, interviewing the famous US philosopher and one of the so-called "new atheists," Daniel Dennett, via Skype. The interview was the first of a whole series of interviews with well-known freethinkers around the globe. These interviews have been put up on the FF website and its YouTube channel under the motto of "Conversations for a Cause," i.e. as a fundraising campaign for the victims of "Yolanda." The interview with Dennett also ended a so-called eighteen-hour "webathon" that FF members conducted on the same day. The show – also accessible via live stream – was supposed "to get the freethinking community in the Philippines and in the world to raise funds to support those affected by this horrific tragedy" (FF 2013).

My ethnographic juxtaposition of these two activities – PATAS' volunteerism at the airbase and FF's "webathon" including the interview with Daniel Dennett – is, of course, not to judge which one has been more effective in actually helping the victims of "Yolanda." Both endeavors, indeed, can be seen as quite successful – each in its own way. What the comparison of both groups' reaction to this tragic disaster illustrates quite well, however, is a general differentiation or distinction between FF and PATAS that was frequently articulated in my interviews and informal conversations with members of both groups. According to the description of some of these members, PATAS represents and is more focused on the "grassroots" level, whereas FF is often seen as the more "elite" and the more "intellectually" inclined group.

While not always expressed exactly in these terms, such a characterization of the two organizations vis-à-vis each other and *beyond* their immediate religion-relatedness seems to play an important part in the discursive construction of their respective collective identities. This can be seen, for example, with regard to PATAS' above-mentioned "Free Medical Clinic." Reflecting on the group's activities, Yek Lai Fatt, at that time PATAS' chairman and the driving force behind the clinic, emphasized in our interview such a focus on the "grassroots" as an important distinguishing factor between FF and PATAS:

> That's why now, PATAS focuses on the grassroots. Like, for example, you can see, Filipino Freethinkers and PATAS are totally two different organizations. Filipino Freethinkers is focused on the common policy, focused on the common regulation, common law, everything . . . for us, PATAS, we want to focus on the grassroots, that means we go down to the community to tell people, they [atheists] are good without God.
> (Interview with Yek Lai Fatt, PATAS 2014)

In order to convey their message – that one, indeed, can be a "moral" person without any religious affiliation – more effectively on the "grassroots" level, the group distributed at the first clinic in February 2014 copies of their mission and vision statement, partly translated to Tagalog. Further, from the start the clinic was seen also as an important potential venue for directly supporting reproductive health (RH). When I talked with Tess Termulo, PATAS' new president, trained medical doctor, and a very outspoken RH supporter, about this issue in our interview, I asked her about the group's engagement and about how PATAS would attempt to have any impact in this regard. She told me that besides "trying to raise awareness online about it" through their website articles, "PATAS does not have the political clout yet to have that very significant effect on political groups concerning this reproductive health law." However, as she added later in the conversation, what PATAS members were planning to do in the context of the "Free Medical Clinic," which the group had launched just a week before our interview, was to "incorporate reproductive health teachings to the community, because these are the people who don't really have access to a lot of information. So we're going to bring the information they need there. At least if we can make significant contributions to a small community, I think that would be a great accomplishment already on the part of the organization" (Interview with Tess Termulo, PATAS 2014). Two months later, in April 2014 during its third Free Medical Clinic, only two weeks after the Supreme Court's final decision on the constitutionality of the RH Law in Baguio, PATAS was already able to include such teaching sessions on RH-related issues. After the lecture, given by a hired social worker, free injectable contraceptives were distributed to interested women living in the neighborhood.

On the other hand, FF's "intellectual" character, as manifest at least to some extent in their social activism described previously, is ascribed to the group in particular with regard to their regular meetups. For instance, in an article on the PATAS website, the author called "Sathepine" referred to FF and "their intellectual discussions." Similarly, another PATAS member, who had attended some FF meetups before, told me that he was not always able to follow the discussions there because of their highly "intellectual" character. PATAS, in contrast, was, as he put it, for "everyone."

As indicated by this short remark, such generalized characterizations of FF and PATAS by local activists are often directly tied to certain differentiations based on the particular "social class" or "milieu" that each group – allegedly – represents and/or caters to. When I was talking to some other FF members in a more informal context, one of them asked me about the differences between FF and PATAS, knowing that I research both groups. While I was sorting my thoughts, not sure back then what answer to give, another FF member chipped in, stating in a similar, but less diplomatic way, that FF was "a bunch of rich kids," while the PATAS guys were the "poor." Although certainly mentioned tongue-in-cheek in this particular situation, I became aware of such socioeconomic depictions and self-portrayals on several other occasions during my fieldwork. At one meetup, for instance, an FF member mentioned that the group is still struggling with its image of being a crowd of "rich students." PATAS in his view somehow managed to cut across different socioeconomic strata with regard to its membership composition.

Thus, the form of each group's activism reflects important differences between them, not only in terms of the specific target group or recipients, but also – or rather particularly – with regard to the respective milieu that

FF and PATAS members themselves represent, or allegedly represent. PATAS' "grassroots" activism – as seen in its "Yolanda" relief operation and its "Free Medical Clinic" – is directed mainly towards the "common" people, or as it is called in Tagalog, the *masa*. That's where members of the group apparently want to spread their ideas and try to counter perceived misconceptions about atheism, particularly by emphasizing and demonstrating that one can be "good without God." It is also from where some of its members, especially in the early phase of the group's existence, came. PATAS thus seems to represent a more diverse membership in socioeconomic terms, and is, as I have shown, characterized as such by members and non-members alike. FF's online fundraising campaign, conversely, was first and foremost directed towards their "peers," i.e. mostly university educated people interested in intellectual issues and discussions – and, one might add, financially able to donate.

The particular forms of the socio-political and humanitarian activism, in which both groups besides their regular meetups frequently engage, and the related "socio-economic mapping"[8] thus illustrate and indicate some important differences between FF and PATAS that seemingly go beyond their immediate stance on religion. They are, however, nevertheless crucial for understanding their overall profiles and agendas, and thus have to be seen as constitutive parts of their mode of nonreligion. In other words, they highlight specific elements of their respective modes, which might not be primarily based on the groups' general relations towards religion as outlined in the previous sections, but which do shape as well as embody them in certain ways, and are thus intimately intertwined with and strongly related to each other.

Summary: on differentiating and comparing local forms of organized nonreligion

> *There are a few important points to bear in mind when one wants to make a comparison. First of all, one has to decide, in any given work, whether one is mainly after similarities or differences. It is very difficult, for example, to say, let alone prove, that Japan and China or Korea are basically similar or basically different. Either is possible depending on one's angle of vision, one's framework, and the conclusions towards which one intends to move.*
> (Anderson 2016, 130)

The terminology and the underlying conceptual framework of this volume are particularly helpful for approaching my empirical observations about the local diversity of organized nonreligion in the Philippines on a more analytical level. As I have described in the very brief contextual overview about the country's historical and contemporary religious landscape, it is the dominance of the Catholic Church – and in particular its influence on political discourses – that constitutes the main object of criticism articulated by (organized) nonbelievers, who, on the other hand, see themselves in a very marginal(ized) position within Philippine society. Thus, it is fair to say that the religious "others" of FF and PATAS are first of all Catholicism and its institutional representations such as the CBCP – or, speaking in the book's terms: they are what the "non" of both *non*religious groups almost exclusively refers to. However, as I have shown, the specific relations of FF and PATAS with religion vary to a significant extent. Drawing on the distinction between four possible ideal-typical kinds of such relations (see Chapter 2), PATAS' generalized overall religion-relatedness – or, its *collective nonreligiosity* – is largely characterized by *conflict* (e.g., "God is dead!") and *competition* (as becomes manifest, for example, in the group's Free Medical Clinic organized under the motto of "Good without God"), while that of FF includes *cooperation* (e.g., with regard to their fight for the RH Bill/Law, during which they joined forces with religious groups in the network RHAN) as well as *dialogue* (e.g., by explicitly welcoming religious persons at the regular meetups). It became clear in my study on what I have called the multi-dimensionality of both organizations' *collective nonreligiosities*, however, that all of these kinds of relations have to be analyzed on different levels or in different contexts, e.g. public discourse vis-à-vis internal articulations and practices. Further, they have to be seen as dynamic, as FF's shift towards becoming a more NGO-like organization fighting for "secularism" instead of focusing on the atheist identity of its earlier days illustrates. This change – what I described as a "normative change," thereby following Müller (2015) – could also be conceptualized as a "moving away from religion-relatedness" (see Chapter 2). As I have argued in my discussion about some of the possible factors triggering such a broader shift, the foundation of PATAS and its public positioning as a more "exclusive" atheist group vis-à-vis FF has certainly played a key role in this regard. Hence, these groups' *collective nonreligiosities* are shaped not only by various relations, or "kinds of relations," to the local religious field, but also by interactions with other nonreligious organizations situated in the same cultural context, as well as by diverse transnational connections with like-minded groups around the world and by global discourses such as the "new atheism."

Their *collective nonreligiosities* are further embedded in what we call "modes of nonreligion," i.e. their overall profile and agenda as constituted, for example, also by their organizational structures and membership composition, their (foundational) history, the social milieu of their members, and their socio-political activism. And while I did not provide more specific "labels" such as the ones described by my colleague in her case study on the differences between the so-called "life stance humanists" and "opinion-making humanists" struggling for discursive dominance inside the biggest Swedish humanist organization *Humanisterna* (see Chapter 3), what became clear in my analysis of FF and PATAS is that in a similar way each of them represents a different local mode of nonreligion.

A detailed empirical analysis and ethnographic description of these groups' specific modes thereby provides the necessary basis for a broader comparative perspective on different nonreligious organizations and phenomena in various national and cultural contexts. The final chapter of this volume (Chapter 6) adopts such a broader perspective by bringing together some observations from our different case studies in Sweden, the Netherlands, India, and the Philippines. While the close-up view on FF and PATAS I have provided in the previous sections mainly focused on and emphasized the *differences* (and differentiations) between these two groups in Metro Manila, this more distant look on organized nonreligion in the Philippines by my colleagues brings into view what I have neglected thereby to some extent: their *similarities*. Comparing the general situation that members of both organizations – whether as self-proclaimed "atheists," "agnostics," or "freethinkers" – face in this country with, for example, the dynamics that humanists in Sweden are confronted with, thus not only underscores or complements but also helps to relativize the picture drawn here of the local diversity of organized nonreligion. As the previously quoted words by the late Benedict Anderson remind us, in the end it depends on the perspective and what one is looking for.

Notes

1 The acronym "PATAS" was intentionally chosen because as a Tagalog/Filipino term it means "equal" or "equality," pointing to what they are fighting for.
2 AFP. 2015. "Pope Francis crowd in Philippines hits record six million." *The Telegraph*, January 18, 2015. https://www.telegraph.co.uk/news/worldnews/the pope/11353443/Pope-Francis-crowd-in-Philippines-hits-record-six-million.html.
3 Paterno, Esmaquel II. 2012. "Making sense of the Nazarene devotion." *Rappler*, January 14, 2012. https://www.rappler.com/nation/841-making-sense-of-the-nazarene devotion.
4 The statistics are taken from Bouma, Ling, and Pratt (2010).
5 For a short historical overview on the separation clause in the different constitutions of the Philippines, see Cornelio (2013).
6 In my doctoral thesis I give a short overview of the history of (organized) nonreligion in the country and of some of its contemporary manifestations (see Blechschmidt 2018, Chapter 2).
7 Names with * are pseudonyms.
8 This notion is taken from Katharine Wiegele's study on *El Shaddai*, where she shows how members of this charismatic Catholic movement in Manila are often similarly framed and frame themselves in terms of social "class" (Wiegele 2005, 80f.).

5 Secularizing politics in the Netherlands

Cora Schuh

Introduction

How God disappeared from the Second Chamber[1]

The Dutch parliamentary elections from 1967 brought relevant power shifts in the political landscape. The Catholic People's Party (KVP) and the Social Democrats, the two parties that had dominated postwar politics, both suffered great electoral losses, and due to the loss of the KVP, the confessional parties – for the first time since 1918 – lost their absolute majority. This political power shift was part of a broader process of deconfessionalization often referred to as "depillarization" (De Rooy 2002; Ellemers 1979; Kennedy [1995] 2007; Knippenberg 1998, 211f; Pennings 1998; Righart 1995, 48–53, 203f). Depillarization means the disintegration of the net of confessional (Calvinist and Catholic) and socialist organizations and institutions that had emerged from the rise of anti-liberal socio-political movements in the late-19th century, and that gave Dutch society a segmented and pluralist organizational structure, referred to as pillarization. This pluralism has never been uncontested. Historically liberals had opposed it, and in the postwar era, social democrats pushed for political depillarization and for "breaking through" to confessional electorates. Ultimately, confessionals and especially the Catholic KVP retained their power position, and the pluralist structure was restored and consolidated in the mid-1940s and 1950s.[2] The depillarization in the 1960s was in the first place a dissolution of the Catholic pillar informed by liberalizations within the global and national Catholic Church. Prominent organizations gave up their former confessional profile or merged with organizations of a different profile.[3] In politics, deconfessionalization manifested in an increase of electoral volatility and a decrease of party membership numbers, a decoupling of religious affiliation and electoral support for religious parties, and consequently a decline of the two main Christian parties (especially the Catholic one) (Pennings 1998). The rules of the political game changed from a focus on tolerance and pacification, elitist decision-making, parity accommodation, and the depoliticization of controversial matters, to one of polarization and politicization (Daalder 1995; Lijphart 2008; Pennings 1998).

New political movements once more claimed a reform of the political system and the old political divides, and a central role was played by the party D66 (Democrats 66 [Democraten 66]), which was founded in 1966 and in the elections of 1967 profiled with a strong criticism of the political system and the established parties.[4] According to the party founders, politics were meant to facilitate the transparent, free, and influential participation of citizens in a process of democratic collective decision-making and efficient governance, and they felt that this was hampered by the confessional parties and the pluralist system. In the elections of 1967, the party gained 4.48 percent and seven seats in the parliament. Liberal and so-called protest parties (among them D66)[5] were the electoral winners of this process, and especially D66 was considered both a manifestation and catalyst of this deconfessionalization. Interrelated with depillarization, the share of non-denominationalism accelerated after the mid-1960s, and also the frequency and relevance of theological references in parliamentary debates declined – an observation that Meijering expressed in the title to his book "How God disappeared from the Second Chamber" (Meijering 2012, 9, 11).

This chapter centers on the party D66 as a collective actor which aimed at the secularization of politics and state. They propagated disentangling the categories of political organization and mobilization, as well as those of governance from religious and religion-like worldview categories for the sake of enabling a more general societal democratization and liberalization. They further used their political power to achieve a respective disentangling of law and state. In reference to Bourdieu (2001), this is framed as a struggle about the political field. The chapter has a strong historical focus, capturing a period from the mid-19th century to the most recent past. This historical account captures the process of pillarization and depillarization as well as the more recent liberalizations. While these developments are generally well known, the chapter contributes to existing research by linking the history of the party D66 with these broader developments and by approaching them from a conceptual perspective on the relationality of nonreligion.[6]

Regarding the outline of the chapter, I first sketch how the political field functions as an arena in which religious and nonreligious actors struggle about secularity as well as the notion of nonreligion. Subsequently I sketch the history of pillarization as the 19th century emergence of a political field as closely entangled with an equally emerging field of religious-nonreligious positions, as well as the contestations about such religion-relatedness. I then sketch the foundation of D66 against this background. I show how the reform aims of the party founders and their criticism of the ideologies of the existing parties entailed an objective of secularizing politics. I further show how they used their political power to push for a further secularization of state and law, this time for the sake of individual liberty and equality. Drawing on this book's notion of a relational determination of nonreligion, I show how the nonreligious character of their initiatives and positioning is itself a constant matter of negotiation. Complementing the party's opposition to principled politics, I point to recurrent attempts of party members to define and promote an epistemic and moral standpoint for politics without becoming ideological themselves. Ultimately, I focus on the party's religion-relatedness by looking at data from election research. I conclude by summarizing and discussing the findings.

The contested religion-relatedness of politics: conceptual elaborations

The book's core interest is how nonreligious actors position and are positioned in relation to religion, and the dynamics that determine the mode of a nonreligious positioning. This chapter pursues this larger goal by focusing on the political field (Bourdieu 2001) as an arena in which the role of religion in society as well as the notion of nonreligion are both the object and outcome of power struggles. In the sense that political struggles concern the relation of religion with politics, law, as well as other fields, they shape the secularity of a given society. The political field is also an arena in which the notion of nonreligion as the "other" to religion is negotiated.[7] The concepts of secularity and nonreligion complement each other in the sense that secularity is understood as a distinction between religion and other (secular/nonreligious) social spheres, while nonreligion is one side of that differentiation and thus synonymous with the secular (Wohlrab-Sahr and Burchardt 2012, 881, 886–8).

Building on Max Weber, Bourdieu describes the political field as an arena for the struggle over symbolic power and legitimate categories and worldviews (the visions and divisions of the world) (Bongaerts 2008, 190, 195f; Bourdieu 2001; Swartz 2012, 168). A further characteristic of the political field is its orientation towards a lay audience. Political capital is the capacity to mobilize electoral support via competing "idées-forces" (fundamental ideas; the worldviews and categorizations of the world) (Bongaerts 2008, 195; Swartz 2012, 163–6, 177).[8] It is gained by transforming other forms of capital into electoral support and thus by reaching beyond the borders of the political field. The mobilization power of ideas is based on their resonance with the position and relation of certain social groups.[9] Interrelatedly, the political field is one of those fields through which the symbolic power of the state is asserted. Here, certain particularistic worldviews are institutionalized as universal and here (as well as in the field of power at large) the different forms of capital (and thus the different fields that exist in a given society) are placed in hierarchical interrelation. In that sense, political struggles not only concern the relative worth of different capital forms within politics, but also within social power relations at large (Swartz 2012, 169f, also Chapter 2).

These general remarks can be fruitful for understanding struggles regarding the religion-relatedness of politics as well as the role of religion in society. I try to illustrate this with a simplified abstract consideration of dynamics central to the case at hand. Some actors might e.g. transform religious capital or religious networks (as a religious form of social capital) into political capital, while others might compete with them by mobilizing voters with other (nonreligious) forms of capital. As part of their mutual struggle for dominance in the political field, these actors might also struggle over the notion of politics and the necessary relation of religion and politics and its nonreligious character. While some might claim a necessary relation of religion and politics, others might claim politics as necessarily not-religious (and religion as not-political). While some might construe nonreligious politics as irreligious, others might frame them as holding a differentiated third-space position, and again others might seek to distinguish between either form of nonreligious politics. Interrelated with such contested notions of politics as such, struggles in the political field might also concern competing religious and nonreligious ideas about organizing society. The struggle for secularizing politics constitutes one possible form of nonreligious political activism and a means to influence the role of religion in other fields and power relations at large (Chapter 2).

As argued in the theory chapter and inspired by the multiple secularities approach, such nonreligious activism can be motivated by different values (Wohlrab-Sahr and Burchardt 2012). Aside from those listed in Chapter 2, the multiple secularities typology distinguishes four possible motives: individual liberty and equality, the balancing of religious-nonreligious diversity, social progress, or the autonomy of spheres (Wohlrab-Sahr and Burchardt 2012).

As indicated, nonreligious political actors can be distinguished by how they position themselves regarding religion, and for the case at hand, the distinction between irreligious or differentiated positionings is central. *Irreligious actors* position themselves in binary competitive and conflicting opposition to religion (as such), seeking to abolish or replace religion (Campbell 1971, in Chapter 2).[10] Actors in a *differentiated position* claim a third-space position with respect to religion, cross-cutting the binary divide between religion and irreligion (Chapter 2). Their positionings give expression to the economic or class-related divides and positions in the social realm. Further, as indicated in the theory chapter, they can also stand in a homologous relation to the positions these actors (or their members) as well as the population groups they represent hold in and in relation to the religious field, the religious and religion-related positions and divides in the social realm of a given society.[11]

Last but not least, this chapter centers on the genre of political polemic and combat rhetoric, and two terms are central: ideology and worldviews. Both concepts are based in the 18th century philosophy of consciousness, which broke with the notion of an objective (Christian) world and rendered the human conscious as that which gave coherence to the world. While the notion of worldviews points to the relativism of all ideas, that of ideology challenges an opponent's ideas as politically irrelevant, or non-realist, and further associates them with rigorism and terror (Mannheim [1929] 2015, 61–9).

The subsequent sections, as mentioned, sketch the process of pillarization in the late 19th and early 20th centuries with a focus on how religious and religion-related divides were translated into the emerging political field, and on how struggles between liberals and confessionals concerned the nonreligious character of politics. Subsequently, I focus on the foundation of D66.

The emergence of a religion-related political field since the mid-19th century

As outlined in Chapter 2, in many societies the 19th century was not only characterized by confessional tensions, but also by the emergence of irreligious worldview movements. This also holds for the Netherlands (Derkx 2002; Gasenbeek and Nabuurs 2006). At the same time, others tried to establish realms, differentiated from religious and worldview differences. The point to make in this section is that the political field, emerging at that time, was co-structured by such religious and religion-related divides. At first liberals dominated and claimed politics as a realm of the common and themselves to stand above particularistic religious divides, but in the latter half of the 19th century, orthodox Christian counter-movements emerged and successfully opposed the dominance of liberalism, claiming politics as necessarily religion-related.[12] Ultimately this resulted in the segmentation (pillarization) of politics and society and the subordination of differentiated secular positions under a confessional logic.

The emergence of a political field had been linked since the mid-18th century with the rise of the bourgeois middle classes who claimed political influence vis-à-vis the Dutch king and aristocracy. Liberalism was the intellectual and political expression of this emancipation movement, aiming at a strong middle-class society in a strong nation-state where rule and liberties were guaranteed via a constitutional system and the control and division of power. Influenced by the French Revolution, liberals also feared mass rule, and this was a second motive for supporting a constitutional system.[13] In the revolutionary year of 1848, the liberal leader J. R. Thorbecke (1798–1872) was tasked by the Dutch king with revising the existing constitution from 1814. The new constitution not only guaranteed the freedom of religion, press, association, and gatherings, but further transferred full political responsibility from the king to the ministers. It gave more control over the government and legislation to the parliament and introduced a system of direct and census-based (district and majority) suffrage for Dutch parliament.[14] The constitution thus not only made it easier to collectively organize but also made the mobilization of electorates conditional to political power – and thus facilitated the emergence of a political field and eventually the mobilization along religion-related and social divides. Liberals were the first to profit from the political changes, and in 1860 they became the dominant party.

To understand how religious divides were translated into political ones, one must first understand the links of liberalism with the religious field and the emerging irreligious movements of the time, as well as its influence on the relations of state and church and the place of religion in society. Since the revolts against Catholic Spain in the 16th and 17th centuries, Reformed Christianity had been the official religion in the Netherlands, with Catholics being the main religious minority. The Dutch Reformed Church was the public church, while Protestant dissenters and minorities, Catholics, as well as non-Christians had limited (but constitutionally guaranteed) religious freedoms.[15] Beyond that, at least since the 17th century, new developments in philosophy and science challenged the authority of the Christian revelation, and were met by assertions of orthodoxy or aims to reform and modernize Christianity. The emergence of nationalism was another development that formulated new demands towards religion, and all these developments led to another form of religious and intellectual diversity, which cut across confessional and church divides.

Liberalism was rooted in the liberal or modernist strands of Dutch Reformed Christianity and found its supporters among Protestant minorities and (until 1870) Catholics. For the members of these minorities, the calls for political influence since the 18th century had been paired with claims to reform the relation of state and church. Eventually, it was in consequence of the French invasion in the late-18th century that the Reformed Church was first stripped from its privileged position, but the liberal constitution from 1848 asserted the separation of church and state.[16] The liberal claim for a separation of church and state was further linked with the ideal of a unified nation and a public-political realm beyond confessional and dogmatic (as well as class-related) divides (Aerts 1997, 129, 197). They conceived the state and politics as having an autonomous responsibility towards the general interest – understood as a combination of universal rights and the continuity and unity of the nation (Aerts 1997, 197, 323f). Churches were meant to be free, but church teachings and interests were to remain outside the political sphere – only at the level of individual inspiration was religion considered legitimately linked with politics (Aerts 1997, 197). Religious diversity was not problematized as such, but a potential segmentation of the public sphere and the nation was to be prevented (Aerts 1997, 190,197). The liberal notion of a national public thereby rendered all those aspects of religion sectarian or particularistic, which did not fit in with liberal notions of a general religion above faith divides. The rise of liberalism, e.g., led to the reduction of religious education in schools and to the teaching of general Christian values and virtues, rather than dogmatic knowledge (De Rooy 2002, 62–2, 72–4).

In the mid-19th century, an orthodox Calvinist "anti-revolutionary" movement constituted itself as a separate fraction in the reformed church and later in parliament, where it replaced the strand of conservatism as the main other of liberals (De Rooy 2002, 64–92; Lucardie 2002, 16–22). At the ideological core of this anti-revolutionary movement was the rejection of the French Revolution and the principle of popular sovereignty, seen as the fundamental reversion of a godly moral and state order, in other words, a revolt against Christ, which inevitably led to radicalism and tyranny.[17] The intellectual and political leaders of the movement were G. W. van Prinsterer (1801–1876) and most importantly Abraham Kuyper (1837–1920). The latter would turn Calvinism into a mass movement and organize it as a separate part of the nation through building a network of Calvinist organizations, including a newspaper (1872), the Anti-Revolutionary Party (ARP 1879), the Free University (1880), and a separate reformed church (1892). Liberals opposed these beginnings of pillarization, and most strongly they objected to the confessional movement in state politics (Aerts 1997, 352). The anti-revolutionary strand was conceived as representing not the general interests, but only their church-related interests; as trying to assert a sectarian and minority program upon the nation rather than being a genuine state party (Aerts 1997, 198, 323f). Kuyper opposed the liberal claim of privatizing confessional divides through reframing politics as fundamentally religion-related and divided in belief and unbelief.

Aside from liberalism and Calvinism, two more political strands emerged during the late-19th and early 20th centuries – political Catholicism and socialism. Catholics had traditionally supported liberalism as a supporter of equal religious freedom, but in the context of the global and national culture wars, they began to oppose liberal rule. Also within Catholic political thought, state centralism was opposed as conflicting with an organic social order, and in the name of a "subsidiarity principle" (De Rooy 2002, 68–72, 81–6; Lucardie 2002, 18–22). The foundation of Catholic organizations started around 1900, and in 1926 the Roman Catholic State Party (RKSP) was founded. Socialism emerged as a fourth political strand in Dutch politics. Unlike liberalism, which was rooted in liberal Protestantism and stood at a distance from atheism and materialism, socialism was the first major carrier of non-denominationalism and unbelief (Aerts 1997, 202, 220, 251, 472; Knippenberg 1998, 211, 213; Lucardie 2002, 25).[18] As a movement, socialism was antireligious but borrowed and transformed elements and symbols of Christianity within and with reference to its own movement and leaders (Groothuizen and Bos 2013; Van Veldhuizen 2013). Religion was portrayed as an ideology and associated with the established interests of king, church, and capital. The Social-Democratic Workers' Party (SDAP) was founded in 1894.[19] Different from liberals, socialists conceived irreligion (or more precisely non-denominationalism and freethought) as necessarily related to politics. Liberals by contrast opposed this; while liberals successfully claimed freethought a mere intellectual project, socialists rendered the party a simultaneously political and irreligious organization (Derkx 2002; Gasenbeek 2007, 5–7).[20]

Generally speaking, the social question and the rise of socialism had a strong influence on the other parties – giving rise to a strand of social liberalism which emerged in counter-distinction from the economically liberal classic liberalism (Pennings 1998, introduction).[21]

By the beginning of the 20th century, four different political strands had emerged. They were rooted in different religious and nonreligious milieus and differed with respect to their religious and nonreligious positioning in politics. While liberals had sought to construe politics as differentiated, such differentiation was (in different ways and for different reasons) countered by both socialists and orthodox Christians. The different positionings thereby echoed the rootedness of the different parties in and with respect to the religious field. The next section centers on the intellectual work of the Calvinist leader, Kuyper, who opposed the liberal claim of privatizing confessional divides through reframing politics as fundamentally religion-related and divided between belief and unbelief.

An antithesis of belief and unbelief

Kuyper's innovative move was to conceptualize Calvinism as a *worldview*, and to further interpret his time as characterized by an encompassing and antithetic worldview conflict – an *antithesis* – between belief and unbelief, between Christianity and modernism. According to Kuyper, a worldview meant a "coherent set of presuppositions and foundational ideas that enabled an individual to interpret reality" (Miller 1999; see also: Sire 2015, 23).[22] The concept implied a simultaneously encompassing and perspectival vision of the world – and Kuyper spoke in similar fashion of life-systems, life-views, and of principles and faith positions that necessarily guided all perspectives on the world. Different worldviews could be compared according to their notions of God, man, and world (Molendijk 2008, 240). From this perspective, immanent and non-orthodox perspectives on the world and religion could be framed as epistemic equivalents and rivals to Christianity. He coined the concept "modernism," first to criticize liberal Protestantism, but later to denote a general and single opponent of Calvinism associated with the Enlightenment and the French Revolution, thus extending the critique beyond the realm of theology (Jellema 1957, 480; Molendijk 2011, 410–12). Modernism is that which "is bound to build a world of its own from the data of the natural man, and to construct man himself from the data of nature" (Kuyper [1931] 1999, 11). A Christian response to such comprehensive modernism would have to be equally comprehensive, with Christianity becoming a life system rather than only a church order or theology, and it was Calvinism that in his view represented such a form of Christianity (Kuyper [1931] 1999, 11). Calvinism and modernism were thus the two antipodes in a worldview struggle between belief and unbelief, or, in other words, of a religious-irreligious worldview field – a frame which took up the theological, intellectual, and political struggles at the time and framed them along a binary divide.

This antithesis left no conceptual space for a differentiated immanent perspective that was not already understood as a direct epistemic other to religion. Kuyper explicitly criticized a "partial" understanding of religion as being confined to a limited sphere, be it that of inner life, of ethics, or sentiment (Kuyper [1931] 1999, 50f.). As a worldview, Calvinism was not merely a theological system but was of relevance for the central (functional) domains of society, a legitimate base for science, politics, art, and family life (Kuyper [1931] 1999; Sire 2015, 33f).[23] In his view, the different social realms were not based on a logic differentiated from religion, but required a foundational principle, which could be found either in belief or unbelief. Regarding science, Kuyper respectively argued that all scientific interpretations were either based on a theistic or atheistic worldview (Kuyper [1931] 1999, 131–4; Kuyper 1880, 31f). There was no conflict between religion and science, but between two different kinds of science, one based in belief, one in unbelief. At the same time, he did not oppose all forms of social differentiation, but rather spoke of the sovereignty of different social spheres or circles, both from each other as well as from the state – examples being churches, the family, business, science, art, and so forth (Kuyper [1931] 1999, 90; see also: Jellema 1957, 482; Molendijk 2008, 244). His Calvinist university was thus independent from the Calvinist Church.

Politics as well, were, according to Kuyper, either based on the authority of God or on human reason and insight; they were either religious or antireligious (De Rooy 2002, 96). From the onset, the self-understanding of anti-revolutionaries had been based on a counter-distinction from mere power-centered politics, and they positioned as politics of witness or principles (getuigenisor beginselpolitiek), as politics of a higher sphere, and as representing the Christian voice in politics (De Haan and Te Velde 1996). The program of principles of Kuyper's party ARP denounced the principles of popular sovereignty and confessed – also in the realm of politics – the "eternal principles" revealed by God (ARP 1918).

The notion of an encompassing antithesis of belief and unbelief allowed Kuyper to attack conservativism, liberalism, and socialism alike as mere variants of a single ideology rooted in the Enlightenment (Jellema 1957, 480). Further, Kuyper's notion of different worldviews allowed him to present Calvinism as genuinely tolerant and accuse liberalism of a "spiritual tyranny" against those of a different mindset (Kuyper [1931] 1999, 78, 109). All in all, his reconceptualization of modernity and Calvinism challenged the claim of liberals to represent a neutral, general position and the nation, and it claimed a future for Calvinism in modernity at a time when liberalism seemed "the wave of the future" (Jellema 1957, 473; also: Miller 1999; Molendijk 2011).

Kuyper's antithesis dwarfed the scope for differentiated nonreligious positions. His ideas served as an intellectual backing of social and political pluralism, and he also introduced a new style of politics and eventually succeeded in changing the rules and divides of the political field. Until 1879 and under liberal dominance, there were no political parties but only so-called chamber clubs. Kuyper was the first to establish a modern party as a representative body of likeminded people with a published program

("Our Program") and shared principles (De Rooy 2002, 89; Tanja 2011).[24] The notion of principled politics as such was far from alien to liberals – liberal intellectuals and politicians spoke of principles of the constitution, and of principles determinant for a certain historical period (Aerts 1997, 193, 2009). The notion of party-specific and thus multiple principles and the notion that parliamentarians should primarily stand for such principles rather than being generally trustworthy, however, conflicted with the liberal ideal of the common good and a national political public beyond religious and worldview divides.

Eventually though, liberals as well, started to found parties and publish election programs and programs of principles.[25] The third program of the Liberale Unie speaks of its own principles, and further claims that "the main principle of our constitutional system: *a government of and through the people* should [shall] more than ever demand complete tribute (huldiging)" (LU 1918). The program of the Liberal State Party is particularly interesting for the case at hand, as it speaks of liberalism as a "strand in the intellectual-spiritual (geestelijk) life," while also stressing that its "political aspirations" and principles were differentiated from (and not conflicting with) "the source from which [. . .] one takes the elements of one's spiritual, moral, or religious world- and lifeview" (LSP 1921). On the one hand thus, the party adapted to the changed terms of political competition and self-positioned as a particular strand; on the other hand, it pertained its positioning as a *third-space* position beyond religious-irreligious divides – the latter being rendered to the private sphere of belief and unbelief. In that sense the program gives a first example of the symbolic subordination of the notion of a differentiated political public under a logic of worldview pluralism. At the same time, the program also gives expression to ongoing struggles between liberals and Calvinists about the religion-relatedness of politics.[26]

Also the political culture changed with the rise of Calvinism, given that Kuyper introduced a more polarizing style to politics than was the custom before (Meijering 2012; Tanja 2011). In the words of De Rooy (2002, 91), parliament now became "less a place [. . .] for making decisions, but a great stage from which the public was addressed," and in which not agreement but at the most compromises could be reached.[27] The antithesis further manifested in the collaboration of Catholics and Protestants in the period between 1888 and 1919.[28] It also manifested in how the left-right distinction in politics was interpreted, with confessionals labeled right, and non-confessionals left. Further, with the foundation of confessional cabinets, references to God and the Bible and theological debates became integral to parliamentary debates. Liberals and socialists objected to the antithesis and the confessional claim of representing the sole legitimate Christian voice as well as the mix of theology and politics (Meijering 2012, 21–5). Irrespectively, these debates inevitably took a theological tone, and among liberals and socialists as well, there were former preachers who engaged in these debates. Aside from such theological tones, the struggles between the different parties in parliament also referenced (predicted) developments in the religious field. Socialists gladly pointed to declining numbers of church affiliation, which they linked with the growth of socialism, while liberals predicted a growth of liberal Christianity rather than religious decline. Their other was not religion as such, but clericalism and the gradual "churching" of the country (Meijering 2012, 47f.).

All in all, thus, by introducing the notion of the necessarily religion-relatedness of politics (their rootedness in principles and worldviews) as well as the notion of a binary divide between religion and irreligion to politics, Kuyper changed the rules of the political game. Even if liberals retained their ideal of a differentiation of politics and worldview positions, they had to do so under changed circumstances and in the form of a particularistic stance.

The institutionalization and contestation of pluralism

According to De Rooy (2001), the period between 1917 and 1965 marked the fourth phase and the completion of pillarization, when the pillars were consolidated and extended to other parts of society. The confessional movements had turned from emancipation movements into holders of political power with access to the means of legislation and administration (Pennings 1998). Complementing their collective (self-)organization, legal and structural preconditions that benefit a pluralist society were now institutionalized. In a prominent political compromise from 1917, the struggles regarding education were resolved with a constitutional guarantee of equal state subsidies for special schools on a par with public ones – a provision that allowed for building a system of religiously based schools and resulted in the segmentation of the educational sector, again rendering secular-public school one particular option in a pluralist setting (Art. 23 GW). The 1917 agreement further introduced general male suffrage and further stabilized the existing party pluralism through the introduction of proportional representation.[29]

The long-term consequence of the confessional pillarization was that large parts of society were organized in a pluralist way. To the present day, diverging evaluations and notions of differentiation echo in scholarly writings on Calvinism and pillarization: the theologian Molendijk (2008, 241, 247) e.g. argues that the Calvinist notion of modernity was more modern than the liberal one, because it recognized pluralism "in various spheres of human life," while liberals only claimed hegemony for their own perspective. The sociologist Ellemers, by contrast, compares pillarization with a functional differentiation as the "normal case." According to him, in consequence of pillarization, "almost the entire Dutch society [was] organized on a worldview base; also those sectors[30] – this is the most relevant characteristic of pillarization – that have not directly something to do with belief and worldviews" (Ellemers 1979, 430).

The German occupation during the Second World War put a pause to most pillarized institutions, but after the war a pluralist structure was rebuilt. At the same time though, the postwar era was characterized by a strong popular movement against pillarization, which was especially carried by the newly founded labor party (PvdA) (Kennedy [1995] 2007, 29–37; Mellink 2011; Van Dam and Van Trigt 2015, 11–13). In its aim to overcome pillarization, the new labor party carried out its own separation of politics and worldviews by giving up its former irreligious profile and opening itself up to Christian members and voters. Different from the liberal notion of differentiation though, they institutionalized confessional and humanist subgroups within the party. Complementing the transformation of social democracy, a newly founded humanist association inherited its former worldview-function (Derkx 2006, 69). Over the course of the 20th century, nonreligious worldviews were gradually granted parity rights with religion, while the differentiation of nonreligious worldviews and secular politics was increasingly institutionalized.

With respect to politics, the postwar order was characterized by a compromise between secular and religious ideas. The labor party had hoped to break though the confessional lines in politics and achieve a new progressive majority, but it failed, and between 1945–1958 ruled in coalition with the Catholic party KVP (Mellink 2011).[31] Political issues, such as the laws on Sunday rest and cremation, which were sensitive to both Christians and secular people alike, were dealt with in a manner of compromise, upholding a Christian public order while tolerating diverging interests, while liberals strongly opposed this and to them the PvdA had betrayed its principled progressive position for equal and individual liberty when becoming a breakthrough party (Van Baalen and Ramakers 2001).

All in all, the postwar era and the 1950s prepared the grounds for a renewed opposition to pillarization with a more liberal profile. In that phase the newly founded party D66 would give a prominent voice to the critique of a pluralist political system and claim the deconfessionalization and secularization of politics.

D66 and the secularization of politics, state, and law

D66 was founded in Amsterdam in 1966, a time of economic growth, suburbanization, gradual transformation into a post-industrialized society, as well as of protests, especially in Amsterdam and most prominently by the so-called Provo movement (Ellemers 1979, 432; Lucardie 1997, 445) – a development which was accompanied by a "regime of self-development" (De Rooy 2002, 238–41), or by what De Jong (2014) calls a "libertarian repertoire" focused on individual freedom and development.[32] After the successful 19th century emancipation movements, now it was the individual (as well as the new groups of women, homosexuals, and migrants) whose emancipation could be aspired for (Lucardie 1997, 447). The founders of D66 were a group of young professionals in their early 30s, belonging to a generation between the political establishment and the Provo movement

(Van der Land 2003, 19–29). Some of them had affiliations with the liberal VVD or the labor party but sought a political path that was more progressive than the VVD and in between liberalism and socialism. Most of them were not active politicians, but scientists, civil servants, business people, working in advertising, and many of them journalists.[33] As such, they were not yet part of the party-political field but were close observers and participants in a public-political debate about what was perceived as a crisis of Dutch politics.

The 1960s so far had been a period of considerable political instability with recurrent cabinet crises and mounting tensions within the main Christian parties.[34] In the period between 1959 and 1965, the Christian parties formed the center of cabinets and mainly governed together with the VVD. Two subsequent cabinets fell early over economic politics as well as the future of the pluralist social institutions. Not only instability as such was criticized, but also the fact that the KVP simply swapped its liberal coalition partner for the labor party after the fall of one of its cabinets and without consulting voters in advance. In the eyes of critics, this was an anti-democratic conservation of political power (Righart 1995, 205–10). The protests of the 1960s further contributed to the perceived urgency with which the political reform was claimed (Van Mierlo 1968). The sense of a political crisis provided an "opportunity structure" for a new party (Lucardie 2004), and the founders of D66 gave a strong voice to this sense, claiming a comprehensive democratization centered on a reform of the political system. They consciously opted for founding a party rather than a social-political movement to assert electoral pressure on the other parties and thus gain factual influence.[35]

Predating the formal party foundation, its initiators published an appeal "to all Dutch who are concerned about the serious devaluation of our democracy" (D66 1966).[36] It contained an assessment of the democratic deficiency, a plan for political and state renewal, as well as a draft program for the future party. From its onset, the focus on equal individual liberty and emancipation constituted a second spear point of the party. The critique of the political system was in the first place one of its pluralism, and further of the central position of confessionals in the political field. The party founders criticized the established parties for their allegedly outdated ideologies, which worked to preserve the political status quo. Against that, they positioned D66 as a "program party" and soon adapted the concept of "pragmatism" to indicate its ideal of making politics.

According to Van der Land (n.d.), it was co-founder Hans Gruijters who had learned about the philosophical strand of pragmatism during a trip to the USA, and who introduced it within the party circles. Also, Glastra van Loon, a legal philosopher who in the 1960s prominently published on the political crisis, who joined D66 in the early 1970s, and whose views seem to have been influential for the party, is said to have been strongly influenced by American pragmatism, and to have introduced such thinking into Dutch legal thought (Schuyt 2003, 43, 46). Pragmatism means thinking in relations rather than in absolute terms, thinking in action and its consequences rather than in abstract principles and values, and understanding concepts via their consequences rather than in any essentialist way (Schuyt 2003, 42–4). Already in the postwar breakthrough movement, pragmatism had been guiding educational reformers, and it was criticized for denying the necessity of founding knowledge and action in a Christian revelation (Biesta and Miedema 1996, 16; De Jong 2014, 259–61). The founders of D66 thus stepped into an established conflict, the party's break-away from the notion of principles-based politics was respectively attacked as opportunistic, as lacking a vision, and as ultimately un-Dutch and dangerous (Van der Land n.d.; Van Mierlo 1968).

The fact that the party clothed its critique in the genre of ideology critique further seems to echo the broader end-of-ideology debate that had concerned European and especially US intellectuals since the 1950s and which gained broad publicity with Bell's 1960 book *The end of ideology*.[37] The end-of-ideology theme was part of a broad debate among Western intellectuals about the future of the Soviet Union and Stalinism (Bell 1988a, 132). In this context, ideological politics were seen as intrinsically linked to totalitarianism because of being based on an ethic of ultimate ends rather than an ethic of responsibility (to use the Weberian distinction) (ibid. 136f). Also in the Netherlands, the end-of-ideology theme seems to have been broadly perceived (De Haan 1997; De Jong 2014, 141–3; Rejai 1971). Here though, it seems to have been linked with the debate about pillarization. In the ideology critique of D66 – but apparently also beyond – the notion of ideologies was associated with the old pillars and seems to have been used in the sense of worldviews, for the ideas and principles central to the different parties. Prominent politicians of the labor party and the KVP problematized the alleged end of ideologies as an end to political ideals and a road towards political indifference (De Haan 1997; De Jong 2014, 141–3). For the founders of D66, by contrast, not the end of ideologies constituted the problem, but the way in which the established parties seemed to clutch the outdated ideologies, mobilizing around the outdated principles and symbolic divisions of the pillarized past, thereby falsely concealing positions and divides which factually mattered with respect to the political problems of the time.

The ideology critique of D66 also had an anti-totalitarian tone, given that the ideological positions of the exiting parties – if taken seriously – were incompatible with democratic politics in a diverse society (Van Mierlo 1968). According to the founders of D66 though, the ideological passion Bell feared had long cooled down in the Netherlands; none of the parties were assumed to aim at realizing their respective utopias. Only during elections, they promoted socialism, liberalism, and confessionalism as the three electoral choices, while not factually basing their political actions on either ideology. Their ideological polarization, though, would block the road for political innovation and the appropriate formation of political camps and majorities. This had turned the historical emancipation parties into obstacles to the complete political emancipation of their followers by keeping them divided and preventing the formation of majorities on genuinely political matters (Gruijters 1967, 59–62; Van Mierlo 1968).

In many ways, the party's ideology critique was a critique against the objectivization of political capital through the established parties, a form of critique, which Bourdieu (2001, 30) called the anticlericalism of politics. The party manifesto claimed, "we are no politicians," and the foundation of a party was explicitly labeled a mere tactical enterprise, a means to reform after which the party itself should not remain. This counter-distinction from the political establishment contrasts with the importance given to politics and the concern with a dysfunctional democracy and political indifference. Neither did the ideology critique imply a rejection of political ideas or visions; rather it was a rhetorical combat strategy in a field where power is electorally upheld and changed through mobilizing ideas. In the next section, I wish to show in what ways the ideology critique implied an objective of secularizing politics.

Disenchanting politics[38]

> D'66 did not emerge from a movement based on a life stance or societal perspective, it emerged out of concern about the direction in which the development had gone.[39]

> D66 is focused on reality.[40]

The first quote from Pieter Fokking's "History of D'66" places the party in distinction from the tradition of pillarization and from both religious and nonreligious worldviews. Rather he states the party's foundation to lie in a particular historical situation. This assessment also fits the party's claim on reality and its self-understanding as secular. In what follows, this section uses the party's ideology critique and its agenda of political and state reform to understand its program of secularizing and disenchanting politics. I subsequently elaborate different aspects of a program of disentangling politics from religion(-like) positions and realms.

Disentangling politics from the problem of (religious-nonreligious) diversity

The party's critique of the political system was in important ways a critique of its pluralism, and a claim to change the function of elections from balancing diversity to enabling collective decision-making. The writings of Van Loon are crucial in that respect. He compared the Dutch election system to that of England and the USA. The Dutch proportional electoral system – for historical reasons – mainly aimed at ensuring the proportional representation of different social groups – allegedly represented by the different parties

(Van Loon and Frederik 1964; Van Loon 1967; also: D66 1966). Consequently, governments and the political course were not directly determined via the democratic choice of voters, but the outcome of coalition formations, inter-party negotiations, and compromises between different ideologies. This was compared negatively to the political systems of England and the USA, in which fewer and broader parties existed, and where elections directly aimed at determining a government and an opposition. The Dutch system had been adequate until the Second World War, but by now the worldview and class divides of the past were bridged by a sense of unity, and this rendered the old system dysfunctional and an obstacle to genuine democracy (D66 1966; Van Loon 1967).[41] It was the sense that the established parties still operated with the by-now outdated categories and divides of a pillarized past, which linked the critique of the pluralist political system with the ideology critique.

Demarcating political reasoning from religious and religion-like principles

A second and related aspect of the ideology critique claims the impracticability of revealed truths and religious principles for politics. Gruijters (1967, 60f) e.g. argued that it was simply not possible to derive concrete political programs by drawing on religious convictions – first because it required an interpretation of religious principles, and second because a godly will could hardly be determined by immanent means. Even those who claimed to hold *religious* positions factually only voiced their *political* views. Gruijters emphasized that his purpose was not to criticize religion, but those who counter-factually claimed that political decisions could be based on articles of faith. The ideology critique thus also has an epistemic focus and marks an insufficient differentiation between two realms and logics. It further frames religious truth claims as something personal only, given that they couldn't be tested by immanent means. Following this private-public distinction and slightly modifying the more general epistemic tone, a party note from 1970 asserts that for individual citizens, it was well possible to base their political goals on principles; only as guideline for collectivities and as a party profile, they had no relevance.[42]

Aside from politics based in religious principles, also those based on a "fixed image of society" were rejected because they upheld a certain course and image "through changing circumstances," which led to a mental inflexibility and incapability of responding to new situations or to pragmatically learn from the effects and faults of certain policy directions (Gruijters 1967, 66f). This critique was mostly directed against the PvdA, which would "preach collectivism" even when there were better solutions at hand (Gruijters 1967, 62f). This word-borrowing from the religious context shows that the ideology concept itself was used in a way that renders ideologies religion-like. According to Weber's sociology of religion, the sermon as a collective teaching about religious and ethical matters was originally the medium of prophets, but has become central to the ethical-religious communities of especially Protestant Christianity (Weber [1922] 1980b, V §6). The metaphorical use points to a process of religious community building and a top-down transmission of authoritative knowledge and suggests a disposition of the political towards the religious (Tyrell 2011) – something which is seen to conflict with open debate and a constant process of collective learning and adaption necessary for genuine politics (D66 1966; Gruijters 1967, 59).

All in all, the counter-distinction from religious principles frames politics as secular, while the lending of words from the religious context frames especially socialism as religion-like. The last point is elaborated again in the next section.

Disenchanting politics[43]

While the previous point centered on the gap between revelation and concrete political positioning, another aspect of the ideology critique is the distinction between politics and a "disenchanted" reality on the one hand, and transcendent and chiliastic hopes on the other hand. Ideological politics are associated with merging the two realms, which is expressed in the word "heilstaat," which Van Mierlo (1968) uses to speak of socialist, liberal, or Christian political utopias. The word links the Christian notion of spiritual salvation (heil) to a worldly social-political order (staat).[44] Here the eschatological dimension of religion is transferred to the political in the sense of making politics a tool or object of ultimate means and absolute states of salvation. Such chiliastic orientation towards ultimate means conflicted with an alleged disenchanted present, the idea of realist politics, and a democratic constitution in a diverse society (Van Mierlo 1968). Mannheim as well linked the concept of ideologies with a narrative of secularization; here though it is a narrative of incomplete secularization, and this was also Bell's idea, considering the emergence of ideologies as a "political expression of eschatological creeds" after the "break-up of chiliastic religious movements as a political force" (Bell 1988b, 324). A different aspect of this theme of disenchantment is the skepticism towards strong securities, and also this was linked to a narrative of secularization. Van Loon (1997) considered ideologies as derived from a "conviction deeply rooted in our culture, which is that history knows fixed principles and securities, which tell us how we have to live our daily lives and how we should face the insecurities therein." Such conviction was inspired on the one hand by the Christian notion of history, and on the other hand, by the 18th century belief in progress.

Ideologies were thus marked as both a secularized expression of Christianity and as religion-like and contrasted with a genuinely disenchanted political perspective. The party manifesto states to not offer an "only saving (alléén-zaligmakende) solution" but possibilities for a solution – this obviously being a reference to the dogma of the Catholic church as only saving

(D66 1966). Breaking with the tradition of the 19th century, the party did not publish a program of principles and announced to recurrently update its program in the light of present developments.

Demarcating a common public realm from sectarian concerns

A fourth aspect of claiming politics as secular is the distinction between public political debates and shared public concerns on the one hand, and particularistic religious and nonreligious worldviews on the other hand. The notion of a common realm is thereby linked with an ethos of collective responsibility for a liveable future, which transcends different material and spiritual expectations (D66 1997, 17). The party note from 1970 rejects party foundations on the base of confessionalism, but also stresses that D66 and other secular parties would leave enough scope for Christian politics. D66 is characterized as a program party, which brought together "people with very different religious and worldview convictions, who found each other in their concern over the shortcomings and dangers of the political and social system and in their shared consciously radical-democratic sentiments" (D66 1980 [1970]). As an individual source of inspiration, religion is accepted, but not as a principle and base for collective organization and action.

Renewing politics in the light of a depillarized and disenchanted present era

A more general point to mention is that the ideology critique of the party founders had a tone of keeping up with the times. They referred to a historical process of deconfessionalization and disenchantment to which established politics still had to adapt. The pluralist politics were not merely denounced as politically inefficient, but as inadequate to a post-pillarized presence (Gruijters 1967, 50; Van Loon 1967). The party manifesto claimed that the ideologies of the current Dutch political parties "give no answers *anymore* to the questions that matter to us" (D66 1966; emphasis mine). The present was "*no longer* marked by truths, securities, by dogmas," and this was "what you had to live with, and also do politics with" (Van Mierlo 1968, emphasis mine; see also: D66 1997, 19). Speaking on behalf of the party founders, Van Mierlo (1968, emphasis mine) stressed that "we no longer wanted ideologies, [. . .] we *no longer* believed in them." The end-of-ideology theme was thus considered a social reality, but both the dynamics of an old political field and the culturally deep urge for meaning made it necessary to claim and keep alive the urge to courageously live in a state of soberness, facing a disenchanted world in life and politics.

In sum, the ideology critique of D66 demarcated politics as secular in four interrelated ways: through disentangling its function from the problem of balancing (religious-nonreligious) diversity, through disentangling political reasoning from religious and religion-like principles as well as from chiliasm, and through demarcating a public political realm against religious and religion-like sectarianism. These claims were made and emphasized by claiming them as a requirement of the time, asked for by a secularized presence. The critique of ideology neither implied a critique of political ideas as such, nor advocated for technocratic solutions. A core motive for the party's aspiration of secularizing politics was the possibility of adequate and efficient collective action, and in that sense it was linked to an ethic of soberness, realism, and responsibility.

At the base of the party's ideology critique is the ideal of a democratic public-political realm in which free and emancipated citizens[45] engage in collective decision-making for the sake of "world mastery" (Weber [1920] 1986, K&T VIII). Governance should not be based on a compromise between different ideologies or worldviews, but on one consistent vision, and this required a public culture of debate and controversy, a (shared) notion of reality, fact-based decision-making, goal-oriented politics, as well as a transparent and efficient way of determining and executing a majority will (D66 1966).[46] Weber linked the concept of world mastery with especially Reformed Christianity, but the founders of D66 placed it in opposition to religious, or better confessional politics (Weber [1920] 1986, K&T VIII).[47] The theme of "actual" problems and threats, which could not be left unaddressed without negative consequences, was central to the ideology critique, and while ideological politics were seen to distract from reality, the founders of D66 made a claim to reality (Gruijters 1967, 66f).

Such an ethic of soberness, realism, and responsibility was most explicitly articulated in a much later party publication titled *From ideology to political responsibility* and an article announcing this publication with the title "survival, and collective responsibility" (D66 1997; Van Loon 1997).[48] The paper sketches a dystopian notion of a technocratic future in which the "survival of man on earth" itself is threatened, and asserts the necessity of an active society and a change of mentality and life style to address this threat. Politics need to lead the debate on the future of society, not only for its own sake, but because it would have negative social effects if it failed to do so. By bringing chiliastic hopes into politics, ideological politics are seen to conflict with both (liberal) democracy and with political realism, both of which were necessary for adequately addressing *real* problems.

All in all, the ideology critique of the party does not directly counter the notion of a necessity to represent a worldview pluralism in politics but claims that the worldviews allegedly represented were no longer relevant in society. They did so as part of and reflection on the general trend of depillarization.

This section pointed to the concern for collective agency as a core motive for secularizing politics. Complementing this, the next section focuses on liberty and equality as a second core motive for this aspiration. It also shows how shifting power relations in politics eventually enabled far-reaching

Secularity and the assertion of individual equal liberty

If collective agency was one central guiding idea of the party's ideal of secularization, a second core focus was the ideal of individual and equal liberty, placed against undemocratic hierarchies as well as horizontal inequalities. This ideal of equality manifested in calls for the democratization of (political and legal) authority – its de-mystification as well as the claim for the equal recognition for nonreligious worldviews on a par with religion (D66 1967; Gruijters 1967). The call for liberty manifested in calls to abolish the laws on pornography, film censorship, and blasphemy, all of which had been issued by different confessional cabinets in the first third of 20th century (D66 1967). All these measures implied a further disestablishment of Christianity.

The 1960s, as mentioned, had given rise to an individual liberty frame that accelerated the emancipative moment of the first breakthrough movement while also challenging the paternalism of its social-political elites (De Jong 2014, 181; Kennedy [1995] 2007, 152–5, 173–9). Individualism had already been a core object of struggle between confessional and secular parties in the 19th century (gender equality being an example in point), and an individual notion of equality and liberty had been placed in conflict with the pillarized model of pluralism and compromise (De Jong 2014; Van Baalen and Ramakers 2001). Since the late 1970s, the party made liberty and individualism key points of its profile – interlinked with the ideal of democracy as a form of governance guaranteeing these two principles (HVMS 2015). With respect to parliament debates and legislative changes, individualism remained contested between religious and secular parties, mainly concerning the so-called "immaterial matters" of reproductive health, end-of-life decisions, and the legal status of homosexuals, as well as the question of Sunday Rest. While D66 strongly advocated legislative changes in the name of individual equality and liberty, this conflicted with the remnants of an institutionalized Christianity as well as with the model of a pluralist organization of diversity. In what follows, I briefly sketch the developments in the political power relations in the party-political field and point to some main legislative initiatives of the party.

The elections of 1967, as mentioned, had significantly changed political power relations in the sense that the Christian parties lost their absolute majority (for the election results see Table 5.6, at the end of this chapter). Almost a quarter of the votes for D66 came from the three main confessional parties (NIWI 1967, 225).[49] In response to this electoral decline, the three main Christian parties (ARP, KVP, CHU) engaged in a merging process in which a Christian Democratic Party (CDA) was founded.[50] Until 1994, the CDA remained at the center of political power – flanked until today by small and more orthodox Protestant parties: the SGP, and two other Protestant parties, which later merged into the current ChristenUnie (CU). The period since the 1960s was marked by a series of liberalizations of immaterial matters and the orthodox parties (and especially the SGP) unsuccessfully opposed these developments (Timmermans and Breeman 2012, 39, 42f). The 1970s debate on abortion was a first and central point of cultural and political polarization, and here the CDA positioned itself in sharp opposition to the social-democratic and liberal policies on abortion.[51] Later the CDA tried to avoid and depoliticize moral controversies to avoid a double attack from secular and orthodox parties alike (Timmermans and Breeman 2012, 39, 42f; see also: De Rooy 2002, 256–8).[52] Due to its central power position, though, the CDA could determine the speed of ethical liberalizations, and this stirred new anti-confessional sentiments, framing the CDA as an obstacle to democratization and liberalization and fueling hopes in an all secular "purple coalition" between liberals, social democrats, and D66 (Derkx 2006; Koenenman et al. 1987, 29f; Rood 1983, 74f; Rosens 2016).[53] D66 once more was a crucial voice for such secular critiques and ambitions.

In 1994, the first of two such purple coalitions was realized after an electoral decline of the Christian Democrats, and an enormous electoral success of D66 (15.5 percent), which left the party in the position to block any other but the intended coalition.[54] Eventually, (especially the second) purple cabinet(s) realized several crucial liberalizations, such as the liberalization of Sunday shop openings (1996), the opening of civil marriage to same-sex couples (2000), and the legal (liberal) regulation of euthanasia (2001).

From their onset, relevant members of the purple cabinets sought to counter the idea of an anti-confessional or antireligious cabinet. Prime Minister Wim Kok (PvdA) e.g. emphasized that it was a "normal cabinet," and he urged his ministers to attend the regular ecumenic church service at Princess Day (Klei and Van Mulligen 2013, 13).[55] Almost the entire cabinet accepted the invitation of the Dutch Bach Association for the annual Passion of Matthew (Derkx 2006, 72).[56] The purple liberalizations alienated orthodox Christians from the purple cabinets and D66, and this still echoes in the party's perception as irreligious among orthodox Christians (Klei and Van Mulligen 2013, PAGE; Timmermans and Breeman 2012, 56). Among the readers of the *Reformatorisch Dagblad*, D66 is considered the most antireligious among all parties (83 percent), and articles recurrently lambast the party for asserting its own particularistic worldview (RD 2013).

In what follows, I point to two different lines of argumentation to defend the legislative changes on same-sex marriage and euthanasia – one referring to the separation of church and state, and the other claiming the compatibility with (liberal) Christianity. Both ultimately position the party as differentiated rather than irreligious.

In the debate on same-sex marriage, an individual equal liberty model was mainly placed against a pluralist model, favored by Christian Democrats, according to which a registered partnership was introduced while marriage remained a heterosexual institution (TK 1993/1994).[57] This granted parity rights to homosexuals but at the same time institutionalized a twofold institutional structure. Under the second purple cabinet, the course was changed towards an explicit break with "traditional" notions of family in the name of individual equal liberty (Boele-Woelki et al. 2006, 4–9).[58] A core argument for opening civil marriage was to grant equal access not only to the material aspects of legal marriage but also for the symbolic aspects of the institution of marriage.[59] This demonstrates a shift away from the course of the earlier Christian-Democratic coalition, and the government explained that it was well aware of breaking a long tradition of Western civilization, and of changing the notion of marriage (TK 2000b, 7). The law on opening marriage was accepted at the end of 2000 by both chambers.[60] Article 30 of Dutch family law now reads:

1 *A marriage can be started by two people of different or the same sex*
2 *The law only focuses on the marriage in its civil meaning.*

The second point is interesting for the case at hand, as the legislative change is explicitly linked to the separation of church and state and respectively that of civil and church marriage. This emphasis needs to be understood against the criticism the bill faced from the Christian parties, and the message seems to aim at appeasing objections, framing the bill as simply conforming to the already established differentiation of religious and civil marriage,[61] and that the law would respect the diversity of ideas on the notion of marriage by exclusively concerning the civil aspects of marriage (TK 2000b, 6). This declared the change an act of differentiation rather than irreligion.[62] In its reference to the separation of church and state, the case of same-sex marriage differed from the case of euthanasia.

Also here, communicative effort was put into making the change less confrontative and countering the idea of an antithesis between religion and irreligion as well as that of a break with the Dutch tradition of respecting minorities and social-religious diversity (Weyers 2010, 404). Prime minister Kok asserted that the euthanasia bill had been prepared and decided in a careful process and with "respect, understanding, and scope given to all societal, lifestance, and political ideas" (TK 70 2001, 4646f). Respect, though, was no longer interpreted as to accommodate law to the reservations of Christian parties, but in the sense of liberalizing and individualizing legislation on moral matters and as accepting a majority vote.

For the position of D66, the assertion of a moral standpoint seems to have been a second core line of reasoning. From the orthodox Protestant side, the legislative change constituted a reversal of the moral order, a shift from a service to life to a providing of death (TK 70 2001, 4649). Spokesmen of D66 by contrast stressed that they acted according to a moral position of their own. As early as 1984, D66 MP Elida Wessel-Tuinstra issued a bill to legalize euthanasia, meant to "humanize society," given that the good death would not always come naturally (Wessel-Tuinstra 1985, 78f). The bill also refers to a prior statement of the Dutch reformed Church (*Nederlandse Hervormde Kerk*), which had "broken the taboo" on the issue, as well as to a party-internal workgroup called "belief and political action," of which she was a member and which had helped to prepare the bill.[63] In a recent documentary movie on the legalization process, she is filmed with a large Bible in the background (Rosens 2016). Somewhat similarly, Els Borst, the D66 minister who had issued the later "purple" bill, said in an interview with NRC that she resented a "formalist" understanding of God's will, which found it legitimate to prolong life for a week but not end it a week earlier (Oostveen 2001).

Both the minister and the MP thus evoked a non-orthodox Christian position on the matter. Other spokespersons simply stressed the idea of an individual moral autonomy and capacity, also with respect to the legislation process itself. Roger van Boxtel, then senator for D66, e.g. argued that during the election one could feel that everyone was making their own conscious choice (Rosens 2016). The legislative change was thus framed as in line with the Dutch tradition of freedom of consciousness as well as the legitimacy and diversity of moral standpoints. This also resonates in a recent article published in the newspaper *Volkskrant* as well as on the party website with the title: "the protection of life is no monopoly of Christian politicians" (Dijkstra 2016). The assertion of an autonomous moral position is placed against the accusation of a mere antagonistic and amoral position.

The encompassing legislative liberalizations of the 1990s and early 2000s were thus advocated with two arguments which placed the changes in line with well-established institutions of Dutch secularity: the separation of church and state, and the freedom and legitimacy of diverse moral and conscious expressions. The bills were framed as further disentangling the state from particularistic religious categories, while at the same time demarcating religious and other forms of moral reasoning as a legitimate but individual or personal part of public life.

Further untold so far is the increased pluralization of the religious field since the mid-20th century as the result of immigration. Especially since 2002, the presence of Islam has become strongly criticized by a populist political movement that has emerged against the purple political elite and the alleged Islamization of the Netherlands as well as immigration in general. In 2002 the second purple coalition ended, and Christian and nationalist perspectives have gained new strength. The CDA had profiled with an anti-purple opposition course on ethical matters and in 2002 started its political comeback with a debate on public morality (P&P n.d.-b). In 2000, after a longer period of acceleration, two of the small orthodox parties merged into the ChristenUnie (CU). The new party has been quite successful and in 2006 joined the fourth Christian-Democratic cabinet of Balkenende together with the PvdA.[64] The heritage of the purple cabinets remains contested between secular and Christian parties – while the former purple parties tend to treat its reforms as an unfinished project and aim at further liberalizations, the latter (at least the small Christian parties) seek to undo or at the least hold such development and to secure certain exemption rights and the autonomy for religious individuals and institutions.

From the side of the new national-populist movement, D66 is now attacked as part of a "left church" and as a carrier of a "multicultural ideology" that supports the assertion of an "Islamic ideology." While individualism has been a guiding principle for integration policies under the purple cabinets, this is now challenged by a new nationalism which claims an essentialized liberal Dutch culture in opposition to Islam. D66 is among those parties that profiles in opposition to this populist nationalist movement – defending state secularity by stressing the individual liberty and equality of Muslims while at the same time countering illiberal notions of Islam.

In the same way as the political contestations, also debates about D66's religion-relatedness continue.[65] Without recalling all arguments made in such evaluations, also now a recurrent point made is that the party would institutionalize and assert an individualist worldview and a radical version of the Enlightenment in a fundamentalist and dogmatic manner, imposing it on others in the Netherlands (see also: Trappenburg 2000, 54f, 65). This challenges the universality the party claims for an individual equal liberty principle and resonates with Kuyper's frame of an encompassing antithesis of belief and unbelief.

In sum, the debates and competing evaluations of the religion-related position of D66 and the purple cabinets show that the divide between irreligious and differentiated third-space positions are used in diverging ways by different actors with different religion-related positions. The notion of a religion-like equivalent to religion, a moral and epistemic rival, is thereby crucial to critics of the secularization course of D66. While so far I have stressed the party's counter-distinction from principled politics, the next section addresses a party-internal countertrend which has gained gradual dominance in the course of the party history. Based on different party publications, I focus on recurrent ambitions of the party to define a moral-epistemic standpoint for politics that avoids the ideology trap.

Defining a moral-epistemic non-ideological standpoint for politics

Political opponents have recurrently accused the party of not having a reliable position, but there were also internal critics of a mere pragmatic course. Already at the beginnings of the party, there was a faction that criticized a mere pragmatic orientation and feared that such would prevent the development of a vision of man and society. For the first years though, this strand remained in a minority position, but similar critiques were recurrently voiced throughout the party's history (Lucardie and Voerman 1991, 2).

Early documents reveal tentative aims to define and articulate an epistemic, ontological, and moral standpoint for politics beyond pragmatism even if this was not meant to be written down in a concise program. Gruijters (1967, 66f) e.g. referred to the ideal of a radical democratization as a starting point and guiding idea for the party. In his mentioned 1968 speech, party leader Van Mierlo engaged with the matter in a procedural way, elaborating the intellectual process of how to derive a "vision" for political action. He tells that while the party founders had developed their program in a pragmatic and case-to-case approach, they then discovered a binding glue and shared motif orienting the different program points. This, goes the argument, was the start of a vision, and such vision, "the spirit of the program," could be used to derive new positions in a more deductive manner. In Van Mierlo's view, this dialectic approach of a constant and mutual influence of action and vision was what distinguished D66 from the other parties, where "rigid vision or ideology was the imperative starting point" and action was forced into that pattern.[66]

Eventually it was only after a strong decline of electoral support in the mid-1970s that the party started to formulate its substantive outlook or standpoint in respective programs, and this seems to be related to or at the least simultaneous with the party's gradual adaption of a social liberal profile under the leadership of Jan Terlouw (1973–1976), who was front runner and fraction leader between 1973 and 1981 and claimed an autonomous position for the party D66.[67] This programmatic shift corresponded with recurrent discussions about adding a label to the party name, but only in the late 1990s, a younger generation of party members succeeded in convincing the member congress of such a move.[68] Also in other respects, the party chair, and especially Van Loon, in collaboration with the party's scientific bureau, began to explicate and articulate what could be called the party's ideological foundation (Lucardie and Voerman 1991; Van der Land 2014; Varkevisser 1998, 26f). From the late 1970s onwards, the attempt to articulate something like guiding principles of a political position are part of the so called "policy papers" of the party.

The political program for 1977–1981 begins with a separate section, which elaborates the party's "principles of action" and sketches a "post-industrial" future. In 1980, another political program renamed this introduction in "starting points (uitgangspunten) for thought and action of D'66." The election programs of the time selectively adapt their ideas (D66 1977b; D66 1981). All such wordings, as well as later ones, and alike those of Gruijters and Van Mierlo, upheld the counter-distinction from dogmas and ideologies. Most striking in that respect is the already mentioned book *From ideology to political responsibility* which aimed to "more specifically formulate the political-substantive perspective for D66" while carrying the counter-distinction from ideologies in its title (D66 1997, 7).

With respect to the policy program from 1980, Lucardie and Voerman (1991, 22f) tell that the term "uitgangspunten" was chosen over the earlier alternative "grondslagen" (starting point, cornerstone, foundation), because the latter was perceived as too dogmatic. In re-articulating the party's ideology critique, these texts as well demarcate politics as a secular realm, differentiated from religion as well as from nonreligious utopias. The election program from 1977 states, "We don't see politics as a battlefield or a pulpit but as a nonpredictable row of big and small problems that have to be solved as well as possible" (D66 1977b, 1); the policy program from 1980 refers to democracy as an "ethical attitude" and as both "goal and means of political action." Further it states: "Our opinions are not irrevocably rooted in dogmatic writings, but are always open for discussion," and:

> D'66 does not magically present principles from a topper but derives at the starting points for its political action via controllable, public procedures. Democracy is no new faith (geloof). Democracy is a hopeful and risky adventure, started in a period in which humans started to emancipate straight against paternalist and oligarchic traditions. In this ongoing emancipation process, we discover at a daily level new aspects that are worth our political attention and that we therefore express in our political program.
> (D66 1980, 3f)

These selective examples suffice to illustrate two interrelated points, which are that first, D66 defines its position in a way that is substantive and generalized in the sense of spelling out a certain vision of man, society, and politics, and that is located at the level of the individual mindset and dispositions – two features that resonate with the notion of worldview positions – while at the same time, the counter-distinction to non-realist and misleading ideologies as well as to religion is upheld. A similar tone is also chosen in most recent publications of the scientific party office. Since 2006, the party is placed in the liberal (vrijzinnig) tradition by borrowing the concept that was used by liberal Protestants and social liberals in the 19th century (D66 2006, 8). A 2009 collaborate volume published by delegates of D66, the VVD, GreenLeft, and the labor party, as well as some prominent humanists, proclaims "the necessity of political liberalism (vrijzinnigkheid)" (Van Boxtel et al. 2009). In the editors' preface, vrijzinnigheid as a political stance is opposed to dogmatism and defined as a recognizable way of thinking and working rather than a recognizable set of standpoints – an "intellectual starting point" central to modern democracy (Van Boxtel et al. 2009, 9). Again thus, a political position is demarcated in counter-distinction to religion, the label vrijzinnig, once used by liberal Protestants and social liberals alike, is only placed in a political context.

Since 2007, the Mr. Hans Van Mierlo Foundation, a think tank associated with the party, is tasked with articulating and detailing the party's social liberal profile and raising its ideological awareness. This was explained to me by the former director of the think tank Frank van Mil, whom I interviewed in 2013. Given the topic of my research, our talk moved from the efforts to revive the think tank to secularism and its relevance in the Dutch public debate. In that context I also asked him about the rise of populist parties in the Netherlands, and he argued that populists had confronted D66 and progressivists more generally with their lacking ideological foundations. For him personally, this confrontation was a core motive for seeking and developing a more concise idea of social liberalism.

His elaborations reveal a different notion of ideology than the one discussed in the context of the party foundation. Aside from the notion of ideology as a false or outdated vision of reality, and that of ideology as a carrier of totalitarianism, there is now also the notion of ideology (or: principles/values) as a view of the world, which might be particularistic or relational, but which is normatively affirmed and defended. Under the condition of a political struggle of ideas and the rise of populist ideologies, the lack of a concise and formulated standpoint constituted a weakness compared to other more elaborated ideas claiming dominance over the social-political realm. Van Mil speaks of a misconstrued liberalism and postmodernism, which misleads many progressives to confuse state neutrality with a relativism of values, and respectively to withdraw from society and public moral debates into a private realm, leaving the floor to those who claimed the state and aimed to increase its powers over the individual. Relativism and withdrawal thus undermine and threaten both democracy and the existing liberties of an open society. I close this section with two related quotes from the interview documenting this line of reasoning:

> And what you do, is that you hand over the public debate about values, about what is good, about what is fair, or what is worthy to strive for to people that do have strong, or that do express their strong values, which quite often are people with a totalitarian state view. [. . .]
> (Van Mil 2013, 378–81)[69]

> I am thinking about Christian organizations, I am thinking about Muslim organizations, I am thinking about also, well this isn't really organization of people, but as a somewhat abstract movement I am thinking about what populists create within the public debate.
> (Van Mil 2013, 427–9)

To sum up, the recent nationalist populism has taken the place of Christian parties as the main other of D66, and this demagogical threat and the understanding of politics as a competition of ideas also renders any omission to self-positioning an expression of a dangerous relativism of values. The assertion of an ideological standpoint does not challenge but reasserts the secular understanding of politics and renders secularism a value and an important aspect of democracy. Throughout this chapter, I have recurrently pointed to D66 as positioning in a third-space position with respect to religion. The final section centers more closely on the religion-related position and positioning of the party by looking at its voters. Drawing on election research, I

Religious and nonreligious affiliations of the party electorate[70]

As recurrently stressed, the party positioned itself as differentiated from religion and irreligion, and this also resonates with the religion-related positions and attitudes of its voters. D66 was never a party of religiously unaffiliated people per se. The percentage of non-church members was about the national average – something the party shared with secular parties like the labor party and the right liberals, but which greatly distinguished them from the communist and socialist parties (CPN, PSP) (Table 5.1). Since the 1960s, the percentage of non-church affiliated party members in D66 has increased and is now above average. Since 1966, the share of non-church affiliated has risen from about a third of the Dutch population to 53 percent in 1996 and to 67.8 percent in 2015 (Bernts and Berghuijs 2016). This compares to 73–87 percent non-church affiliated among the voters of D66 in 2012. Still, 35 percent of D66 voters consider themselves religious. Based on data from 1979, D66 voters over-proportionally identified with humanism, also when compared to other secular parties (Table 5.2) (Goddijn, Smeets, and Van Tillo 1979). This link between social liberalism and humanism also manifests in the fact that since the foundation of the Humanist Association, five out of twelve times, the chairperson was affiliated with D66.[71]

To a certain extent, survey data also gives information on people's normative ideas regarding the relation of religion, worldviews, and politics. In the 1960s e.g., the voters of D66 were far less inclined to consider their party choice a principled one, something which resonated especially well with the voters of the Protestant parties (NIWI 1967, 99). According to recent data, D66 voters stand out with a particularly high level of support for

Table 5.1 Non-church affiliation; party comparison

Non-church-affiliated voters (%)	VVD	D66	PvdA	CPN	PSP	CDA	CU	SGP
1967 (NIWI)[72]	29	34	38	64	50			
1979 (GNL)	51	49	69	100	82	9		0
2011/12 (DANS)	70	73	63	SP: 69		31	8	0
2012 (Nat KO)	75	87	82	80		27	10	9

Table 5.2 Relatedness with humanism; party comparison

1979 (GNL) (%)	Ø	ND	VVD	PvdA	D66	CPN	PSP	CDA	SGP
Strong relatedness with humanism[73]	9	15	9	12	18	15	52	2	0

secular politics in the sense of disagreeing with the idea of religion being a good guide in politics (Table 5.3). Still, 43 percent of D66 voters state that their faith greatly influences their political attitudes, a score which more than doubles the support for religion-based politics. Faith might have been understood as a personal inspiration rather than a collective ideology and doctrinal course.

The importance given to matters of secularity was only measured in the 1960s. Then, the voters of D66 stood out with an over-proportional concern about the relations of religion and nonreligion in the country. As Table 5.3 shows, this distinguished D66 voters from all established parties while rendering them alike to the voters of socialist/communist as well as the reformed parties.[74] With respect to religion-related conflict issues polled at the time – the need to limit the scope of antireligious propaganda – the voters of D66 found themselves at the opposite pole compared to those of the Christian parties, and they stood out with highly under-proportional support rates. They were also significantly different from the group of non-church-affiliated voters in general (Table 5.4).

If judged by its voters, D66 is not positioned in a binary opposition to religion, but its focus on political and state secularity is carried by non-affiliated, irreligious, and religious and religiously affiliated people alike. In parts and at least in the sense of a personal inspiration, they also give relevance to religion in politics. What its voters share is a strong orientation towards the values of liberty and political and/or state secularity.

While in 1967, D66 was one of the parties giving expression to the political dissatisfaction of a non-church-affiliated and liberal population, this picture has been reversed (NIWI 1967, 185, 188).[75] According to current data

Table 5.3 Religion and politics; party comparison

2012 (NaKO)	Ø	VVD	PvdA	SP	D66	CDA	CU	SGP
Religion is a good guide in politics (fully/agree)	24	17	15	13	12	63	90	89
Fully disagree	34	35	40	39	47	8	0	0
Faith has great influence on political attitudes (fully/agree; DANS 2011/12)	43	37	38		43	50		100

Table 5.4 Perceived religious-nonreligious conflict

1967 (VU) (%; values not exact)	Ø	ND	VVD	PvdA	D66	CPN	PSP	Q	ARP	SGP
Main conflict religious/nonreligious	7	9	3	6	15	9	10	4	11	14
Too much freedom for propaganda against religion	32	17	23	28	5	20	4	37	41	79

on satisfaction with the political system, moderate satisfaction is quite high among nearly all voters. If one looks at the more extreme answers (very/ not satisfied at all), D66 voters stand out as the most satisfied, while voters for orthodox parties (especially SGP, but also CU) are less satisfied.[76] This echoes the changing power relations outlined before (Table 5.5). Geert Wilders' populist party PVV represents the most unsatisfied voters. In sum, one may say that the religion-related frustration with politics has somewhat reversed since the 1960s.

Table 5.5 Satisfaction with Dutch democracy

2012 (NaKO)	Ø	VVD	SP	PvdA	D66	CDA	CU	SGP	PVV
Very satisfied	17	19	9	18	29	17	8	10	2
Very/ fairly satisfied	83	90	78	86	91	89	71	76	50
Not at all satisfied	1	1	2	1	0	1	0	7	6

Table 5.6 Election results, Second Chamber

Selected election results Second Chamber (%; rounded)	1963	1967		1994		2002	2006	2012
KVP	32	27	CDA	22		28	27	9
ARP	9	10						
CHU	9	8						
PvdA	28	24		24		15	21	25
VVD	10	11		20		15	15	27
D66		4		15		5	2	8
SGP	2	2		2		2	2	2
GPV	1	1		1	CU	3	4	3
PVV							6	10

Table 5.7 D66 electoral strength and government participation

Year	Seats Second Chamber (D66)	D66 participation in cabinets
1967	7	
1971	11	
1972	6	Den Uyl
1974 (PS)	1%	
1977	8	
1981	17	Van Agt II
1982	6	
1986	9	
1994	24	Kok (Paars) I
1998	14	Kok (Paars) II
2002	7	
2003	6	Balkenende II
2006	3	

Summary and concluding remarks

The overall interest of this book is to understand the discourses and practices that constitute phenomena as irreligious, religion-like, or differentiated, and this chapter centered on the political field as an arena in which the place of religion in politics and other fields, as well as the notion of nonreligion, is negotiated. Mainly the chapter focused on the Dutch party D66 and framed it as a carrier of political and state secularization. As a historical background to the party formation, it sketched the historical defeat of 19th century liberalism in consequence of the rise of confessional organizations. Liberals had aimed at excluding confessionalism from the political public, which they construed as neutral to confessional divides. Calvinists attacked this notion of neutrality by construing politics as necessarily religion-related as well as divided by a binary divide of belief and unbelief. This rhetorically paved the way for a pluralist organization of politics and society and the subordination of the liberal notion of a differentiated secular realm under the confessional logic of competing worldviews. In consequence of the success of confessionalism, the divides in the political field came to echo the religious and nonreligious positions and divides of the time. Until far into the 20th century, politics remained committed to the balancing of religious-nonreligious diversity.

Against this background, the chapter sketched the foundation of D66 and its entry in the political field, which corresponded to the more general break with the pillarized and confessional era in the 1960s. I further showed how in the 1990s, D66 used its strategic position in the political field to achieve the first all-secular government. Once in power, they pushed for a further disestablishment of Christianity and the secularization of state and law. Last but not least, the chapter briefly pointed to the rise of a nationalist movement which is based on its own criticism of ideology, now challenging D66 as part of a "left church."

Two central and interrelated sets of values served as motives for the party founders' secular ambitions and shaped the profile of the party. A first motive was that of collective, responsible, and democratic agency. The party founders felt that the established and propagated religion-relatedness of politics would hamper its function of facilitating collective decision-making, and they attacked the other parties for holding on to outdated ideologies. I showed how the party's criticism of ideology framed politics as secular and differentiated from religion. A second core motive was that of individual equality and liberty rights. Part of the party profile from the onset, it gained particular importance in the 1990s. In the conceptual language of this book, their objective was to influence society.

Complementing the historical perspective, two further sections dealt with the party's nonreligious positioning, first by sketching its gradual adaption and articulation of a moral-epistemic standpoint for politics, and second by focusing on the religiosity and nonreligiosity of its voters. Both sections point to the party's asserted notion of politics as disenchanted and differentiated from religion (and irreligion). Kuyper's antithesis denaturalized an immanent conception of politics and rendered it as a worldview. For the founders and current members of D66, such an immanent perspective on politics and social life as such is taken for granted. From such a perspective, religion is also an immanent phenomenon and an aspect of human culture, rooted in the capacity and urge to build worlds and to associate institutions and acts with (partly ultimate) meanings and hopes. Such an immanent perspective on religion also informs the notion of certain phenomena being insufficiently disenchanted and religion-like, an accusation made towards the old opponents of confessionalism, liberalism, and especially socialism.

All in all, the distinction between irreligion and third-space positions organizes the interrelation of liberals, socialists, and orthodox in the sense that liberals distinguish themselves from irreligious and religion-like socialism while they are themselves perceived as irreligious from the orthodox perspective. While Kind demonstrated how some Swedish humanists consider a direct competition with religious faith groups, seeking to enter and extend the religious field, such debates play no role within D66 despite its links with Dutch humanism (see Chapter 3). This positioning of D66 as differentiated from religion and irreligion matches its electoral rootedness within diverse religious and nonreligious milieus as well as the general institutionalized differentiation of worldviews and politics in the Netherlands.

Since the party foundation, recurrent phases of electoral loss have stimulated attempts to formulate a standpoint. Recently it is the rise of a new nationalist movement that has renewed the necessity of principled politics, and it is against this challenge that the party has recently articulated and asserted its standpoint. The theory chapter of the book introduced the schematic distinction between NR 1 and NR 2 to systematize competing modes of nonreligion, and themes or aims of moving away from specific relations with religion (Chapter 2). The position of the party at the time of its foundation might be considered an aim to move away from religion and religion-likeness alike, and to also constitute politics respectively. In that sense it can be said to have taken a NR 2 position vis-à-vis confessionalism (R 1) and socialism (NR 1). Questions might emerge as to whether the recent articulation of a social liberal standpoint constitutes a shift inside the formerly rejected ideological field, or as becoming religion – like and from an NR 2 to a NR 1 position. While to a certain extent this is plausible; not only a substantive profile and mentality is increasingly articulated, but at times even the word ideology is used. At the same time though, the counter-distinction from unreal ideologies, dogmas, and religious politics is upheld, and in that sense the party still positions in a similar way and along the old conflict line. The shift might thus be a change towards articulating a third-space orientation rather than leaving it.

Notes

1 This is the title of a book by Eginhard Meijering (2012), who has written on the decreasing relevance of Bible-based and theological references in Dutch parliament. The title echoes that of the prominent book *How God disappeared from Jorwerd* by Geert Mak.
2 According to Van Dam (2011, 47), it is only in the 1950s that the term pillarization was used.
3 Core examples are the collaborative federation between Catholic and socialist workers' organizations and the "secularization" of a formerly Catholic newspaper.
4 At the time of its foundation, the abbreviation still carried an apostrophe (D'66), which was later removed.
5 Aside from D66, this was also the Boerenpartij (Farmers' Party) founded in 1958, as well as socialist and communist parties PSP and CPN.
6 A few books on the process of depillarization and the cultural changes in the second half of the 20th century, though, mention the party foundation (De Jong 2014; De Rooy 2002; Kennedy [1995] 2007; Righart 1995), and there is a detailed history of the party, which however has a more party-internal focus (Van der Land 2003). These books, however, are not interested in conceptualizing secularity or nonreligion. In a previous collective article, we have placed the history of pillarization and depillarization in the broader context of long-term shifts in the notion of secularity in the Netherlands, then placing central focus on the ideal of individual liberty that gained importance with the 1960s (Schuh, Burchardt, and Wohlrab-Sahr 2012). Regarding the conceptual approach to secularity, Van Dam and Van Trigt (2015) have apparently at the same time developed a somewhat similar approach based on prior work of Van Rooden.
7 The conceptual sections of this chapter have been thoroughly reworked after peer review, and I thank the anonymous reviewer for pushing me to work out my conceptual ideas and arguments in more clarity.
8 Swartz states that the mobilization power of ideas is that which Bourdieu considers to be specifically about ideas in the political field.
9 This does not imply a pre-political self-understanding as a collective; rather the process of political mobilization can explicate latent notions and create such collectives.
10 Irrespective of their oppositional stance to religion, such actors can be considered part of the same field rather than religious ones. Weir (2014) e.g. has analyzed such groups as being part of a confessional field.
11 Bourdieu speaks of a structural homology between fields, and points to the structural affinity of actors in homologous positions of different fields or the social structure (Bourdieu 1985; Hilgers and Mangez 2014). These homologies are the consequence of the fact that each semi-autonomous field is co-determined by the relations in the field of power. As stated in the theory chapter, Bourdieu understands the field of power to be structured by the opposition between dominated cultural capital and dominant economic capital, while Mangez and Liénard argued that it could be co-structured by additional divides, including that between religious and secular positions (Mangez and Liénard 2014, 185f).
12 De Rooy (2001) considers the period between 1830 and 1860 as a phase of pre-pillarization.
13 The term liberalism, which was known in Dutch language since 1820, had a pejorative notion.
14 Liberals were constitutionalists, not democrats.
15 The Union of Utrecht (1579), which served as a constitution for the early republic, guaranteed basic religious freedom in the sense of a freedom of consciousness.

16 In the first place, this gave equal organizational freedom to the Catholic Church in the Netherlands, put into law by the first liberal cabinet, which led to massive protests and the eventual fall of the cabinet.
17 In anti-revolutionary thought, God was the sole legitimate authority and the precondition and guarantee of human liberty. The revolutionary act of giving authority to man was conceived as a reversal of the legitimate order and as ultimately subjecting man to the illiberalism of mass rule and totalitarianism (Jellema 1957, 481; Kuyper [1931] 1999, 87f).
18 It was only at the end of the 19th century that non-denominationalism became an urban and upper-class phenomenon (Knippenberg 1998, 214f).
19 De Rooy (2001) considers the period between 1830 and 1860, marked by the self-organization of Calvinists and the eventual adaption of liberals to the new situation, as the second phase of pillarization. The buildup and mutual competition of Catholic and socialist organizations fell in the third phase between 1890 and 1917.
20 Derkx (2002) speaks of the party becoming also the cultural and possibly spiritual home for the non-church affiliated left. This only changed with its transformation into the labor party (PvdA) after the second World War when Christian socialists were explicitly addressed as potential party members.
21 Kuyper's relation with socialism seems to have been ambivalent: on the one hand, also he was opposed to the social costs of capitalism and even spoke of the need of a "Christian socialism" (Jellema 1957, 477). On the other hand, he considered Marxism the most consistent heir of the French Revolution and thus as a central antagonist. In the early 20th century, it was his cabinet that harshly suppressed a socialist workers' strike (Jellema 1957, 477, 480). For social liberals, state intervention into the social and economic realm was necessary to guarantee equal chances and counter class struggle and capitalist exploitations (De Rooy 2002, 59, 62–4, 66f, 72–6, 92–6; Dudink 1997; see also: Aerts 1997, 482f).
22 The concept of worldviews originated in 18th century German philosophy and was broadly used in the 19th century.
23 This explicit reference to social or functional differentiation distinguished Kuyper from other Christian thinkers of his time.
24 The ARP did not remain the only party in the Protestant camp. In 1908, the Christian Historic Union (CHU), a right-economic split off from the ARP, was founded, and in 1918 the Reformed Political Party (SGP) was founded, which differed from Kuyper and objected to the separation of state and church.
25 The first liberal party (Liberal Union, LU) was founded in 1885. In the liberal camp, various parties resulted from schisms or mergers: such as the Alliance of Free Liberals (BVL), the Liberal State Party (LSP), and the Liberal Democratic Union (VDB).
26 Based on the party programs, the positioning of socialists is more difficult to assess. The characterization of the SDAP as a cultural or spiritual home refers to its, more or less implicit, humanist and atheist profile (Derkx 2002). The programs of principles of the SDAP from the end of the 19th century as well as from 1912 and 1937 do not make any reference to worldview positions, to religion, science, or materialism. They are centered on the social question and a transnational class struggle. Since 1937, the program names democracy as its core principle. Only the PvdA program of principles from 1947 explicitly states that the party is open to "persons with very different life-convictions that agree with its program of principles" and further recognizes "the intimate relation of life-convictions and politics."
27 With respect to their confrontative style of politics, socialist leader Ferdinand Domela Nieuwenhuis has been compared to Kuyper, as someone who took political divides and conflicts seriously; like the Calvinist party, also the socialist

Secularizing politics in the Netherlands 139

one was based on a particular propagated ideology (Tanja 2011, 68, 71; Van Veldhuizen 2013).
28 Between 1888 and 1919, liberal and confessional cabinets alternated.
29 In 1918, female suffrage was introduced.
30 Ellemers does not specify which sectors he means.
31 The main confessional parties (the Catholic people's party KVP, the Calvinist Anti-Revolutionary Party ARP, and the Calvinist Christian Historical Union, CHU) were reestablished, and the former liberal parties ultimately merged into the current VVD. Social Democrats (the SDAP) for the first time in 1939 participated in a short-lasting cabinet with confessionals and social liberals.
32 For a history of the party see: Menno van der Land (2003), Lucardie (2002, 86–90), and Lucardie and Voerman (1991).
33 Bourdieu spoke of the journalistic field as part of the political field, a notion which has also been challenged (Bongaerts 2008, 199f).
34 The political developments of the time are summarized well in the following short articles of the website *parlement en politiek*: Kabinetscrisis 1960: de bouwcrisis, Kabinetscrisis 1965: de omroepcrisis, Kabinetscrisis 1966: de Nacht van Schmelzer, Kabinet-De Quay (1959–1963), Kabinet-Marijnen (1963–1965), and Kabinet-Cals (1965–1966) (www.parlement.com/).
35 D66 was not meant to become an institutionalized party, but only temporarily serve to blow up the political system. This was followed by a considerable period in which the party collaborated with the labor party and other small left parties to realize a progressive political front (Van der Land 2003, 73). Only then it would start positioning as an autonomous party in the political field.
36 Aside from this manifesto and the first party program, this chapter draws on the following documents: two early speeches of the long-term party leader Hans van Mierlo (1931–2010), an early party note on its political positioning, and selected writings of intellectuals who were related with the party and influenced its course and which are by now considered part of the historical canon of the party. With respect to the third point, these are a book by co-founder Hans Gruijters (1931–2005) in which he elaborated his choice for D66, and two early articles by the legal philosopher Glastra van Loon (1920–2001), who in the 1960s prominently published on the political crisis, whose ideas were taken up by the party founders, and who in the early 1970s joined D66. I also integrate one later publication of the party's program commission central for the issue at hand from 1997, as well as an article in which this publication is announced in the party's member magazine.
37 The end-of-ideology debate was associated with the works of Daniel Bell, Martin Lipset, Edward Shils, and Raymond Aron.
38 The title is not only a reference to Weber, but mostly borrowed from Quack's (2012) monograph on Indian rationalists, titled *Disenchanting India*. This, however, is not meant to suggest an equally rationalist agenda for D66.
39 Pieter Fokking (1980, 1) "The History of D'66 [De Geschiedenis van D'66]," Fokking is a former university teacher of Philosophy and member of the D66's program commission.
40 Hans Gruijters (1967, 67), "Daroom D66."
41 Somewhat surprising on that background is that the appèl states that the rules of the political system would date back to 1848, and not e.g. 1917, when proportional representation was introduced. In my understanding, the year of 1848 is associated with the double structure of Dutch parliament and the only indirect vote of the First Chamber, which D66 aimed to abolish. The First Chamber, meant to balance potentially extreme results of the more democratic Second Chamber, was/is thus in conflict with the party's ideal of more direct democracy. Some authors criticize that the Dutch political system has

accommodated to the prior monarchical rule too much. (Compare: D66 1967; Gruijters 1967, 32f, 43.)

42 The same note also stressed that the party, despite its rejection of confessionalism, left sufficient scope for the political activism of Christian party members.

43 Weber uses disenchantment for the declining faith in magical relations and meanings which set in with the ancient Jewish prophecies, was furthered by Hellenic scientific thought, and was completed in the Puritan reformation and later empirical scientific developments (Weber [1919] 2002, [1920] 1986, 94f, 564). In this context, disenchantment means a state of soberness vis-à-vis ultimate truth claims and salvation hopes.

44 The word *heil* (literally: health, wellbeing) carries a religious connotation by also referring to the Christian concept of salvation from sin, and is still used in a somewhat spiritual meaning in compound words such as *Leger des Heils* (Salvation Army) (EWN 2004–2009a). The word "staat" literally translates to status, condition, status groups, politics, and government of a people (EWN 2004–2009b). The compound word "heilstaat" can be used as a state of devotion towards God – thus in an 18th century verse-composition of Psalm 119: 37 ("Al wie U vreest , zal op mijn' heilstaat letten"). Today it is most commonly used for somewhat eschatological political utopias.

45 De Jong (2014, 178) writes that, in contrast to the earlier breakthrough movement, D66 portrayed the citizen as already emancipated, emphasizing that this is also why they claimed an abolition of the then still existing electoral duty.

46 In similar terms, also Bell spoke of a new pragmatic consensus.

47 Also Weber discussed the tensions between the rationalisms of different value spheres (Schluchter 1976, 275). Schluchter (1976, 280) also linked the notion of conscious world mastery with Weber's notion of an ethic of responsibility, which again was central to Bell's thinking and fits in with the ideas of the party founders.

48 Again this was also central to the work of Bell (1988a, 136f).

49 Another quarter came from the left parties and one third came from the right liberals and a right Protest party; almost 7 percent were new voters.

50 It no longer positioned itself as directly based on the gospel, but as representing a "political conviction" that had been developed as a response to the appeal of the gospel (Ten Napel 2012).

51 The first program of D66 had already called for an open debate on abortion.

52 Later also the CDA liberalized its position. The abortion law passed under the first cabinet of Lubbers (CDA, 1982–1986), which granted impunity for abortions under certain conditions without legalizing it (P&P n.d.-a). Assisted reproduction, embryo, and stem-cell research and same-sex marriage received much less consideration by parties in electoral struggles (Timmermans and Breeman 2012, 42).

53 Others, like old VVD leader Dijkstal, claim that there was no secular reason for the purple cabinets as the CDA had sufficiently liberalized. In any case, the contrasting picture of the envisioned purple coalition was the so-called "staphorster Variant" – a possible minority cabinet of Christian Democrats and right liberals with support (gedoogsteun) from the small orthodox parties (Klei 2011, 232).

54 Internationally, the purple coalition was mostly famed for its so-called polder model, an institutionalized dialogue of employers, unions, and politics for determining economic and loan policies, commonly regarded as part of the third way movement in European social democracy (The Economist 2002, for a more critical analysis see: Van Apeldoorn 2009). In fact, this structure has its origins in the more corporatist policies of the prior CDA-PvdA cabinet, but it was continued under the purple cabinet and then gained international prominence.

Secularizing politics in the Netherlands 141

55 Also such gestures however were contested. According to Klei, Van Mierlo refused to go to the mentioned church service.
56 Respective evaluations, in any case, seem to depend on different political strategies and interests, both past and present. In a recently published book on the purple cabinets, prominent VVD members decline the relevance of the secular, non-Christian face of the coalitions, claiming that also with the CDA the most important reforms could have been achieved (Van Weezel and Zonneveld 2002, 18–21, 111f). The authors, however, argue that this evaluation seems to reflect rather the party's current position towards the CDA than that of the mid-1990s.
57 The bill foresaw such partnerships for all those living together but being exempted from the entitlement to marriage, something which would include people being closely blood related such as siblings as well as parents or grandparents with their children. This desexualized these partnerships and symbolically reemphasized the exclusive tie between marriage and (hetero-)sexuality. Before the bill was passed, the elections of 1994 brought the purple cabinet into power. This desexualization was reversed even prior to the opening of civil marriage.
58 Within D66, Boris Dittrich (MP for D66 from 1994 to 2006), together with an MP from the labor party, pushed for the opening of marriage, apparently also against partial objections within his own fraction (NRC 2001; TK 1996, 1997/1998). In its 1994 election programs, D66 still claimed a revised version of the partnership model, but in 1998 it focused on marriage. Dittrich brought the opening of marriage into the coalition agreement for the second purple government in 1998 in consequence of which it became the official government position (TK 1993/1994, 2000a, 2000b).
59 The institution of a registered partnership, which had been in place since 1998, should not be abolished, but kept in place, equally accessible to all couples and serve those who wished to avoid exactly that symbolism associated with marriage.
60 VVD, D66, PvdA, GL, and SP voted in favor, as did some second chamber members of the CDA. One MP of the labor party voted against.
61 Art. 68 of Dutch family law forbids religious marriages if no civil marriage has been conducted priorly.
62 Ultimately, the legal change was only a temporary stage in the struggle. The crucial and contested question has been whether registrars may claim conscientious objections if asked to conduct a same-sex marriage. State secretary Job Cohen (PvdA) had granted the small Protestant parties that registrars would not be forced if the conduct of marriage was assured through other means in every municipality (NRC 2007; TK 2000a). In 2014 a D66 bill was put into law, which makes it illegal for registrars to discriminate against homosexual couples (Staatsblad 2014).
63 The Church spoke in favor of the legitimacy of passive euthanasia but stated to be divided with respect to active euthanasia.
64 Between 2002 and 2010, there were four Christian-Democratic cabinets (Balkenende I–IV). The right liberals were the main coalition partner, and both the populist LPF (party of Pim Fortuyn) and later D66 were smaller coalition partners.
65 I searched via lexis nexis in five Dutch newspapers for the following word-combinations: D66 + godsdienst/ christen/ Islam. The newspapers consulted were: the orthodox reformed *Reformatorisch Dagblad*; the once Protestant resistance paper *Trouw*, which used to be close to the ARP and still has a special focus on religion and philosophy; the once Catholic *de Volkskrant*; the liberal NRC *Handelsblad*, and the liberal weekly paper *Elsevier*. The search was limited to articles between 2013 and 2016, which brought around 500 hits.

66 The speech seems to have been an early and important occasion to reflect on the original aims and positions of the party and to decide its future course, and possibly it was also directed at the internal critics of the pragmatist course, offering something like an intellectual compromise. Beyond this, Van Mierlo explained that in parliament, they constantly had to take positions on matters that had not been addressed in the program and that here, one could draw on "a combination of: the spirit of the program, common sense, and if possible the expertise of working groups" (Van Mierlo 1968).

67 Aside from party chairs and fraction leaders, Dutch politics also knows the unofficial position of political leaders who are considered the face of a party, but who are not officially elected. Terlouw is commonly seen to have succeeded Van Mierlo as the political leader of D66 (see: "politiek leider van een partij" at: wwww.parlement.com). Van Loon would in a similar tone position D66 as a fourth strand in Dutch politics (Van der Land 2003, 144f).

68 The party name, however, still has no additional label. In 2006 the party program committee formulated five guiding principles for social liberal politics, and since 2007 the party think tank has began to formulate and develop an ideological base for the party (Van Mil 2013). The think tank is now called "Hans van Mierlo Stichting: Scientific Bureau D66 for social liberal ideas [gedachtegoed]."

69 After rereading this quote, Van Mil added that it would have been more precise to speak of "people with a more etatist, perhaps even totalitarian state view."

70 This section presents survey data on the religious and nonreligious affiliations of the voters of D66, drawing on the following studies: a study by the Free University (VU), including the data set conducted after the 1967 elections (NIWI 1967), the 1979 data set from God in Nederland (GNL), a study by DANS on religion in Dutch society from 20011/12 (Eisinga, Kraaykamp and Sheepers. 2012), and the National Voter Research (NKO) from 2012 (Kolk et al. 2012). All numbers given in the following tables are rounded to the nearest natural figure. Concerning the data set of the VU study (VU 1967), parts of it were lost before digitalization and the numbers are not exact but still highlight inter-party differences.

71 In 1969, succeeding the founder Jaap van Praag, Max Rood became chair of the humanist association, leading the organization until 1977. He had also been a member of D66 since 1966 and in 1982 was Minister for the Interior in the Van Agt cabinet. The second social liberal chair of the HV was Jan Glastra van Loon (1987–1994), who had been among the party founders and was State Secretary and senator for D66. Liesbeth Mulder held the chair from 1998 to 2000, and Roger van Boxtel from 2003 to 2005. Since 2012, Boris van der Ham, also a former member of parliament for D66 (2002–2012), has been chair of the humanist association.

Conversely, D66 is among those parties that get positive reviews by the Humanist Association before elections. Criteria in 2010 were: liberty rights, the separation of church and state, care and education, immigration and integration policies, and medical-ethical matters, privacy, and sustainability (HA 2010).

72 (NIWI 1967, 256).

73 This does not mean membership in the Humanist Association.

74 D66 voters also over-proportionally considered their vote a protest vote, alike to the voters of the socialist and communist parties and the new farmers' party (NIWI 1967, 34).

75 Voters opting for belief as a main principle were the most satisfied with politics at the time, while voters opting for liberty were the most unsatisfied (NIWI 1967, 185).

76 If all church members and non-members are compared, however, there is no great difference. Mainline Christian Democratic voters are highly satisfied, and the orthodox parties are numerically very small.

6 Comparison
Normativities and contested relations

Susanne Kind, Cora Schuh, and Johannes Quack[1]

This book's primary aim was to illustrate the analytical advantages of a relational conceptualization of nonreligion based on three case studies. The book provided a conceptual outline of our understanding of nonreligion (Chapter 2) as well as three empirical case studies (Chapters 3–5) that applied and illustrated this approach. In this final chapter, we summarize some key arguments and observations, which complement our arguments from a comparative perspective. In other words, we conclude this book by highlighting the ways in which a relational approach to nonreligion designed to research different religion-related positions helps to establish new perspectives on contested understandings, roles, and meanings of religion in a specific research setting.

This concluding chapter begins with a summary of our conceptual concerns (Chapter 2), bringing together the central observations from our case studies and the religious and socio-political contexts that inform the nonreligious activism and identities of the respective groups. It then highlights how the activism we studied – notwithstanding the obvious and substantive differences between the case studies – is directed against an apparently privileged status and norm-giving role of religion, something we call *religio-normativity*. Subsequently, we turn to the central characteristics of the different modes of nonreligion we researched. Here, our focus is the respective religious and nonreligious others, the key foci, which inform relationships with them as well as competing modes of nonreligion, particularly how modes of nonreligion shift against the backdrop of organizational and social changes. The chapter concludes with the main aims and benefits of a study of nonreligion by addressing two questions: (1) In what way do our case studies further scholarly understanding of the societies in which they are located? (2) In what ways do our case studies contribute to the study of the diversity of nonreligion?

Summary of the concepts and case studies

Conceptual concerns

This book presents an understanding of *nonreligion* that builds on an analysis of the contestations around positions and borders of fields rather than on a substantial definition of religion or an essentialist characteristic of people, groups, or worldviews that may be seen as cultural and existential equivalents to religion. We employ a relational definition of nonreligion that shifts the focus from the question regarding whether something should be considered religious or nonreligious, to the discourses and practices that constitute a certain phenomenon in relation to or in distinction from religion. The book introduces the notion of a religion-related surrounding (*Umfeld*) that heuristically includes any position outside a specific religious field that stands in determinable relation with positions inside of this field (Quack 2014, 445–6), or, in other words, comprising that which is related to and co-constitutive of a religious field. To achieve this, the case studies analyzed positions and positionings at the periphery and the contested boundaries of the religious field (Chapters 3 and 4), as well as in other fields with contested relations with the religious one (Chapter 5).

All three cases studies drew on the relational approach to explore the positioning of different groups and organizations that self-position as nonreligious in diverse ways and settings. Accordingly, they exemplify the four aspects central for understanding modes of nonreligion. First, they pointed to the various others to which the *non* of their nonreligiosity refers and to which the actors relate as well as the different notions of religion at stake here. Second, the groups refer to different themes and values, most centrally those of truth, social justice and equality, individual liberty, worldview pluralism, and community formation. Third, the case studies underscore the degree to which all groups and subgroups have different objectives for their activism, most centrally those of weakening the organizations' presumed (religious) opponents, strengthening one's identity, encouraging, and gaining (lay-)members, and influencing society at large. Collective actors can also be internally divided in terms of their prime objectives or the means by which they should be reached. For a party like D66, the central goal is to influence society, even if objectives like the notion of reality (not genuinely truth claims) or identity formation can become important and instrumental to achieving this. By contrast, Swedish Humanists are divided over placing their primary focus either on identity and social work, including community formation, or on political activism. Fourth, this book has depicted the ways in which respective actors in each of the case studies can stand in diverging kinds of relations with different religious and nonreligious others. Specifically, the case studies demonstrate how particular actors shape and potentially wish to change their positions in relation to the religious field by engaging in, refraining from, or terminating certain relationship forms. Two such aims were particularly important: moving away from religion-likeness and moving away from religion-relatedness. Both resonate with a central question that motivated this book: which nonreligious positions are shaped by or reproduce logics and rules of their respective religious fields?

Even within an organization, activists at times try to realize different objectives through their social activism and collective self-organization.

While all attempted to weaken the organizations they presumed to be their opponents, the actors differed in denoting who or what is central in this respect. While some focus particularly on strengthening their own identities, others focus more on attracting (lay-)members or voters. One difference in this regard lies in discrepancies between those who see the organization partly as an end it itself (e.g., some representatives of life stance humanism) as opposed to those who see it as a means to different ends, such as to influence the respective society at large (e.g., proponents of opinion-making humanism as well as the D66 party). To highlight the different approaches to nonreligion, we introduced the concept of religio-normativity, which emphasizes the context-specific explicit and implicit normative expectations carried by certain religious traditions and actors, which go beyond traditional and acknowledged forms of institutionalization.

Case studies

The three case studies in this book are located in very different national settings and focus on different kinds of groups. In all case studies, the research constantly oscillated back and forth between, first, the groups' religion-related positioning(s) and orientations, and, second, their objective position in relation to the role of religion in the given society. In the following, we briefly highlight important points with respect to the groups, their relations, and the respective societies. In all case studies, the groups we focused on struggle against and find their religious other in some form or residuals of a religious establishment in the sense that a religious other not only holds, claims, or is attributed a dominant position in the religious field but also beyond, in other fields or with respect to the state. Such establishments might be quite encompassing in some cases, while in other cases there are mere relics of a past establishment. Still those relics can echo and symbolize a continuous claim for dominance and inform forms of opposition, ranging from explicit claims of disestablishment to claiming minority rights.

How individuals and groups position themselves in terms of religion tells us something about the society at large and how it deals with religious phenomena. To connect the case studies with a greater understanding of the societies in which they are located, we start with a national frame, qualified below by the acknowledgement of specific milieus as well as international and global contexts and influences.

Sweden

Sweden is commonly depicted as "one of the most secular(ized) countries in the world" in public as well as academic discourse (Jäntera-Jareborg 2010; Norris and Inglehart 2004; Therborn 1995; Zuckerman 2008). The case study highlights several on-going processes of secularization, like the disestablishment of the Church of Sweden from the state, decreased church membership, and a steadily declining number of people who believe in the traditional Evangelical Lutheran theology, attend church services, and use Christian life-cycle rituals. It is nevertheless important to consider that there is still a high percentage of Swedes (46 percent) who believe in "some sort of spirit or life force" (Willander 2013, 124; with reference to the EVS 2010). Furthermore, as the case study illustrated, despite the official separation from the state, the Church of Sweden maintains a partial and "semi-official" (Cavallin 2011, 45; Bäckström, Beckman, and Pettersson 2004, 20; Pettersson 2011, 123) monopoly position. Yet, the country's multifaceted religious change has pluralized the religious field through, e.g., the establishment of new religious studies and health centers and religious fairs outside the institutional context of the Church of Sweden (Frisk and Åkerbäck 2013).

Against this background, the case study focused on the Swedish Humanist Association (SHA), an organization with around 5,300 members, and its identity politics and activism in the urban settings of Uppsala and Stockholm. While the Church of Sweden is the traditional other of organized humanism, its recent disestablishment, and the fact that it became more liberal and according to critics theologically vague, has resulted in a situation where it no longer seems to be the most relevant religious opponent to some humanists. Others, by contrast, point out that the Church of Sweden continues to hold an influential position, e.g., concerning the provision of life-cycle rituals and communal forms of belonging. For such actors, the Church continues to be perceived as the biggest player in the field. These different evaluations are based on different constructions of a collective identity and related foci as well as aligned strategies and relations, which is evident in the case study in two distinct forms: *life stance humanism* (LSH) on the one hand, and *opinion-making humanism* (OMH) on the other. The study showed that these two forms, related to diverging perceptions of the groups' identity, are negotiated in comparison to each other.

In Sweden, secular humanists develop and offer nonreligious alternatives to religious ones and thereby established mirroring and competitive relationships with the Church of Sweden and other religious actors. At the same time, they increasingly position themselves as a non-governmental political and opinion-making organization in public debates, where they oppose and criticize not only new religious phenomena but also actors they consider to be representatives of postmodernism, New Age thinking, or racism. With respect to members' changing context and different foci, they are engaged in on-going internal discussions about their organizational identity: what work should secular humanists do, and which occupational field is in this regard the "natural" or right ones for them? Which problems and opponents are the most urgent and harmful, and, thus, which of their relationships – competitive or conflictual – are the most effective, suitable, and legitimate? Should their future development include a more comprehensive life stance community, or should they evolve into an even more influential political and public player?

In its attempts to answer such questions, the SHA has found itself split across two different humanisms. First, supporters of LSH refer to the Church's relatively strong position in offering rituals and communal belonging, and seek to become its competitor by attempting to attract potential members as a nonreligious life stance, promoting a universal humanist morality through ceremonial offerings, and consolidating a humanist community. They seek a competitive relationship that is functionally closer to the Church of Sweden than ever before. By contrast, advocates of OMH, the second position, aim to fight religion-related harm primarily through critical observation. From their point of view, humanists are meant to be an opinion-making force that promotes humanist values in the public sphere and engage in conflict and functionally distant competitive relationships. They refrain from entering into functionally close competitions with religious actors and their norm-setting practices that, according to them, reach down to the very details of personal ways of living.[2]

While representatives of OMH think that the quite liberal church does not represent an urgent opponent, they perceive the normative role of rituals and normativity within faith communities as problematic in a more general sense. This critique, then, also applies to humanist rituals and the establishment of a community which is based on a shared humanist life stance. Furthermore, this standpoint leads to claims of outsourcing or abolishing life-cycle rituals from humanist activism. LSH includes humanists who do not perceive alternative humanist offerings as norm-setting as well as those who perceive the same as norm-setting, but as far less dogmatic, dangerous, and exclusive than religious ones.

The Philippines

In contrast to Sweden and the Netherlands (introduced later), the Philippines is commonly considered a highly religious country. It has been extensively shaped by the strong hegemony of the Catholic Church throughout its history. Spanish colonial rule lasted more than 300 years and concurrently resulted in the Christianization of large parts of the Philippine population. Still today, more than 80 percent of the population is considered a member of the Roman Catholic Church. For many, Catholicism became part of their national identity, part of what it means to be a Filipino. Religion, respectively Catholicism, is very much present in the public realm, shaping time through rituals and public gatherings, and also has considerable influence on political decision-making. The respective case study focuses on two groups critical of the Catholic Church: the Filipino Freethinkers (FF) and the Philippine Atheists and Agnostics Society (PATAS). Both groups are based out of urban Manila, while the inter-group divides also give expression to milieu differences.

Despite the differences in terms of the groups' objectives and positions, both echo the dominance of Catholicism as a carrier of community, morality, and ontology. Both groups seek to provide a community, public platform, and voice to marginalized nonbelievers, and they also engage in critiques on the Church's dominant position and political influence (FF), and in the atheist critique of religion (PATAS). The political commitment of both groups, e.g., in their alignment with the LGBT movement, shows their activism in the field of reproductive health matters, as well as state secularity – something obviously linked with the emancipation of the nonreligious. There are also, however, significant differences between the groups regarding differences in foci and relations, which might also be an expression of class differences both between and within the groups.[3]

PATAS stands in a critical, conflict-oriented relation with the Catholic Church, and understands itself to be its antipode. At the same time, PATAS also operates with a more generalized notion of religion and Christianity, whereby its atheism is portrayed as the better alternative to religion as such. The resulting relational assemblage entails PATAS' competition with the Catholic Church. It offers nonreligious conceptualizations of morality and personal integrity, a form of activism that is also directed at countering the stigmatizing effects of religio-normativity on the nonreligious as mentioned previously. It not only challenges the normative expectation of being religious, but also seeks to disembowel the notion of religion, or in other words to cut away the positive associations linked with religion and the negative associations linked with nonreligion.

FF, in contrast, positions itself not as atheist but as freethinkers, which signals a more inclusive position towards personal beliefs (PATAS has also indicated that it might pursue such a strategy as well by placing greater emphasis on the notion of *humanism* in the future). They claim a position alongside Catholicism on the basis of which relationships of dialogue and cooperation could be possible, in addition to those cooperative relationships that they established with members of some other religious minorities, such as the Episcopalian church. They do not oppose religion or Catholicism as such, but argue against the Church as a hierarchical institution, as dogmatic and violating secularism, as oppressive to women and minorities – especially with respect to the freedom to choose in reproductive health matters. This position accepts religion as an individual freedom in a society marked by religious and worldview diversity.

To some degree, both groups' social activism – PATAS' charity project but also FF's fundraising project – further competes with the Church's own charity activism. It draws on a nonreligious and progressive-liberal value base. A core example is reproductive health rights – a public conflict where the complex dynamics of religion, politics, morality, and modernity intersect. Representatives of both FF and PATAS aim to establish a stable identity and a safe harbor and community independent of the Catholic Church and partly in opposition to religion in general. This establishment is perceived as a necessary first step, on the basis of which they want to engage with the larger society by addressing discursive themes such as truth, worldview pluralism, liberty, and equality, e.g., with respect to the debates around the reproductive health bill.

The Netherlands

Similar to Sweden and in contrast to the Philippines, the Netherlands is a second rather secular research setting – a large majority of the Dutch are neither affiliated with any church nor consider themselves religious, the state has officially cut ties with churches, and Christian influences on laws, particularly exemption rights for religious groups, have increasingly been reduced. Still, there is also an important difference in comparison to the Swedish case (and the Philippines): religious diversity has been a key feature of Dutch society since the Dutch Revolt against Spanish rule, and liberty and tolerance for diversity have been central values of Dutch political thought. Such a basic consensus, however, does not preclude competing notions of the scopes and limits of liberty and diversity and the adequate role and notion of religion in state and society. These notions have always been contested and linked to competing claims on and struggles about the categories and divides of social organization. It is also possible to speak of a twofold religious past in the Netherlands, the residuals of which still stir social and political debates: first, the past and for some still relevant notion of the nation as Protestant; and, second, the pluralist institutionalization of religious and worldview diversity, dubbed pillarization.

This case study conceptualized the political field as one through which the role of religion in state and society can be influenced, and while it mainly centers on the political party D66 and its struggle for the secularization of politics and state, it provides a historical background for this by focusing on the emergence of a political field in the mid-19th century as well as the process of pillarization. The process of pillarization involved the pluralization of politics and implied the subordination of a liberal notion of a neutral (secular) political public to a confessional and pluralist system. D66 by contrast was founded in opposition to the remains of this pluralist system and the dominant role of confessionals therein, struggling to secularize the political field and law.

It centered, first, on the party's struggle to secularize politics in the sense of disentangling it from religious and nonreligious worldviews and ideologies. Second, the case study showed how the party in the 1990s used its political power to further secularize politics as well as state and law. Moreover, the study pointed to two motives for the party's concern with secularity: first the value or guiding idea of collective action and responsibility was the core, and second, individual liberty and equality.

The party's secular ideal of politics is based on the distinction between public and private or particularistic realms, and further on an immanent notion of religion as part of the cultural and meaning-making aspects of human life. Religion is not problematized as such, but only in certain forms – if applied to the wrong social questions, if institutionalized in a way that challenges the state's power monopoly, the autonomy of law, or the principle of equal citizenship, and if religion works to fragment the public political realm as the institution through which democratic collective agency is realized. As demonstrated by election research from different periods of time, this ideal of secular politics is carried by an electorate of people with religious and avowedly nonreligious affiliations as well as religiously unaffiliated people. The electorate also diverges from the general group of religiously non-affiliated people in relevant ways and finds its common denominator in the importance given to liberty.

An immanent perspective on religion can at the same time be used to undermine or challenge a secular ideal of politics, when, e.g., religion is framed as culture or a fundamental world perspective and thus as something that is inevitably part of politics. Conversely, such a perspective also works to challenge and relativize secular claims on a common public, rendering them as culturally and worldview-particular as well. In that sense, the distinction between religion, irreligion, and a third space structured the positions and interrelations of parties in the political field while the notion of each concept differed. While liberals since the 19th century aimed to differentiate politics from religion (or confessional diversity), they were framed as irreligious by their orthodox contenders.

Within the political arena, D66 finds its religious others in the different Christian parties. In all cases, these parties stand in conflict with its secular and non-pluralized ideal of politics. Christian parties were criticized for blocking the political process by obscuring genuine political categories and ideas. "Ideological" tensions were greatest with the orthodox Christian parties – at least with respect to the so-called immaterial matters of gender, sexuality, and life/death related matters. The large confessional parties and later mainline Christian Democrats are further criticized for their central power position in the political field, through which they can, flanked by orthodox competitors, block liberalizing reforms.

Relations between parties can be based on (at least) two different forms of competition – direct (for the same voters) as well as indirect (for the greatest share of votes). Furthermore, there are both formal and informal forms of cooperation (such as coalitions or more informal agreements). In the Dutch pluralist context, even small parties can have relevant influence if they are necessary for coalitions, which recurrently stirs concerns among secular liberals with respect to the small orthodox parties. At least at the time of its foundation, D66 competed with the confessional parties in both direct and indirect ways. The combination of electoral wins and particular strategies of coalition forming helped to oust Christian Democrats from political power in the early 1990s. At the beginnings of its history, D66 had supported a so-called progressive coalition with the social democrats and small left parties. While such collaborations are no longer actively pursued at the national level, they can still be seen in some local settings.[4] Still, also in the period after the purple coalitions, there are certain inter-party collaborations and agreements on secular-social liberal matters.

Aside from inter-party relations and despite the institutionalized differentiation of secular politics and nonreligious worldviews, different traceable relations in the liberal strands of the religious and nonreligious worldview field are also evident in the affiliation or activism of party members as well as in the form of informal exchanges or collaborations.

Inter-party competition implies the necessity to formulate a standpoint. At the time of their foundation when it was based on the opposition to confessionalism, the party profiled as non-ideological, but in the course of time, the relations in the political field have changed. Gradually the counter-distinction from fixed principles lost its importance while the demonstration of a genuine position of one's own became important to gain visibility. In the most recent context of rising populism, it has become central to defend social liberalism against the accusation of promoting a relativistic ideology of multiculturalism.

Local, national, global

While a national frame is in many respects central, we do not want to fall into the trap of methodological nationalism and therefore also acknowledge specific milieus as well as international and global contacts and influences. With regard to the case study from the Philippines, the nonreligious groups in question emphasize questions and concerns of members of urban Manila in contrast to the ways of life and perspectives of many people in other parts of the country. Moreover, while their position is crucially shaped by the national legal and socio-political context, it is also embedded in global international relations. For the Netherlands as well, regional and local differences are crucial even if they are not at the center of the respective chapter. It is not by chance that D66 was founded in Amsterdam, the center of the 1960s cultural changes which is positioned as a city of both sexual and lifestyle liberty. The urban center has its other in the so-called Dutch Bible Belt, a region with greater support for orthodox Protestant parties. This regional diversity also manifests itself in different party-internal perspectives on the national organization of secularity.

All three case studies deal with a specific urban and, roughly, middle-class milieu. Secular humanists in Sweden are part of the well-educated elite, and they are most active in urban areas such as Stockholm, Göteborg, and Malmö.[5] Representatives of life stance humanism in Sweden emphasize that addressing individual and social needs, especially by offering life-cycle rituals, provides an opportunity to reach a larger share of the Swedish population than those who advocate a solely opinion-making humanism. They criticize the latter for representing an "elitist club" (Gran 2013, quoting Irene Rune, a member of the SHA), and for remaining intellectually and practically within their milieu. The two groups in Manila represent different milieus in this city, but take similar positions with respect to the rest of the country, knowing that they are sometimes accused of being part of "Manila imperialism." D66 also self-consciously understands itself as a particularly educated and intellectual party, but also self-critically reflects on its elitist position (Trouw 2006).

Debates on religion and nonreligion have a long global history, not only as well-known reference points for nonreligious activism, but also for relations of solidarity or cooperation that can transcend national borders. In both the Filipino and the Swedish cases, global discourses, primarily those related to the so-called "New Atheism," were strongly perceived by nonreligious activists and adapted to their own aims and contexts. In Sweden, the popularity of "New Atheism," among other factors, helped the SHA become a visible public actor (Thurfjell 2015, 98). Furthermore, both the Filipino Freethinkers and the Swedish humanists joined like-minded transnational networks or umbrella organizations like the International Humanist and Ethical Union (IHEU), Atheist Alliance International (AAI), and the European Humanist Federation (EHF). These ties constitute a valuable resource as well as a means to stimulate change. The Swedish Humanist Association is furthermore decisively influenced by what members refer to as their "sister organization," the Norwegian Humanist Association, which functions as a role model and offered to fund the expansion of humanist ceremonial work in Sweden.

In addition to networking with other nonreligious organizations, references to religion beyond the national border play an important role: several SHA members found motives for activism in the situations in other countries like the United States, India, or Bangladesh. Pointing to the ills and wrongs of religion beyond the Swedish context serves not only to illustrate the necessity of global mutual support but also, more generally, that of humanist activism. As Quack (2012, 290) already observed, the influence of like-minded movements in other parts of the world are also manifested in terms of the organizational or formal structures, including their many meetings, publications, and magazines as well as terminology and narratives.

Finally, an international or global perspective has from the beginning also been central to D66's party profile, and the party also operates at the European level, where it also holds a secular and progressive pole position but faces much stronger (religious) conservative opposition than at the national level. In terms of the role of religion, the secular legislation at home might be argued for in the light of international events (Van der Ham and Zunderdorp 2013).

In sum, as this section depicts, nonreligion is not solely placed in a national context but is part of interrelating local, national, and transnational contexts. Global references and relations can be an asset in national religious-nonreligious contestations. On the other hand, they might also be an indicator of globalized religious-nonreligious discourses and exchanges.

Religio-normativity

Despite obvious differences, we find similarities in all our studies in the ways in which the groups are concerned with and significantly related to religion. To explain this, we draw on our discussion of *religio-normativity*. As previously mentioned, religion can carry and support as well as undermine certain symbolic-cultural orders in a given society. Additionally, particular forms of being religious or being "religious" as such might themselves be set as a norm. In what follows we summarize how this concept helps to explain the nonreligious activism dealt with in the different case studies.

Religious or conservative orders: competing symbolic divides

In all case studies, the opposition to an institutionalization of religion goes or has gone hand in hand with a concern for liberal values of individual equality and liberty (and respectively a critique for religious support of conservative orders). Only in the Swedish case such a critique is somewhat of the past, at least with respect to the mainline church.[6] The concern for liberty and equality as central values manifests among other things in support for gender issues and the LGBT movement. The fact that religiously non-affiliated (or liberal) people hold a similar position vis-à-vis religious orthodoxy also manifests itself in expressions like "coming out" as not-religious (Chapter 4). All groups further discussed shared interests with certain religious actors. They all develop at least in part a third-space profile in the sense that they did not merely focus on the binary opposition between atheism vs. theism or unbelief vs. belief, e.g., by placing certain values and notions of secularity at the center without concentrating on personal religiosity. In the case of D66, this position is very much part of the (social-)liberal tradition which has central roots in liberal Protestantism. In the case of the two Philippine groups, this is different, as PATAS and FF have positioned themselves as the main other to religion as such, but have also partly turned towards a third-space profile. From an orthodox position, such a third-space position might be non-recognized and framed as just another version of anti-religiosity – something that points to the recurrently mentioned relationality of what constitutes religion and its others.

Debates on religious conservativism further facilitate a focus on the competing divides with which social-political differences can be framed – with a binary divide between religion and nonreligiosity being only one option. Given that religiously affiliated and dis-affiliated people can be found on either side, the distinction between religion and nonreligiosity runs counter to the divide between liberal and orthodox/conservative positions – especially with respect to notions of gender, sexuality, race, class, age, etc. A second core divide between religiosity and nonreligiosity is that between private and public positions – a position which renders personal religiosity as well as personal anti-religiosity compatible with public secularity – a distinction, which on the other hand might only be plausible for specific religious and nonreligious commitments. Furthermore, the distinction between religion and "culture" might be used to relativize orthodox or conservative "religious" positions, thereby functioning similarly to that between liberal and conservative/orthodox positions while at the same time upholding a singular notion of religion.

Even if religion functions as a carrier of certain symbolic-cultural orders, opposition to it can be based on different distinctions. Such opposition is also likely to be at least framed in some cases along a binary divide of religion and anti-religiosity. The interrelation and relative relevance of these different divides might also be contested, not only in social-political debates at large, but also within nonreligious organizations.

In both Sweden and the Netherlands, a certain individualization and liberalization of immaterial or ethical matters had already occurred over the course of the 20th century. By contrast, respective changes in the Philippines are more recent (to remind the reader, the long-debated reproductive health bill was passed into law in 2012 after long and vehement opposition from the Catholic Church). At present, the Catholic Church in the Philippines constitutes a major opponent to reproductive rights while at least some minority Protestant churches represent a religious counter voice on that matter. The Church of Sweden has become liberal to a degree that this relativizes its conflict line with the Swedish Humanist Association on moral matters and other problems and opponents move into the focus of some members of the SHA. In the Netherlands and in Dutch politics, there is a threefold distinction on ethical matters between liberal-secular positions, mainline Christian Democracy, which favors compromises on such matters, and orthodox Christian positions. D66 spokespersons and members in any case aim to counter a binary opposition between religious and nonreligious positions and tend to frame respective debates in terms of the principle of individual equality and liberty or the separation of church and state. Orthodox political opponents by contrast position them in line with such binary antithesis.

In the Netherlands, orthodox reformed groups and parties constitute a central and traditional other to liberal-secular politics. Additionally, the role of Islam and Muslims has been discussed in Sweden and the Netherlands under the aspect of its alleged conservativism, and partly also fundamentalism and extremism. For Swedish humanists, Islam constitutes a relevant other with regard to, e.g., questions of gender equality. D66 relates to Islam similarly to how it relates to religion in general – with a focus on individual liberty and the separation of church and state, both in opposition to the rising anti-Islamic and nationalist populism and Islamism, or Islamic orthodoxy/conservativism. While D66 is partly criticized as favoring multiculturalism and being too soft on Islam, Swedish humanists have been criticized for portraying "religion" in a simplistic, negative, and essentialist way that risks being understood as xenophobic and Islamophobic or at least as playing into the hands of such thinking and tendencies among the population (Gerle 2010, 92f; Olsson and Sorgenfrei 2011, 96). The humanists in turn reject such comparisons and criticize them for contributing to a dangerous climate of limiting religious criticism.

This short discussion is connected to the earlier point of how certain values and themes provide the orientation for nonreligious activism. It also relates such orientations to the capacity of religion to support social symbolic orders and the diverse and competing frames with which religion-related social struggles can be framed. Based on the different case studies, we have further shown how this links with competing divides and distinctions – with a binary divide between religion and nonreligiosity being only one of the competing divides that shape both public-political debates as well as those within nonreligious organizations.

Religion(s) as the norm

As explained previously, particular religious traditions as well as religion as such can be institutionalized and experienced as an implicit normative expectation for how people are or are supposed to be, which in turn can create nonconformists and stigmatized nonreligious identities. Such a normative role of religion seems strongest in the Philippines, manifesting in the tacit and explicit presupposition that being a good Filipino implies being a good Catholic, which brings in further moral expectations. By no surprise, therefore, nonreligious activism counters both stigmatized nonreligious identities and conservative moralities. In Sweden as well, this aspect of religio-normativity plays a role when Swedish humanists are in part concerned that the apparently uncontroversial and liberal position of the Church of Sweden might conceal its still dominant normative position, manifest in ritual practice, and might further feed into widespread perceptions of religion being the source of values and ethics. Furthermore, the question of humanist rituals raises concerns regarding a potential sacralization of family and marriage, which can be seen as merely a means to reproduce religious normativities. Regarding religion as a norm, the study of D66 in the Netherlands is situated in an almost reverse setting, with non-affiliation becoming at least a statistical normality. In a certain way, however, legislative initiatives that curtail previous religious exemption rights are based on a similar opposition to an underlying specialness of religion. In sum, religio-normativity expresses ways in which individuals and groups experience religion as a normative force within their lives and societies. The enforcing aspects of this normativity are often difficult to grasp by those who fit in easily. In different ways – and to different degrees – nonreligious activism can be understood as a reaction to experienced religio-normativities.

Different modes of nonreligion

As the introduction (Chapter 1) establishes, a mode of nonreligion is necessarily (though not sufficiently) characterized by different foci (values, themes, and organizational objectives), which orient nonreligious activism and inform the kinds of relations (competition, cooperation, conflict, and dialogue) that actors engage in with particular religious and nonreligious others. While different nonreligious actors can collaborate, they can also stand in opposing camps when, e.g., certain nonreligious phenomena are seen to function similar to religion – to be religion-like – and thus just as much the focus of criticism. Nonreligious identities are thus, as this book underscores, negotiated against the background of such front lines, cutting across the divide between religion and nonreligion.

What the "non" refers to

The groups introduced in this book position themselves against different religious others, mostly different strands and institutional forms of Christianity, as well as – in some cases – against Islam as an immigration-related new religion. Moreover, such positionings occur against rather generalized notions of religion in different ways.

As demonstrated in the previous section, opposition was mainly raised against an alleged privileged or institutionalized role of religion, what we call "religio-normativity" as well as against illiberal positions perceived to be backed by certain religious positions or associated with religion in a more general sense. For some Swedish Humanists and the Philippine PATAS, a more generalized counter-distinction from religion is also central to their self-understanding as an organization of religiously non-affiliated. This differs from D66, which, even if by now a great majority of its members are religiously non-affiliated, considers religious and nonreligious worldview affiliations private things distinct from party commitment. Its self-positioning as nonreligious is based on a counter-distinction from religious parties, which also operates with a generalized notion of religion but is confined to the specific realm of politics and the notion of state-church separation and a general public.

Foci

The previous section has already mentioned some of the foci that provide the orientation for the different forms of activism we observed. In terms of the different objectives of nonreligious activism, the greatest structural tension lies between, on the one hand, a focus on building a collective identity and community, and, on the other hand, influencing society in a broader sense. The positioning of the two Philippine organizations can be understood through the lens of such tension. This section complements the previous ones by engaging with two clusters of values central in all three case studies in more detail: first, that of individual and collective emancipation, equality, and liberty; and, second, that of reason and rationality.

Emancipation, equality, and liberty

As explained previously, the activism we focus on is directed in important ways against (perceived) religious dominance and/or privilege. This is oriented by a notion of a right to status equality and liberty, which can motivate movements of solidarity among different yet more-or-less marginalized groups. The aspect of solidarity and emancipation emerged the strongest in the research on the Philippines. Both FF and PATAS aim to provide support to marginalized non-believers, counter their stigmatization, and advocate for their concerns. The solidarity with the LGBT movement and the identification with their coming out show the centrality of such an emancipative function. It is also these values that provide the orientation for their solidarity with the LGBT movement (cf. Cimino and Smith 2014, 4f).

In Sweden as well, emancipation is important. The Swedish Humanist Association is divided between those humanists whose main objective is the equal recognition and emancipation of institutionalized secular life stances with religious ones, and those who primarily focus on defending individual freedoms and rights against religiously legitimized collective rights and freedoms in society. The latter perceive fighting for the SHA's official recognition as a collectively organized life stance community as conflicting with their focus. At the same time, though, SHA representatives regard the Swedish context as one based on a majoritarian nonreligious and potentially humanist population. Accordingly, the people of Sweden must be freed from the last remaining, outdated regulations, reminiscent of the former, restrictive state-church system, and the special status that religions and religiously legitimized rights enjoy in Swedish society. Potentially more important than a perceived marginalization of secular life stances, however, is a strong ideal of social egalitarianism and individual diversity as something that legitimately constitutes social reality, and which thus creates the normative ground on which the religious establishment is challenged. Any frame that grants a status apart from religious distinctions ultimately conflicts with the primacy of social equality and individual liberty (Schenk, Burchardt, and Wohlrab-Sahr 2015).

For D66 in the Netherlands, liberty, diversity, and tolerance have also been central political values and are core to the party's political position. Collective, pluralist emancipation on the one hand, and individual equal liberty on the other hand, have been placed against each other as two competing models of social organization. While the pluralization of politics and society at the turn of the 19th century has partly resulted from various emancipation movements, 19th century liberals as well as currently D66 oppose such a pluralist model. They prefer instead a general public realm as well as supporting emancipation movements that cut across the established pluralist boundaries – in the first place that of women and homosexuals – and thus render the individual the ultimate minority (Van der Ham 2014). While at the time of its foundation, the party mobilized those marginal to the pluralist confessional order, members of the orthodox Reformed minorities now criticize D66 for institutionalizing a secular liberal order.

In all case studies, the focus on equality and liberty vis-à-vis certain religious others and social orders goes hand in hand with the attempt to determine a standpoint for one's own position, which shows certain forms of religion-relatedness. PATAS, for example, wants to be recognized as "good without god," highlighting their difference ("without god") as well as moral grounds ("good") that transcend such differences. Some Swedish humanists offer rituals that express both their universalistic claim of individual and social needs, which from their point of view makes an alternative to religion necessary, as well as the right to individual diversity. Other humanists fear that positioning secular humanism as an alternative to religion would mean that they frame and communicate universal individual rights and rationality as one possible position among several others. For them, this is a step towards a "life stance relativism" (Holst 2013) that questions the universality of these rights and undermines their fight for them. D66's ambitions to define a standpoint that is not ideological also echoes the opposition to pluralism and worldview-based politics, as well as the (pragmatic and identitarian) need to define a standpoint in a factually pluralist political system.

Science, rationality, reason, and truth

In the context of his research in India, Quack (2012) documented how the rationalist organization ANiS (Organization for the Eradication of Superstition in Maharashtra) attempts to unmask superstitious beliefs with a scientific program in the countryside of India. Ideologically, they display the basic conviction that in principle all human problems and questions can be solved and answered through science, and the belief – described by Max Weber as central to processes of disenchantment – that the world is (in principle) explicable and therefore controllable to the limits of scientific knowledge at the time, and that there are no incalculable, mysterious, or supernatural forces. Such convictions are intimately linked to the organization's claim that societal reform and progress can only be achieved by tackling the abundance of irrational beliefs, fraud and deceit, and credulity and gullibility on the part of the general public with "education and reform" programs. These are conducted in rural parts of the country to both "eradicate superstition" as well as spread a rationalistic spirit of inquiry (Quack 2012, 109–43). Such insights into the crucial role assigned to science, as well as the debates about "New Atheism," pose interesting questions about the importance and usage of science, rationality, reason, and truth among nonreligious actors in countries like Sweden, the Philippines, and the Netherlands. Although references to science have only been discussed briefly in the individual chapters, it is obvious that for all the actors at the center of these case studies, such references are relevant to their self-understanding and positioning vis-à-vis religion. At the same time, there are some considerable differences in how such references are expressed.

For some actors, arguably most important for representatives of PATAS, science constitutes a central comprehensive single frame of world perception while religion is seen to be giving competing but false explanations of the world. Here, science is a central part of their identity and worldview. PATAS' conviction that science and atheisms necessarily go hand in hand resonates with arguments of likeminded organizations in other parts of the world. In the context of the Philippines, though, it is only PATAS that applies a genuine atheist stance against religious beliefs. Conversely, FF shifted the focus to "politics" rather than epistemologies.

Members of the Swedish Humanist Association as well place science at the basis of what they call the "descriptive part" of their life stance, the way in which they understand and view the world, which is supplemented by the "normative part," which comprises humanist ethics and values. Aside from epistemological questions, they are interested in the political promotion of science. Rationality and critical thinking are important for all members of the SHA, but it is the proponents of an opinion-making focus who place them more centrally in their concrete activism than other members. For them, ceremonial work is not compatible with a focus on rationality, critical thinking, and good arguments. Members in favor of a life stance concept of humanism, on the other hand, are concerned about and reject a one-sided focus on rationality and science and emphasize in this regard the individual and social emotional needs of people. A competing position considers emotions and rituals central to forging a community within which secular morality and rationality can ultimately blossom. This provides the grounds for arguing against an exclusive rationalism, which has a false idea of man and overlooks the importance of emotions and bonds between people as a base for a humane society.

The relation with science is not as central to the case study on the Netherlands even if similar historic shifts and dynamics can be traced with respect to the relations between science, religion, and worldviews.[7] For D66, science and research constitute a source of authoritative knowledge for political reforms and governance. This, however, does not come down to an encompassing unlimited notion of science and rationalism in the sense of a comprehensive frame for life as such. Instead, D66 ascribes great value to inspiration and creative realms of expression and comprehension, such as art. Religion is not considered to simply be false and opposed to science; instead, it is positioned as something that is differentiated from science as a functionally different social realm, undergoing change and reform similar to any other part of human culture. Religion is not the other to an immanent (and potentially rational and ethical) world, but part of it. All in all, the notions of realism and pragmatism seem of greater "ideological" relevance than that of science. Scientific studies are important to base politics and education (and through that: society) on social reality and prepare for future realities.

Regardless of the centrality of science or rationality, these case studies also indicate that such positionings are also made in relation to nonreligious others. This is evident in the Swedish Humanist Association's activism, which places science and rationality against religion as well as postmodernism and other "pseudo-sciences." With respect to D66, both political realism and pragmatism are placed not only against confessionalism but also socialism.

In sum, science, rationality, reason, and realism were important reference points for nonreligious activism in each of the case studies presented here, as epistemological, ontological, and moral arguments are interrelated (see also Quack 2012, 272–4). Reference to reason is thereby not necessarily identical to an antireligious or atheist position, but can be compatible with notions of religion as a differentiated realm as well as a general commitment to reform – including that of religion.

Shifting others

Members of nonreligious organizations have their own perspective on the religious field, sometimes exceeding what is commonly considered to be at the heart of a religious field. While some humanists in Sweden mainly focus on institutionalized religious traditions and their respective experts, others rather place phenomena such as pseudo-science, New Age thinking, esotericism, and relativism at the center of opposition. In relation to secularization processes and religious change, secular humanists' perspective on the Church of Sweden has changed throughout the years since the founding of the SHA, although in different ways. On one hand, some argue that, especially in such a secularized country as Sweden where people would still turn to the Church for the lack of sufficient attractive ceremonial alternatives and social communities, it is time for secular humanists to establish nationwide known, comprehensive, and engaging offers. On the other hand, others emphasize that the competitive relation to the Church might have been the right strategy when it was still very dominant and hegemonic, but since the Church has lost a lot of its influence, other issues have come to the fore and thus the former focus is outdated. In the case of the Philippines, the re-orientation of one of the organizations, the Filipino Freethinkers, towards a more inclusive identity correlates with their recognition and integration of liberal modes of religion, and the building of collaborative relations with liberal religious actors. Regarding D66, the main religious others were first the confessional parties, and later the Christian Democrats, given their central power positions in the political field. Regarding ideological divides, the small orthodox parties, especially the SGP, constitute its main other. Even if there is no Islamic party, Islam has emerged recently in the party's policy making and positioning in the political field.

Whether such debates are best described by highlighting different perspectives on a religious field or whether religiously related issues are but one manifestation of more general phenomena is an empirical question. If a group's overarching values are truth and rationality, different social fields and various others might be of equal concern: esotericism in the religious, postmodernism in the scientific, and alternative health practices in the medical fields. From the perspective of such actors, then, arguments in the fields of science and medicine are to be seen as religious-like or quasi-religious.

Contested relations with religion

Central to all the case studies in this book are actors in positions that not only have tensions with certain religious others but also with positions deemed nonreligious – be it within or outside the respective organization. Contestations between nonreligious positions concern different kinds of relations with religious others. In the conceptual chapter (Chapter 2), we introduced two themes of opposition to a particular nonreligious other: moving away from religion-likeness or religion-relatedness.

In the case of Swedish humanists, a "life stance" position that presupposes at least a minimal conceptual and functional similarity between secular and religious life stances has become a contested position between those who favor a functionally close competition and those who primarily aim at a form of religious criticism that allows them to position themselves as differentiated actors in comparison to religion, somewhat independent of certain religion-related or life stance-related logics. Those who favor the further development of humanist rituals as one of their main objectives are accused of being religion-like, given their aim to establish humanism as a comprehensive life stance community. It is these objectives that opinion-making humanists perceive as religion-like and wish to move away from. At the same time, it is not religion-relatedness they wish to avoid, since they claim a position of critique for themselves, arguing that it comes from a position of universality (rational and moral). In this book (Chapters 1 and 2), we speak of nonreligion 1 and nonreligion 2 to highlight that certain forms of nonreligion oppose other forms of nonreligion on the same grounds (in reference to the same themes and values) upon which they oppose certain religious others. With reference to this distinction, life stance humanists could be labeled as nonreligion 1, while opinion-making humanists could be labeled as the latter, nonreligion 2.

The chapter on the Netherlands (Chapter 5) showed how broader social-political contestations refer to two competing ways of relating to religion: an irreligious position (understood as binary opposition to religious positions or religion as such) and a differentiated third-space position. The chapter shows that the struggles between liberals, respectively D66 and orthodox Christian parties, are not so much concerned with the religion-related character of the party, but the organization of the state and a social-political public. Nineteenth-century confessionals introduced the notion of a binary divide between religious and irreligious politics, a frame which is in parts still deployed by the orthodox party. Liberals challenge such an exclusive claim and encompassing notion of religion, while D66 also defends the notion of politics as an ontologically immanent realm and third space with regard to religion at the same time. This is expressed in the party's ideological critique. The category of ideology can stand for religious, religion-like, religion-related, and areligious ideas, but the concept itself seems to be placed in a religion-related genealogy. Socialism as an alleged nonreligious version of Christian chiliasm constitutes a position seen as a religion-like other. In both cases, ideology marks the alleged transgression of nonpolitical ideas into politics.

Against that background, the party claimed a pragmatic and non-ideological position both as a party and with respect to politics as such – an aim to move away from religion-likeness, and a position described as a nonreligion 2 positioning in the chapter. The chapter pointed to the party's recurrent attempts to articulate a moral and epistemic standpoint for politics. While this might be seen as a shift to a nonreligious 1 position, the conflict line in the sense of a counter distinction from ideology and dogma is upheld. In that sense, the shift might rather be a change within a third-space orientation. Recurrently, the party has pursued legislative changes to increase the separation of church and state, that is, religion and legislation. While this could be seen to render its politics religion-related, its position differs from that of the Swedish proponents of opinion-making humanism as the party has, at least according to its own positioning, no particular focus on religion, and only removes remaining forms of institutionalized religion in order to realize genuine individual equality.

With regard to the Philippines, tensions between the two groups are less prominent even though they develop in different directions. The positioning of FF can thereby be seen to constitute a move away from religion-likeness. In comparison to the situation in the Netherlands and Sweden though, the Philippine case differs in the sense that there is no state-sponsored structure in which nonreligious positions are formally recognized as equivalents to religion or have reasonable hope to achieve such status, so that there is less a formalized option of being classified in the same category as religion. Possibly this reduces the ways in which struggles about a nonreligious positioning are overtly expressed. Furthermore, there might be less a divide between universalist and pluralist politics in general. Similar to the Dutch case, though, a central divide seems to exist between antireligious positions and those that focus on political secularity only and could thus be described as a differentiated third-space position. The aim of at least FF is to move away from an antireligious atheist position, which is partly formulated in direct distinction from PATAS. For PATAS as well, becoming less antireligious might be a potential future option – due to some relations with players within the international humanist community described previously. In that sense, the schematic distinction between nonreligion 1 and 2 is also applicable to the Philippine case. It is possible to speak of FF as nonreligion 2 by rejecting the ontological and epistemological focus on the status of god, which is characteristic for both PATAS (nonreligion 1) and the Catholic Church (religion 1), which then again enables collaboration with another religious actor (religion 2). Nonetheless, there appears to be a certain kind of coordinated "division of labor" between the two groups, and several people are members of both organizations. This qualifies the opposition highlighted previously, while the Swedish case suggests that it is more difficult to organize such a "division of labor" within one group.

The case of the SHA contrasts and complements the other two cases in the sense that the organization is internally divided over whether a nonreligious life stance community or secularism should be the core organizational identity of Swedish Humanists. There are voices that argue that atheism is a central part of their collective identity. Others, however, promote the view that they should communicate to potential members that every person, regardless of being an unbeliever or believer, are welcome as long as they want to advocate for human rights and the separation of church and state.

Shifting positions

While the last section illustrated how positions can be contested, this section discusses the different reasons for such contestations and shifts of positions deemed nonreligious. In the case of secular humanism in Sweden, it was the interplay of social and religious as well as organizational changes that provided the grounds for the current struggle within the organization. With the separation of church and state in 2000, and although they themselves were not able to contribute much to this development at the time, humanists reached one of their central goals. Furthermore, the Church of Sweden, because of its liberalization in matters such as gender equality and homosexuality, lost its importance as a moral opponent of secular humanism. In the eyes of humanists, this made it partly necessary to re-orient the movement. Evidence also suggests that the organization experienced an increase in members who focus on opinion-making. The media-prominence of "New Atheists" and the focus of SHA chairman, Christer Sturmark, on religious criticism in the years after 2005 were apparently crucial factors here. It is the interplay between these and other factors that are at the base of and fuel the struggle for the organization's future course. At the same time, as the previous section illustrated, the question of what kind of members – and which objectives – will be mobilized for the organization is part of that struggle.

Regarding the Philippines, there are several interrelated factors that have contributed to the organizations' (potential) shift in focus. One seems to be the growing self-consciousness of the groups, which makes them focus not only on building a community, but also on social outreach and activism. For the Filipino Freethinkers, another factor is the changed perspective on the religious field and the discovery of like-minded religious organizations. A third reason that partly explains PATAS' position seems to be their differentiation from each other. Finally, the organization's relations with international humanist and other nonreligious organizations set incentives for a more humanist and less atheist self-positioning.

In terms of D66, while the shift in the nonreligious position is not explicit, the party has consoled its pragmatic tradition with a more recent turn towards social liberalism and towards an explicated "ideology." This shift was catalyzed by several developments: first, the growing importance of the once subdominant social liberal strand within the party, due to leadership changes, internal criticism, and the rise of a younger generation within the party; electoral losses and the perceived need to develop a clearer party profile provided a second incentive to change. More recently, it seems that the debate on public morality and especially the rise of populism has motivated a movement towards explicating social liberal (or better: vrijzinnig) principles.

In sum, the actors and their activism differ from each other with respect to the particular struggles, front lines, and commonalities that link them to religious actors. Different themes might be positioned at the center of the debate by one actor but rejected or ignored by others. The distinction between nonreligion 1 and nonreligion 2 as well as the aims of moving away from religion-likeness or religion-relatedness show that when we speak of distinctions from religion, the very notion of religion is a placeholder for different (alleged) characteristics, that is, institutional forms of religion, and that religious as well as nonreligious positions might be rejected on the same grounds (cf. Campbell 1971). The notion of religion-likeness does not constitute a clear-cut label to be attributed to certain actors and positions, but rather helps to understand the emic religion-related perspective of agents in the field and various forms and relations for which nonreligious actors might strive. Competing modes of nonreligion imply negotiations of what constitutes religion and its respective other (see Quack 2011 on the debate between Bradlaugh and Holyoake). In some cases, struggles between competing modes of nonreligion might concern the borders of the religious field in the sense that what seems a mode of nonreligion to some is rendered a mode of religion by others.

Concluding remarks

In this book, we developed a relational understanding of nonreligion to empirically research distinct but contested positions in a religion-related surrounding. Our empirical focus was on certain forms of social and political activism. The relational approach drew attention to the contested positions, borders, and margins of a religious field, and showed that from different perspectives, the notion of what constitutes a position inside a religious field differs.

We conceptualized modes of nonreligion through four main aspects: the foci (values, themes, and organizational objectives) of nonreligious activism, the respective (religious and nonreligious) others, and the kinds of relations with those others. Together values and objectives constitute two axes along which the foci and position of an organization can be reconstructed. A mode of nonreligion can be understood as a specific assemblage of certain characteristics of these dimensions with regard to different religious and nonreligious others. The positions of collective actors we researched can be distinguished along those lines. In particular, Kind (Chapter 3) has identified LSH and OMH as two competing and conflicting ideal types of humanism in Sweden, exemplifying how ideal types of nonreligion can be gained from empirical analysis via the different dimensions named.

We further explained the heuristic advantages of conceptualizing a religion-related surrounding (*Umfeld*) and discussed its relations with other fields outside the religious field as well as possible transformations of the religious field towards a religious-nonreligious field, and the potential of the surrounding itself developing characteristics of a field (in the Bourdieusian sense). We have argued that nonreligious activism can be seen to challenge the borders of the religious field by either seeking to widen it to include nonreligious positions under an extended frame, or to contain the religious field and differentiate it from other fields (Chapter 5). Such religious-nonreligious struggles can thereby take place at the borders of the religious field, at the borders of related (or differentiated) fields, and in the field of power.

By understanding the ways in which individuals and groups position themselves in terms of religion, we learn something about the respective societies at large and how they deal with religion, for example, the different moral and symbolic orders to which both religion and nonreligion are linked. This also enables us to understand the religion-relatedness of matters like sexuality, gender, rituals, and dying. Conversely, by understanding how religion is institutionalized in specific societies, we can better comprehend how and why individuals and groups position themselves in critical or competitive relations vis-à-vis different forms of religion and in what way they draw on certain secular ideals and specific (interpreted) experiences with such institutionalizations.

In all three case studies, activism is fueled by the idea of containing religion in its "proper field," while its social influence is much more far reaching. This means that the actors have implicitly or explicitly taken a secular state and social differentiation as an ideal form of social organization. The case study on the Netherlands was the main example here, placing the political field central as one arena in which the borders of state, politics, and religion are negotiated. The notion of nonreligious equivalents to religion, which was prevalent in the Netherlands at least since mid-19th century, constitutes a further unique aspect of the case. The D66 party was introduced as struggling for the disentanglement of politics from both religious and nonreligious worldview positions, while at the same time claiming state recognition for nonreligious religion-like positions as being equal to religious ones. At least from the perspective of the state, religion and its equivalents were to be treated alike, subordinating the concept of religion into the broader one of worldviews. The freedom of worldviews is thereby paired with their privatization – not in the sense of banning them from the public or banning worldview parties – but still as something that disturbs the functioning of politics.

In the other two case studies as well, actors struggle to contain the influence of religion by trying to influence the political field with respect to, e.g., certain legislative measures or at least to establish nonreligious counter voices in various fields such as charity (Philippines), education (Sweden), or even the realm of those social institutions that shape private life course and apparently personal bonds and identities (Sweden).

The Swedish case in particular shows that state policies may act as incentives for nonreligious parity claims, when such arrangements are institutionalized for faith communities and paired with subsidies. Such policies might in this regard pave the way for an extension of the existing religious field through the (partial) inclusion of nonreligious positions. In the near future, proponents of life stance humanism in Sweden would like to establish humanist counseling in hospitals, prisons, and the military – something that is also practiced in countries like the Netherlands and Belgium, two countries that function as role models in this regard. Conversely, however, in places like the Philippines where religious organizations and not the state are the main providers of welfare, this might as well set an incentive for establishing nonreligious equivalents, an example being the PATAS-established "Free Medical Clinic."

All this goes to show that our understanding of *nonreligion* denotes a position both distinct and related to the specific manifestations and forms of religion in a given social context. There is no simple binary that divides religion and nonreligion; they are interrelated with each other and entangled in larger social dynamics and discourses. As such, nonreligion cannot be researched without understanding religion and its societal role. Nonreligion denotes not only a self-positioning as "not religious," but is also based in certain values and themes, paired with certain objectives. Such value positions can be linked to different emancipative and egalitarian (political) movements, or to the alleged requirements and functions of certain social realms or fields. What constitutes a mode of nonreligion can be understood by focusing on the relations with other positions in and outside a religious field. With respect to phenomena claiming differentiated or third-space positions vis-à-vis religion, a relational frame of nonreligion is thus helpful to analyze remaining entanglements. Taking all this together, the book accordingly highlights the fruitfulness of taking a new look at religion, its others, and secularity from a relational focus on the diversity of nonreligion.

Notes

1 The Introduction, Chapter 2, and Chapter 6 of this book were jointly written by Kind, Quack, and Schuh, and all three authors have made more or less similar contributions to the different chapters. Rather than listing the authors always in alphabetical order we decided, however, to mix the order of authors.
2 Some proponents of the latter view emphasize more generally that they would prefer to focus on problems they consider more urgent than the Church of Sweden's remaining monopolies, such as New Age thinking, postmodernism, or racism.
3 Another open question is why the membership structures of all explicitly atheist, rationalist, or secularist organizations seem to consist of a very large male majority, no matter whether we look at the 19th or 20th centuries and no matter

whether we look at Sweden, India, Germany, Great Britain, the Philippines, or the United States (Quack 2012, 290–2). By contrast, the Dutch political party, D66, is more or less gender balanced, less so than the Green party though (Kolk et al. 2012).
4 This is dealt with in more detail in Schuh's PhD thesis.
5 Members of the Swedish Humanist Association have on average a high educational level, with 81 percent having attained a university education (Jansson 2013).
6 This obviously does not preclude that nonreligious activism could go hand in hand with conservative positions as well.
7 This was sketched in a talk Schuh gave at the 2017 spring conference of the DGS department for sociology of religion at WZB, Berlin, Germany, titled "Politische Verhältnisbestimmung von Wissenschaft und Religion in den Niederlanden" (Politically relating science and religion in the Netherlands).

Bibliography

Aerts, Remieg. 1997. *De letterheren: liberale cultuur in de negentiende eeuw: het tijdschrift De Gids*. Meulenhoff: Amsterdam.

Aerts, Remieg. 2009. "Nationale beginselen? Een transnationale geschiedenis van politiek en grondwet in de negentiende eeuw." *BMGN-Low Countries Historical Review* 124 (4): 580–98.

AFP. 2015. "Pope Francis crowd in Philippines hits record six million." *The Telegraph*, January 18, 2015. https://www.telegraph.co.uk/news/worldnews/thepope/11353443/Pope-Francis-crowd-in-Philippines-hits-record-six-million.html.

Alberts, Wanda. 2010. "Religionskritik, Alternative zu Religion oder säkulare Religion? Der Human-ethische Verband Norwegens." In *Religionspolitik, Öffentlichkeit, Wissenschaft. Studien zur Neuformierung von Religion in der Gegenwart*, edited by Martin Baumann and Frank Neubert, 219–50. Zürich: Pano-Verlag.

Amarasingam, Amarnath. 2010. *Religion and the New Atheism: A Critical Appraisal*. Leiden: Brill.

Anderson, Benedict R. O'G. 2016. *A Life Beyond Boundaries*. London: Verso.

Andersson, Lena, Hans Bergström, Eva Dahlgren, Christer Fuglesang, Sven Hagströmer, P. C. Jersild, Morgan Johansson, Sara Larsson, Nina Lekander, Stellan Skarsgård, Christer Sturmark and Björn Ulvaeus. 2009. "Därför är det viktigt med ett sekulärt samhälle." *Dagens Nyheter*, June 18.

Antonio ~ [pseud.]. 2012. "Inside an Atheist Diary." *PATAS Website*, June 25. http://patas.co/2012/06/atheistdiary/ (site discontinued).

Apilado, Digna Balangue. 2009. "The Issue of HIV/AIDS in the Philippines: The Roman Catholic Church and the Philippine Government." In *Christianity and the State in Asia: Complicity and Conflict*, edited by Julius Bautista and Francis Khek Gee Lim, 131–54. London: Routledge.

Asad, Talal. 2003. *Formations of the Secular: Christianity, Islam, Modernity*. Stanford: Stanford University Press.

A. U. 2012. Interview by S. Kind.

Bäckström, Anders. 2014. "Religion in the Nordic Countries: Between Private and Public." *Journal of Contemporary Religion* 29 (1): 61–74.

Bäckström, Anders, Ninna Edgardh Beckman and Per Pettersson, eds. 2004. *Religious Change in Northern Europe: The Case of Sweden: From State Church to Free Folk Church*. Final Report. Stockholm: Verbum Förlag.

Batista, Treb. 2012. "My Journey to Godlessness." *PATAS Website*, July 10. http://patas.co/2012/07/my-journey-to-godlessness/ (site discontinued).

Bautista, Julius. 2010. "Church and State in the Philippines: Tackling Life Issues in a 'Culture of Death'." *SOJOURN: Journal of Social Issues in Southeast Asia* 25: 29–53.
Beaman, Lori G., and Steven Tomlins. 2015. *Atheist Identities: Spaces and Social Contexts*. Heidelberg: Springer.
Bell, Daniel. 1988a. "The End of Ideology Revisited (Part I)." *Government and Opposition* 23 (2): 131–50.
———. 1988b. "The End of Ideology Revisited (Part II)." *Government and Opposition* 23 (3): 321–31.
Berglund, Jenny. 2012. Interview by S. Kind.
Bernts, Ton and Joanitne Berghuijs. 2016. *God in Nederland 1966–2015*. Utrecht: VBK Media.
Biesta, Gert J. J. and Siebren Miedema. 1996. "Dewey in Europe: A Case Study on the International Dimensions of the Turn-of-the-Century Educational Reform." *American Journal of Education* 105 (1): 1–26.
Bjerkhagen, Michael, Mohammad Fazlhashemi, Eskil Franck, Philip Geister, Erna Möller, Ute Steyer and Christer Sturmark. 2016. "Nytt livsåskådningsforum för öppnare samtal." *Dagens samhälle*, January 18. Accessed February 8, 2016. www.dagenssamhalle.se/debatt/nytt-livsaskadningsforum-foer-oeppnare-samtal-21677.
Blankholm, Joseph. 2014. "The Political Advantages of a Polysemous Secular." *Journal for the Scientific Study of Religion* 53 (4): 775–90.
———. 2017. "The Limits of Religious Indifference." In *Religious Indifference: New Perspectives from Studies on Secularization and Nonreligion*, edited by J. Quack and C. Schuh, 239–58. Cham: Springer.
Blechschmidt, Alexander. 2018. "The Secular Movement in the Philippines: Atheism and Activism in a Catholic Country." PhD. diss., University of Zurich, Switzerland. https://doi.org/10.5167/uzh-157305.
Blom, Agneta, Staffan Gunnarson, Fredrik Idevall, Carl-Johan Kleberg, Anneli Noréus, Peder Palmstierna, and Magnus Timmerby. 2013. "Motion 2. Ceremoniernas roll och Humanisterna som folkrörelse." *Humanisterna Kongresshandlingar 2013*: 49–52.
Boele-Woelki, Katharina, Ian Curry-Summer, Miranda Jansen and Wendy Schrama. 2006. "Huwelijk of geregistreerd partnerschap?: Een evaluatie van de Wet openstelling huwelijk en de Wet geregistreerd partnerschap." *Dutch Ministry of Justice*. Alphen aan den Rijn: Kluwer.
Bongaerts, Gregor. 2008. *Verdrängungen des Ökonomischen: Bourdieus Theorie der Moderne*. Bielefeld, Germany: Transcript Verlag.
Borg, Annika and Christer Sturmark. 2011. "Kyrkan måste sluta fred med religionskritikerna." *Dagens Nyheter. DN Debatt*, September 10.
Bouma, Gary D., Rodney Ling and Douglas Pratt. 2010. *Religious Diversity in Southeast Asia and the Pacific: National Case Studies*. Dordrecht: Springer.
Bourdieu, Pierre. [1971] 2000. *Das religiöse Feld. Texte Zur Ökonomie des Heilsgeschehens*. Edited by Stephan Egger, Andreas Pfeuffer und Franz Schultheis. Konstanz: UVK.
———. 1979. "The Disenchantment of the World: The Sense of Honour: The Kabyle House or the World Reversed." In *Algeria 1960*. Cambridge: Cambridge University Press.
———. 1985. "The Social Space and the Genesis of Groups." *Information (International Social Science Council)* 24 (2): 195–220.

———. 1987. "Die Auflösung des Religiösen ['The Dissolution of the Religious'] (Original 'La Dissolution du Religieux,' Choses Dites [In Other Words], Paris, France, Editions de Minuit)." In *Religion: Schriften zur Kultursoziologie 5*, edited by F. Schultheis and S. Egger, 117–23. Frankfurt am Main: Suhrkamp.

———. 2001. *Das politische Feld: Zur Kritik der politischen Vernunft*. Konstanz, Germany: UVK.

Bourdieu, Pierre and Loïc J. D. Wacquant. 1992. *An Invitation to Reflexive Sociology*. Chicago: University of Chicago Press.

Bowler, Peter J. 2007. *Monkey Trials and Gorilla Sermons. Evolution and Christianity from Darwin to Intelligent Design*. Cambridge, MA: Harvard University Press.

Bräunlein, Peter. 2008. "'Passion' Als Idiom von Kritik Und Widerstand Im Philippinischen Katholizismus." In *Religionsinterne Kritik Und Religiöser Pluralismus Im Gegenwärtigen Südostasien*, edited by Manfred Hutter, 231–49. Frankfurt am Main: Peter Lang.

———. 2012. "'We are 100% Catholic': Philippine Passion Rituals and Some Obstacles in the Study of Non-European Christianity." *Journal of Religion in Europe* 5 (3): 384–413.

Brown, Wendy. 2009. "Introduction." In *Is Critique Secular? Blasphemy, Injury and Free Speech*, edited by Talal Asad, Wendy Brown, Judith Butler and Saba Mahmood, 7–19. Berkeley: University of California.

Burchardt, Marian. 2017. "Collective Memory and Religious Indifference in Immigration Societies: Secular Resurrections of Catholicism in Quebec." In *Religious Indifference: New Perspectives from Studies on Secularization and Nonreligion*, edited by Johannes Quack and Cora Schuh, 83–99. Wiesbaden: Springer.

Campbell, Colin D. 1971. *Toward a Sociology of Irreligion*. London: Macmillan.

Cavallin, Clemens. 2011. "After the State Church: A Reflection on the Relation between Theology and Religious Studies in Contemporary Sweden." *Journal for the Study of Religions and Ideologies* 10 (29): 43–63.

Cimino, Richard and Christopher Smith. 2007. "Secular Humanism and Atheism Beyond Progressive Secularism." *Sociology of Religion* 68 (4): 407–24.

———. 2010. "The New Atheism and the Empowerment of American Freethinkers." In *Religion and the New Atheism: A Critical Appraisal*, edited by Amarnath Amarasingam, 139–56. Leiden: Brill.

———. 2014. *Atheist Awakening: Secular Activism and Community in America*. Oxford, NY: Oxford University Press.

Claudio, Lisandro E. 2013. *Taming People's Power: The EDSA Revolutions and Their Contradictions*. Quezon City, Philippines: Ateneo de Manila University Press.

Cornelio, Jayeel Serrano. 2013. "Religious Freedom in the Philippines: From Legalities to Lived Experience." *The Review of Faith & International Affairs* 11 (2): 36–45.

Cotter, Christopher R. 2015. "Without God yet Not Without Nuance: A Qualitative Study of Atheism and Non-Religion Among Scottish University Students". In Atheist Identities: Spaces and Social Contexts, edited by Lori G. Beaman and Steven Tomlins, 171–93. New York, Springer.

D66. 1966. Appèl. Amsterdam, the Netherlands.

———. 1967. Politiek Program van de Democraten'66 [election program].

———. 1977a. Beleidsprogram 1977–1981 [political program].

———. 1977b. Election Program (Programma D'66 Tweede-Kamerverkiezingen 1977) [election program].

———. 1980. Beleidsprogram 1977–1981 [political program].

———. 1980 [1970]. De program-partij D'66 en de beginsel-partijen. In *De geschiedenis van D'66*, edited by Pieter Fokking. Den Haag: D66.
———. 1981. Verkiezingsprogramma Democraten'66 1981–1985 [election program].
———. 1997. *Van ideologie tot politieke verantwoordelijkheid: Pleidooi voor een aktieve betrokkenheid bij rechtsstaat en democratie*. Den Haag: Stichting Wetenschappelijk Bureau D66.
———. 2006. Het gaat om mensen [election program].
Daalder, Hans. 1995. *Van oude en nieuwe regenten: Politiek in Nederland*. Amsterdam: Bert Bakker.
Damaschke, Ralf and Johan Ericsson Qvist. 2013. "Till gemenskapens försvar." *HumanistInfo. Humanisternas medlemstidning* 15 (1): 16–17.
Dannefjord, Per. 2012. "Gemenskapens baksida." *HumanistInfo. Humanisternas medlemstidning* 14 (4): 16–17.
David. 2013. Interview by S. Kind.
Davie, Grace. 2000. *Religion in Modern Europe: A Memory Mutates*. Oxford: Oxford University Press.
———. 2007. "Vicarious Religion: A Methodological Challenge." In *Everyday Religion: Observing Modern Religious Lives*, edited by Nancy T. Ammerman, 21–36. Oxford: Oxford University Press.
———. 2012. Interview by S. Kind.
Dawkins, Richard. 2006. *The God Delusion*. London: Bantam Press.
De Haan, Ido. 1997. "De maakbaarheid van de samenleving en het einde van de ideologie. 1945–1965." In *Maakbaarheid. Liberale wortels en hedendaagse kritiek van de maakbare samenleving*, edited by J. W. Duyvendak and I. de Haan, 89–103. Amsterdam: Amsterdam University Press.
De Haan, Ido and Henk Te Velde. 1996. "Vormen van politiek. Veranderingen van de openbaarheid in Nederland 1848–1900." *BMGN-Low Countries Historical Review* 111 (2): 167–200.
De Jong, Wim. 2014. "Van Wie Is de Burger? Omstreden Democratie in Nederland, 1945–1985." Radboud Universiteit Nijmegen.
Derkx, P. 2002. "Modern Humanism in the Netherlands." In *Empowering Humanity: State of the Art in Humanistics*, edited by Annemie Halsema and D. J. van Houten, 61–79. Utrecht: De Tijdstroom.
———. 2006. *I'm still confused, but at a higher level: over niet-confessionele politiek en de humanistische beweging. Georganiseerd humanisme in Nederland: geschiedenis. visies en praktijken*. B. D. P. Gasenbeek, 60–85. Utrecht/Amsterdam, The Netherlands: Humanistisch Archief/SWP.
De Rooy, Piet. 2001. "Voorbij de verzuiling?" *BMGN-Low Countries Historical Review* 116 (1): 45–57.
———. 2002. *Republiek van rivaliteiten: Nederland sinds 1813*. Amsterdam: Mets & Schilt.
Dijkstra, Pia. 2016. *Bescherming van leven geen monopolie christenpolitici*. edited by D66.
Dudink, Stefan. 1997. *Deugdzaam liberalisme. Sociaal-liberalisme in Nederland 1870–1901*. Amsterdam: Amsterdam University Press B.V.
The Economist. 2002. Model makers.
Eisinga, Rob N., Gerbert Kraaykamp and Peer Sheepers. 2012. *Religion in Dutch Society: Documentation of a National Survey on Religious and Secular Attitudes and Behaviour in 2011–2012*. Amsterdam: Pallas Amsterdam University Press.
Ellemers, Jo Egbert. 1979. "Nederland in de jaren zestig en zeventig." *Sociologische Gids* 26 (6): 429–51.

Engelke, Matthew. 2015. "Humanist Ceremonies: The Case of Non-Religious Funerals in England." In *The Wiley Blackwell Handbook of Humanism*, edited by Andrew Copson and A. C. Grayling, 216–33. Chichester: Wiley Blackwell.

———. 2015. "On Atheism and Non-Religion: An Afterword." *Social Analysis* 59 (2): 135–45.

Equmeniakyrkan's Webpage. 2016. "Vår historia." Accessed November 16, 2016. http://equmeniakyrkan.se/kyrka/var-historia/.

Erik. 2014. Interview by S. Kind.

European Humanist Professionals. 2016. "Mission." Accessed November 21, 2016. www.humanistprofessionals.eu/mission-2/.

FF (Filipino Freethinkers). n.d.-a. "About FF." Accessed May 22, 2018. http://filipinofreethinkers.org/about-ff/.

———. n.d.-b. "Affiliates." Accessed May 22, 2018. http://filipinofreethinkers.org/about-ff/affiliates/.

———. 2013. "Filipino Freethinkers Livestream and Meetup for a Cause." *FF Website*, November 13. http://filipinofreethinkers.org/2013/11/13/filipino-freethinkers-livestream-and-meetup-for-a-cause/.

Finn. 2013. Interview by S. Kind.

Fitzgerald, Timothey. 2003. *The Ideology of Religious Studies*. New York: Oxford University Press.

Fligstein, Neil and Doug McAdam. 2012a. "Grundzüge einer allgemeinen Theorie strategischer Handlungsfelder." In *Feldanalyse als Forschungsprogramm 1: Der programmatische Kern*, edited by Stefan Bernhard and Christian Schmidt-Wellenburg, 57–97. Wiesbaden: VS Verlag für Sozialwissenschaften.

———. 2012b. *A Theory of Fields*. Oxford: Oxford University Press.

Fokking, P. 1980. *De geschiedenis van D'66*. Den Haag, the Netherlands: D66.

F. R. 2012. Interview by S. Kind.

Fragell, Levi. 2002. "The Future of International Humanism and the IHEU." In *International Humanist and Ethical Union 1952–2002: Past, Present and Future*, edited by Bert Gasenbeek and Babu Gogineni, 112–20. Utrecht: De Tijdstroom uitgeverij.

Francisco, Jose Mario C. 2014. "People of God, People of the Nation: Official Catholic Discourse on Nation and Nationalism." *Philippine Studies: Historical and Ethnographic Viewpoints* 62 (3–4): 341–75.

———. 2015. "Letting the Texts on RH Speak for Themselves: (Dis)Continuity and (Counter)Point in CBCP Statements." *Philippine Studies: Historical and Ethnographic Viewpoints* 63 (2): 223–46.

Frisk, Liselotte and Peter Åkerbäck. 2013. *Den mediterande Dalahästen. Religion på nya Arenor I Samtidens Sverige*. Stockholm: Dialogos.

Gasenbeek, Bert. 2007. "150 jaar vrijdenkersbeweging in Nederland (1856–2006)." In *Denkers zonder dogma's: voordrachten en foto's van het jubileumcongres 'God noch autoriteit' gehouden ter gelegenheid van het 150-jarig bestaan van de vrijdenkersbeweging De Vrije Gedachte op 13 en 14 oktober 2006*, edited by B. D. P. Gasenbeek. Utrecht: Het Humanistisch Archief.

Gasenbeek, Bert and J. W. M. (Jo) Nabuurs. 2006. "Op zoek naar'het ware, het goede en het schone': 150 jaar vrijdenkersbeweging in Nederland (1856–2006)." In *Georganiseerd humanisme in Nederland: geschiedenis, visies en praktijken*, edited by Bert Gasenbeek and Peter Derkx. Utrecht: Humanistisch Archief.

Gerle, Elisabeth. 2010. "Farlig förenkling. Religion och politik utifrån Sverigedemokraterna och Humanisterna." Nora: Nya Doxa.

Bibliography 173

Glaser, Barney G. and Anselm L. Strauss. 2009. *The Discovery of Grounded Theory: Strategies for Qualitative Research*. New York: Transaction Publishers.

Goddijn, Walter H. Smeets and G. van Tillo. 1979. *Opnieuw: God in Nederland: Onderzoek naar godsdienst en kerkelijkheid ingesteld in opdracht van KRO en weekblad de Tijd*. Amsterdam: De Tijd.

Gomez, José Edgardo A., Jr. and Marie Stephanie N. Gilles. 2014. "Worship and Urban Structure in Unconventional Locations: The Spatial Features of Religious Group Diversity in Metro Manila." *Philippine Sociological Review* 62 (Special Issue): 85–113.

Gomez, Jose L. 2015. "Freethinkers Too Few to Deserve a Space in the Inquirer." *Philippine Daily Inquirer*, January 27. http://opinion.inquirer.net/82038/freethinkers-too-few-to-deserve-a-space-in-the-inquirer.

Gran, Even. 2013. "Reportasje: Blått lys for humanistiske seremonier i Sverige?" *Fritanke.no*, February 10. Accessed September 24, 2014. http://fritanke.no/src/popup.php?page=utskrift&NyhetID=9212.

Groothuizen, Jolijn and Dennis Bos. 2013. "Religious Aspects of Socialist Imagery, c. 1890–2000: A Visual Essay." In *Political Religion Beyond Totalitarianism*, edited by Joost Augusteijn, Patrick G. C. Dassen and Maartje J. Janse, 101–14. Hampshire: Palgrave Macmillan.

Gruijters, J. P. A., Hans. 1967. *Daarom D'66*. Amsterdam: De Bezige Bij.

Gunnarson, Staffan. 2009. "Ceremonierna ger mänskligt ansikte åt humanism." *Humanisten. Tidskrift för Kultur-och Livsåskådningsdebatt* 15 (4): 26–9.

———. 2012. "Historiska perspektiv på humanismen. Del 4. Upplysning, kritik och nydaning." *HumanistInfo* 14 (4): 12–13.

———. 2013. "Humanism är mycket mer än religionskritik." *Newsmill*, January 2.

———. 2016. "Humanisterna har nu chansen att ta nästa steg." *Humanisten. Humanisternas medlemstidning* 17 (2): 11–12.

HA, Humanistische Alliantie. 2010. "CDA en PVV scoren slechtst op humanistische meetlat." Accessed December 11, 2017. www.humanistischealliantie.nl/nieuws/humanistische-meetlat/.

Hilgers, Mathieu and Eric Mangez. 2014. "Introduction to Pierre Bourdieu's Theory of Social Fields." In *Bourdieu's Theory of Social Fields: Concepts and Applications*, edited by M. Hilgers and E. Mangez, 1–36. Abingdon and New York: Routledge.

Holst, Sören. 2013. "Humanismen – en tro bland andra?" *HumanistInfo* 15 (2): 12.

Holyoake, George J. and Charles Bradlaugh. [1870] 1987. "Is Secularism Atheism?" In *A Second Anthology of Atheism and Rationalism*, edited by Gordon Stein Buffalo, 345–69. New York: Prometheus Books.

Humanists UK Webpage, December 11, 2018. https://london.humanistchoir.org.

HVMS, Mr. Hans Van Mierlo Stichting. 2015. "Grondslagen-debat 1978." In *Historische canon van D66* (website with published sources). Accessed May 14, 2019. https://vanmierlostichting.d66.nl/fundamenten-sociaal-liberalisme/de-historische-canon-van-d66/grondslagen-debat-1978/.

Ida. 2013. Interview by S. Kind.

Inglehart, Ronald and Wayne E. Baker. 2000. "Modernization, Cultural Change and the Persistence of Traditional Values." *American Sociological Review* 65 (1): 19–51.

Inglehart, Ronald and Chris Welzel. 2015. "Live Cultural Map: WVS (1981–2015)." *World Value Survey*. Accessed July 20, 2017. www.worldvaluessurvey.org/WVS Contents.jsp?CMSID=Findings.

Jacoby, Susan. 2004. *Freethinkers: A History of American Secularism*. New York: Metropolitan Books.
Jana. 2013. Interview by S. Kind.
Jansson, Urban. 2013. *Humanisterna Medlemsenkät. Rapport – kompletta versionen*, March 20. Accessed November 2, 2016. www.humanisterna.se/pdf/enkat.pdf.
Jänterä-Jareborg, Maarit. 2010. "Religion and the Secular State: National Report of Sweden." Paper presented at the 18th International Congress on Comparative Law, Washington, DC, July–August. www.crs.uu.se/digitalAssets/55/55502_Religion_in_the_Secular_State.pdf.
Jellema, Dirk. 1957. "Abraham Kuyper's Attack on Liberalism." *The Review of Politics* 19 (4): 472–85.
Karstein, Uta. 2012. "Auseinandersetzungen in und zwischen Feldern. Vorschläge zur Spezifizierung des Bourdieu'schen Begriffs sozialer Kämpfe am Beispiel des Staat-Kirche-Konfliktes in der DDR." In *Feldanalyse als Forschungsprogramm 2: Gegenstandsbezogene Theoriebildung*, edited by Stefan Bernhard and Christian Schmidt-Wellenburg, 257–79. Wiesbaden: VS Verlag für Sozialwissenschaften.
———. 2013. *Konflikt um die symbolische Ordnung. Genese, Struktur und Eigensinn des religiös-weltanschaulichen Feldes in der DDR*. Würzburg: Ergon Verlag.
Kennedy, James C. [1995] 2007. *Nieuw Babylon in aanbouw: Nederland in de jaren zestig*. Amsterdam: Boom.
Kenneth Keng (FF). 2012. GMA interview.
———. 2014. Interview by A. Blechschmidt.
Kettell, Steven. 2013. "Faithless: The Politics of New Atheism." *Secularism and Nonreligion* 2: 61–72.
Kirmer, Stephanie. 2002. "Organizing Humanism." In *International Humanist and Ethical Union 1952–2002: Past, Present and Future*, edited by Bert Gasenbeek and Babu Gogineni, 112–20. Utrecht: De Tijdstroom uitgeverij.
Klei, Ewout. 2011. *'Klein maar krachtig, dat maakt ons uniek': een geschiedenis van het Gereformeerd Politiek Verbond, 1948–2003*. Amsterdam: Bert Bakker.
Klei, Ewout and Remco Van Mulligen. 2013. *Van God los: het einde van de christelijke politiek?* Amsterdam: Nieuw Amsterdam.
Knippenberg, Hans. 1998. "Secularization in the Netherlands in Its Historical and Geographical Dimensions." *Geo Journal* 45 (3): 209–20.
Koenenman, L., et al. 1987. "Kroniek 1987: overzicht van partijpolitieke gebeurtenissen van het jaar 1987." In *Jaarboek Documentatiecentrum Nederlandse Politieke Partijen 1987*, edited by R. Koole, 16–57. Groningen, the Netherlands: Documentatiecentrum Nederlandse Politieke Partijen.
Kolk, H., et al. 2012. *The Dutch Parliamentary Election Study 2012*. S. K. N. S. C. B. v. d. Statistiek.
Kolk, H., J. N. Tillie, P. van Erkel, M. van Welden and A. Damstra. 2012. *The Dutch Parliamentary Election Study 2012–DPES 2012*. Stichting Kiezersonderzoek Nederland SKON; Centraal Bureau voor de Statistiek. Accessed October 27, 2016. https://easy.dans.knaw.nl/ui/datasets/id/easy-dataset:57353.
Krech, Volkhard and Hartmann Tyrell. 1995. "Religionssoziologie um die Jahrhundertwende. Zu Vorgeschichte, Kontext und Beschaffenheit einer Subdisziplin der Soziologie." In *Religionssoziologie um 1900*, edited by V. Krech and H. Tyrell. Würzburg: Ergon Verlag.
Kuyper, Abraham. 1880. *Souvereiniteit in eigen kring: rede ter inwijding van de vrije universiteit*. Amsterdam: J.H. Kruyt.

———. [1931] 1999. *Lectures on Calvinism*. Grand Rapids, MI: Eerdmans Printing Company.
Kyrkan på Pride. 2016. Accessed November 11. www.kyrkanpapride.se.
Lahiri, Smita and Deirdre De La Cruz. 2014. "The Philippines." In *Figures of Southeast Asian Modernity*, edited by Joshua Barker, Erik Harms and Johan Lindquist, 19–22. Honolulu, Hawai'i: University of Hawai'i Press.
Langseth, Marissa. 2011. "The Rise of Atheism in the Philippines." *PATAS Website*, July 12. http://patas.co/2011/07/the-rise-of-atheism-in-the-philippines/ (site discontinued).
Larsson, Göran. 2016. "Sweden." In *Yearbook of Muslims in Europe*, Volume 7, edited by Oliver Scharbrodt, Samim Akgönül, Ahmet Alibašić, Jørgen S. Nielsen and Egdūnas Račius, 549–61. Brill: Leiden.
L. E. 2012. Interview by S. Kind.
LeDrew, Stephen. 2012. "The Evolution of Atheism: Scientific and Humanistic Approaches." *History of the Human Sciences* 25 (3): 70–87.
———. 2013. "Discovering Atheism: Heterogeneity in Trajectories to Atheist Identity and Activism." *Sociology of Religion* 74 (4): 431–53.
———. 2015. "Atheism versus Humanism: Ideological Tensions and Identity Dynamics." In *Atheist Identities: Spaces and Social Contexts*, edited by Lori G. Beaman and Steven Tomlins, 53–68. Heidelberg: Springer.
———. 2016. *The Evolution of Atheism: The Politics of a Modern Movement*. New York: Oxford University Press.
Lee, Lois. 2011. "Glossary." *Virtual Conference: Non-Religion and Secularity Research Network*, May 27: 1–4.
———. 2012. "Research Note: Talking about a Revolution: Terminology for the New Field of Non-Religion Studies." *Journal of Contemporary Religion* 27 (1): 129–39.
———. 2015. *Recognizing the Non-Religious Reimagining the Secular*. New York: Oxford University Press.
Leon. 2014. Interview by S. Kind.
Leviste, Enrique Nino Panaligan. 2011. "Catholic Church Hegemony Amidst Contestation: Politics and Population Policy in the Philippines." Thesis, National University of Singapore. http://scholarbank.nus.edu.sg/handle/10635/25826.
Lijphart, Arend. [1967] 2008. *Verzuiling, pacificatie en kentering in de Nederlandse politiek*. Amsterdam: Amsterdam University Press (dbnl).
Lindenfors, Patrik and Christer Sturmark. 2015. *Sekulär Humanism. Förnuft, Omtanke, Ansvar*. Stockholm: Humanisterna.
Lucardie, A. P. M. (Paul). 1997. "Een luchtkasteel voor logocraten: Nieuw Babylon en de jaren zestig in Nederland." *Sociologische gids* 44 (5–6): 440–52.
———. 2002. *Nederland stromenland: een geschiedenis van de politieke stromingen*. Assen, the Netherlands: Koninklijke Van Gorcum.
———. 2004. "M.S. van der Land, Tussen ideaal en illusie. De geschiedenis van D66, 1966–2003." *BMGN: Low Countries Historical Review* 119 (2): 299–301.
Lucardie, A. P. M. (Paul) and Gerrit Voerman. 1991. "Worstelen met ideologie: het verhaal van een pragmatische partij." *Idee: tijdschrift van het Wetenschappelijk Bureau van D66* 12 (6): 19–25.
Luckmann, Thomas. 1967. *The Invisible Religion: The Problem of Religion in Modern Society*. New York: MacMillan.
Mahmood, Saba. 2005. *Politics of Piety: The Islamic Revival and the Feminist Subject*. Princeton: Princeton University Press.

Malte. 2013. Interview by S. Kind.
Mangez, Eric and Georges Liénard. 2014. "The Field of Power and the Relative Autonomy of Social Fields." In *Bourdieu's Theory of Social Fields: Concepts and Applications*, edited by M. Hilgers and E. Mangez, 183–97. New York: Routledge.
Mannheim, Karl. [1929] 2015. *Ideologie und Utopie*. Frankfurt am Main: Klostermann.
Martin, David. 2005. *On Secularization: Towards a Revised General Theory*. Aldershot: Ashgate.
Martin, John L. 2003. "What Is Field Theory?" *American Journal of Sociology* 109: 1–49.
Mats. 2013. Interview by S. Kind.
Mattsson, Jonatan. 1995. "Humanistisk andlighet?" *Humanisten* 1 (1): 11–12.
Meijering, Eginhard. 2012. *Hoe God verdween uit de Tweede Kamer: De ondergang van de christelijke politiek*. Amsterdam: Uitgeverij Balans.
Mellink, Bram. 2011. "Tweedracht maakt macht. De PvdA, de doorbraak en de ontluikende polarisatiestrategie (1946–1966)." *BMGN: Low Countries Historical Review* 126 (2): 30–53.
Miller, Glenn T. 1999. "Review Peter Heslam: Creating a Christian Worldview: Abraham Kuyper's Lectures on Calvinism." *Church History* 68 (2): 479–81.
Molendijk, Arie L. 2008. "Neo-Calvinist Culture Protestantism: Abraham Kuyper's Stone Lectures." *Church History and Religious Culture* 88 (2): 235–50.
———. 2011. "'A Squeezed Out Lemon Peel:' Abraham Kuyper on Modernism." *Church History and Religious Culture* 91 (3–4): 397–412.
Moreno, Antonio F. 2006. *Church, State, and Civil Society in Postauthoritarian Philippines: Narratives of Engaged Citizenship*. Quezon City, Philippines: Ateneo de Manila University Press.
Müller, Dominik M. 2014. *Islam, Politics and Youth in Malaysia: The Pop-Islamist Reinvention of PAS*. Milton Park, Abingdon and New York: Routledge.
———. 2015. "Islamic Politics and Popular Culture in Malaysia: Negotiating Normative Change between Shariah Law and Electric Guitars." *Indonesia and the Malay World* 43 (127): 318–44.
Natividad, Maria Dulce Ferrer. 2012. "Reproductive Politics, Religion and State Governance in the Philippines." Dissertation, Columbia University. http://hdl.handle.net/10022/ACP:13126.
Nilsson, Per-Erik and Victoria Enkvist. 2016. "Techniques of Religion-Making in Sweden: The Case of the Missionary Church of Kopimism." *Critical Research on Religion* 4 (2): 141–55.
NIWI, Netherlands Institute for Scientific Information Services. 1967. "Verkiezingsonderzoek Vrije Universiteit."
Norris, Pippa and Ronald Inglehart. 2004. *The Sacred and the Secular: Religion and Politics Worldwide*. New York: Cambridge University Press.
Nosti, Helena. 2016. "Ökat behov av borgerliga ceremonier." *SVT Nyheter*, June 20.
NRC/Handelsblad. 2001. "Kabinet verstrekt desinformatie."
———. 2007. "Bij homostel kan mijn hart niet spreken."
Olsson, Susanne and Simon Sorgenfrei. 2011. "Svensk religionskritisk diskurs." *Din: tidsskrift for religion og kultur* 2011 (3–4): 82–98.
Oostveen, Margriet. 2001. "Ik kan me goed voorstellen dat artsen stervenshulp niet melden." *NRC Handelsblad*, April 14. Accessed September 29, 2016. http://retro.nrc.nl/W2/Nieuws/2001/04/14/Vp/01a.html.
Palmstierna, Peder. 2012. "En uppgift för Humanisterna!" *HumanistInfo* 14 (4): 19.

Paraiso, John. 2011. "Science." *PATAS Website*, June 27. http://patas.co/2011/06/science/ (site discontinued).

Paras, Junn D. 2011. "To God or No to God: The Story of My Atheism." *PATAS Website*, August 17. http://patas.co/2011/08/to-god-or-no-to-god-my-story-of-my-atheism/ (site discontinued).

PATAS (Philippine Atheists and Agnostics Society). n.d. "About PATAS." *PATAS Website*. Accessed August 23, 2012. http://patas.co/patas/about-patas/ (site discontinued).

Paterno, Esmaquel II. 2012. "Making sense of the Nazarene devotion." *Rappler*, January 14, 2012. https://www.rappler.com/nation/841-making-sense-of-the-nazarenedevotion.

Pennings, P. J. M. (Paul). 1998. "Verzuiling en ontzuiling: Het ontstaan van ontzuiling." *Parlementair Documentatie Centrum van de Universiteit Leiden (PDC)*. Accessed October 4. www.politiekcompendium.nl/id/vh4valoy6suf/het_ontstaan_van_ontzuiling.

Pettersson, Per. 2011. "State and Religion in Sweden: Ambiguity between Disestablishment and Religious Control." *Nordic Journal of Religion and Society* 24 (2): 119–35.

———. 2012. Interview by S. Kind.

Pettersson, Per and Annette Leis-Peters. 2015. "Religion i Sverige: Kontinuitet och förändring." In *Sociologiska Perspektiv på Religion i Sverige*, edited by Mia Lövheim and Magdalena Nordin, 37–52. Malmö: Gleerups.

Philippine Atheism, Agnosticism, and Secularism (PATAS). *Website*. Accessed December 20, 2018. http://patas.org.ph/.

Plessentin, Ulf. 2012. "Die Neuen Atheisten als religionspolitische Akteure." In *Religion und Kritik in der Moderne*, edited by Ulrich Berner und Johannes, 83–114. Berlin, Münster: LIT.

P&P, Parlement & Politiek. n.d.-a. "Mr. J. (Job) de Ruiter." Accessed October 26. www.parlement.com/id/vg09llignjpe/j_job_de_ruiter.

———. n.d.-b. "Prof. Dr. J.P. (Jan Peter) Balkenende." Accessed October 26. www.parlement.com/id/vg09lljrp5z5/j_p_jan_peter_balkenende.

Quack, Johannes. 2011. "Is to Ignore to Deny? Säkularisierung, Säkularität und Säkularismus in Indien." In *Religionspolitik, Öffentlichkeit, Wissenschaft: Studien zur Neuformierung von Religion in der Gegenwart*, edited by Martin Bauman and Frank Neubert, 291–317. Zürich: PANO-Verlag.

———. 2012. *Disenchanting India: Organized Rationalism and Criticism of Religion in India*. New York: Oxford University Press.

———. 2013. "Was ist 'Nichtreligion'? Feldtheoretische Argumente für ein relationales Verständnis eines eigenständigen Forschungsgebietes." In *Säkularität in religionswissenschaftlicher Perspektive: Studien zur Neuformierung von Religion in der Gegenwart*, edited by Peter Antes and Stefen Führding, 87–107. Göttingen: Vandenhoeck & Ruprecht.

———. 2014. "Outline of a Relational Approach to 'Nonreligion'." *Method & Theory in the Study of Religion* 26 (4–5): 439–69.

Quack, Johannes and Cora Schuh. 2017. "Conceptualizing Religious Indifferences in Relation to Religion and Nonreligion." In *Religious Indifference: New Perspectives from Studies on Secularization and Nonreligion*, edited by Johannes Quack and Cora Schuh, 1–24. Wiesbaden: Springer.

Quilop, Raymund J. G. 2011. "Religion and Politics in the Philippines." In *The Politics of Religion in South and Southeast Asia*, edited by Ishtiaq Ahmed, 157–73. London: Routledge.

Racelis, Mary. 2012. "Technology and Morality in Women's Lives: And Deaths: The Reproductive Health Debate." *Philippine Sociological Review* 60: 257–90.

RD, Reformatorisch Dagblad. 2013. "RD-lezer vindt D66 meest antichristelijk." January 12. Accessed November 28, 2017. www.rd.nl/rd-lezer-vindt-d66-meest-antichristelijk-1.279599.

Red Tani (FF). 2014. Interview by A. Blechschmidt.

———. 2016. Interview by A. Blechschmidt.

Rejai, Mostafa. 1971. *Decline of Ideology?* Aldine: Atherton.

Remmel, Atko. 2017. "Religion, Interrupted? Observations on Religious Indifference in Estonia." In *Religious Indifference: New Perspectives from Studies on Secularization and Nonreligion*, edited by Johannes Quack and Cora Schuh, 123–42. Wiesbaden: Springer.

Righart, Hans. 1995. *De eindeloze jaren zestig: Geschiedenis van een generatieconflict*. Amsterdam Antwerpen: De Arbeiderspers.

Rood, M. 1983. "Niet met zeloten." In *Tussen droom en daad: D'66 en de politieke crisis*, Meningen bijengebracht door Joris Backer, M. H. Bakker, J. J. Peters, D. J. Pot, J. G. Upmeijer and K. M. Paarlberg, 69–81. Baarn, the Netherlands: Uitgeverij In den Toren.

Rosens, Nan. 2016. *De strijd om het einde*. Video, online available at VIMEO. Accessed May 14, 2019. https://vimeo.com/155574649.

Rudolph, Kurt. 1985. *Historical Fundamentals and the Study of Religions: Haskell Lectures Delivered at the University of Chicago*. New York: Macmillan.

Rune, Irene. 2013. "Självklart att Humanisterna ska ha officianter och ceremonier." Disskussionsunderlag om Humanisternas ceremoniverksamhet. Inför höchstkonferensen 26–27 oktober 2013, 4–6, September 30. Accessed October 13, 2013. www.humanisterna.se/wp-content/uploads/2013/09/Diskussionsunderlag-ceremonier-2013.pdf.

Sanchez, Korina. 2008. "Atheists in Foxholes." *PhilSTAR* (The Freeman, Opinion). Last Updated July 16, 2008. Accessed June 15, 2012 (page deleted). Personal print-out only.

Santiago, Katrina S. 2012. "Food for Free thought: An Interview with Red Tani and Kenneth Keng." *GMA News Online*, April 4. www.gmanetwork.com/news/opinion/content/253832/food-for-free-thought-an-interview-with-red-tani-and-kenneth-keng/story/.

Sapitula, Manuel Victor J. and Jayeel Serrano Cornelio. 2014. "A Religious Society? Advancing the Sociology of Religion in the Philippines (Foreword)." *Philippine Studies: Historical and Ethnographic Viewpoints* 62 (Special Issue: Sociology of Religion): 1–9.

SCB. 2014. "Statistika centralbyrån. Folkmängden efter region, civilstånd, ålder och kön. År 2014." Accessed November 16, 2016. www.statistikdatabasen.scb.se/pxweb/sv/ssd/START__BE__BE0101__BE0101A/BefolkningNy/table/tableViewLayout1/?rxid=393b628d-0497-498d-a39e-20ef8c3d3658.

———. 2015. "Statistika centralbyrån. Foreign/Swedish background 2015." Accessed November 2, 2016. www.statistikdatabasen.scb.se/pxweb/en/ssd/START__BE__BE0101__BE0101Q/UtlSvBakgTotNK/table/tableViewLayout1/?rxid=646305d2-852a-48ab-b11d-c1cf9555d023.

Schenk, Susanne, Marian Burchardt and Monika Wohlrab-Sahr. 2015. "Religious Diversity in the Neoliberal Welfare State: Secularity and the Ethos of Egalitarianism in Sweden." *International Sociology* 30 (1): 3–20.

Schluchter, Wolfgang. 1976. "Die Paradoxie der Rationalisierung: Zum Verhältnis von Ethik und Welt bei Max Weber/the Paradox of Rationalization: On the Relations of 'Ethics' and 'World' in Max Weber." *Zeitschrift für Soziologie* 5 (3): 256–84.
Schröder, Stefan. 2013. "Dialog der Weltanschauungen? – Der Humanistische Verband Deutschlands als Akteur im interreligiösen Dialoggeschehen." In *Säkularität in religionswissenschaftlicher Perspektive*, edited by Steffen Führding and Peter Antes, 169–85. Göttingen: V&R unipress.
Schuh, Cora, Marian Burchardt and Monika Wohlrab-Sahr. 2012. "Contested Secularities: Religious Minorities and Secular Progressivism in the Netherlands." *Journal of Religion in Europe* 5 (3): 349–83.
Schuyt, K. 2003. "Het pragmatisme in de filosofie van JF Glastra van Loon." *Netherlands Journal of Legal Philosophy* 1: 41–53.
SFS. 1988:950. Kulturmiljölag.
———. 1990:1144. Begravningslag.
———. 1998:1591. Lag om Svenska Kyrkan.
———. 1998:1593. Lag om trossamfund.
———. 1999:932. Lag om stöd till trossamfund.
SHA Humanisterna webpage. 2016a. "Ministerdeltagare på den officiellt erkända sekulära ceremonin vid Riksmötets öppnande," August 29. Accessed September 5, 2016. www.humanisterna.se/news/ministerdeltagare-pa-den-officiellt-erkanda-sekulara-ceremonin-vid-riksmotets-oppnande/.
———. 2016b. "Riksmötets öppnande." Accessed November 7. www.humanisterna.se/riksmotets-oppnande/.
———. 2017. "Humanitär hjälpverksamhet." Accessed July 23. http://humanisterna.se/hjalpverksamhet-2/.
SHA Kongresshandlingar. 2013.
———. 2014. Accessed Novembers 22, 2016. http://humanisterna.se/pdf/KH2014.pdf.
———. 2016.
SHA Kongressprotokoll. 2013.
SHA program of ideas. 2016. [Humanisternas idéprogram]. Accessed November 2. http://humanisterna.se/pdf/ip.pdf.
Simmel, Georg. [1908] 1992. *Soziologie. Untersuchungen über die Formen der Verge-sellschaftung*. Frankfurt am Main: Suhrkamp.
Sire, James W. 2015. *Naming the Elephant: Worldview as a Concept*. Downers Grove, IL: InterVarsity Press.
Sofka, Michael D. 2000. "Mythen des Skeptizismus." *Skeptiker* 13 (1): 18–28.
SST Statistik. 2014. "Swedish Commission for Government Support to Faith Communities (SST)." Accessed October 4, 2016. www.sst.a.se/statistik/statistik2014.4.1295346115121ad63f315d2a.html.
Staatsblad. 2014. *Wet van 4 juli 2014 tot wijziging van het Burgerlijk Wetboek en de Algemene wet gelijke behandeling met betrekking tot ambtenaren van de burgerlijke stand die onderscheid maken als bedoeld in de Algemene wet gelijke behandeling*. Staatsblad van het Koninkrijk der Nederlanden, Ministerie van Justitie.
Stolz, Jörg. 2010. "A Silent Battle: Churches and Their Secular Competitors." *Review of Religious Research* 51 (3): 253–76.
Sturmark, Christer. 2014. "Förslag till utredning om lagändring angående statligt stöd till livsåskådnings-organisationer." Letter to the Government: To the Ministry of Justice, Ministry of Culture, Stockholm, October 24.

Sturmark, Christer, Bengt Westerberg, Levi Fragell and Désirée Liljevall. 2012. "Se över lagen om statligt stöd till trossamfund." *Dagens Nyheter*, June 13.
Svenska Kyrkan. 2015. Svenska kyrkans medlemsutveckling år 1972–2015.
———. 2016a. Medlemmar i Svenska kyrkan i förhållande till folkmängd den 31.12.2016 per församling, pastorat och stift samt riket.
———. 2016b. Inträden i och utträden ur Svenska kyrkan år 1970–2016.
———. 2016c. Besök i Svenska kyrkans gudstjänster 1990–2016.
———. 2016d. Döpta, konfirmerade, vigda och begravda enligt Svenska kyrkans ordning år 1970–2016.
Svenska Kyrkan i siffror. 2015 and 2016. www.svenskakyrkan.se/statistik.
Sveriges grundlagar. Successionsordningen, from 1810, revised 1979, §4.
Swartz, David L. 1996. "Bridging the Study of Culture and Religion: Pierre Bourdieu's Political Economy of Symbolic Power." *Sociology of Religion* 57 (1): 71–85.
———. 2012. "Grundzüge einer Feldanalyse der Politik nach Bourdieu." In *Feldanalyse als Forschungsprogramm 2*, edited by S. Bernhard and C. Schmidt-Wellenburg, 163–94. Wiesbaden: VS Verlag für Sozialwissenschaften.
Tani, Red. 2009. "FF Meetup 8." *FF Website*, April 21. http://filipinofreethinkers.org/2009/04/21/ff-meetup-8/.
———. 2015. "Why I don't like Pope Francis." *Philippine Daily Inquirer*, January 19. http://opinion.inquirer.net/81837/why-i-dont-like-pope-francis.
Tanja, Erie. 2011. "'Dragers van beginselen'. De parlementaire entree van Abraham Kuyper en Ferdinand Domela. Nieuwenhuis." In *Waar visie ontbreekt, komt het volk om: Jaarboek parlementaire geschiedenis*, edited by Carla Van Baalen, H. Goslinga, A. van Kessel, J. van Merriënboer, J. Ramakers and J. Turpijn. Amsterdam: Boom.
Taylor, Charles. 2007. *A Secular Age*. Cambridge, MA: The Belknap Press of Harvard University Press.
Ten Napel, H.-M. 2012. "CDA partijgeschiedenis." Accessed June 30, 2017. http://dnpp.ub.rug.nl/dnpp/pp/cda/geschied.
Terrier, Jean. 2012. "'Auch in unserer Zeit werden Götter in den Massen geboren'. Emile Durkheims Erklärungsansätze zur Entstehung gesellschaftlicher Ideale in der Moderne." *Berliner Journal für Soziologie* 22 (4): 497–516.
Tess Termulo (PATAS). 2014. Interview by A. Blechschmidt.
Therborn, Göran. 1995. *European Modernity and Beyond: The Trajectory of European Societies, 1945–2000*. London: Sage.
———. 2012. *Världen: En inledning*. Stockholm: Liber.
Thurfjell, David. 2015. *Det gudlösa folket. De postkristna svenskarna och religionen*. Stockholm: Molin & Sorgenfrei Akademiska.
Timmerby, Magnus. 2018. "Personal communication via e-mail." November 28.
Timmermans, Arco and Gerard Breeman. 2012. "Morality Issues in the Netherlands: Coalition Politics under Pressure." In *Morality Politics in Western Europe: Parties, Agendas and Policy Choices*, edited by Isabelle Engeli, Christoffer Green-Pedersen and Lars Thorup Larsen, 35–61. Hampshire: Palgrave Macmillan.
TK, Tweede Kamer der Staten-Generaal. 1993/1994. Wijziging van Boek 1 van het Burgerlijk Wetboek en van het Wetboek van Burgerlijke Rechtsvordering in verband met opneming daarin van bepalingen voor de registratie van een samenleving.
———. 1996. Leefvormen Motie van de Leden M.M. van der Burg en Dittrich.
———. 1997/1998. Leefvormen: Brief van de Staatssecretaris van Justitie.
———. 2000a. Wijziging van Boek 1 van het Burgerlijk Wetboek in verband met de openstelling van het huwelijk voor personen van hetzelfde geslacht (Wet openstelling huwelijk): Brief van de Staatssecretaris van Justitie.

———. 2000b. Wijziging van Boek 1 van het Burgerlijk Wetboek in verband met de openstelling van het huwelijk voor personen van hetzelfde geslacht (Wet openstelling huwelijk): Nota naar aaanleiding van het verslag.

———. 2001. 70 (Interpellatie uitspraken minister van VWS over de pil van Drion).

Tomasson, Richard F. 2002. "How Sweden became So Secular." *Scandinavian Studies* 74 (1): 61–88.

Trappenburg, M. J. 2000. "Paarse ethiek." In *Zeven jaar paars*, edited by B. Tromp, et al., (2001), 53–78. Amsterdam: Arbeiderspers.

Trouw. 2006. "Van der Laan: D66 is te veel partij voor elite geweest." *Trouw*, February 10. Accessed November 1, 2016.

Tyrell, Hartmann. 2011. "Religion und Politik – Max Weber und Émile Durkheim." In *Religionen verstehen: Zur Aktualität von Max Webers Religionssoziologie*, edited by Agathe Bienfait, 41–91. Wiesbaden, Germany: Verlag für Sozialwissenschaft, Springer.

Van Apeldoorn, Bastiaan. 2009. "A National Case-Study of Embedded Neoliberalism and Its Limits: The Dutch Political Economy and the 'No' to the European Constitution." In *Contradictions and Limits of Neoliberal European Governance*, edited by Bastiaan Van Apeldoorn, Jan Drahokoupil and Laura Horn, 211–31. Hampshire: Palgrave Macmillan.

Van Baalen, C. and J. Ramakers. 2001. *Het kabinet-Drees III, 1952–1956. Barsten in de brede basis*. Den Haag: Sdu Uitgevers.

Van Boxtel, Roger, Wim Dik, Thom De Graaf, Alexander Ronnoy Kan and Hans Wijers. 2009. *Open en onbevangen. De noodzaak van politieke vrijzinnigheid*. Amsterdam: Uitgeverij Balans.

Van Dam, Peter. 2011. *Staat van verzuiling: Over een Nederlandse mythe*. Amsterdam: Wereldbibliotheek.

Van Dam, Peter and Paul Van Trigt. 2015. "Religious Regimes: Rethinking the Societal Role of Religion in Post-War Europe." *Contemporary European History* 24 (2): 213–32.

Vandenberghe, Frédéric. 1999. "'The Real Is Relational': An Epistemological Analysis of Pierre Bourdieu's Generative Structuralism." *Sociological Theory* 17 (1): 32–67.

Van der Ham, Boris. 2014. "De ultieme minderheid is het individu." Idee (paper of Van Mierlo Stichting, Think Tank D66).

Van der Ham, Boris and Rein Zunderdorp. 2013. "In het godslasteringsdebat staan levens op het spel." *de Volkskrant*, December 9. Accessed October 29, 2016. www.volkskrant.nl/politiek/-in-het-godslasteringsdebat-staan-levens-op-het-spel~a3558943/.

Van der Land, Menno. 2003. *Tussen Ideaal en Illusie: De Geschiedenis van D66, 1966–2003*. Den Haag: SDU.

———. 2014. "D66 partijgeschiedenis." *Documentatiecentrum Nederlandse Politieke Partijen (DNPP)*. http://dnpp.ub.rug.nl/dnpp/node/1306.

———. n.d. "Een on-nederlandse partij: De Verenigde Staten als inspiratiebron voor D66." www.mennovanderland.nl. www.mennovanderland.nl/Een%20on-Nederlandse%20partij.pdf.

Van Loon, Glastra Jan. 1967. "Democratie in Nederland." *Acta Politica* 3: 185–209.

———. 1997. "Overleven., een collectieve verantwoordelijkheid." *IDEE* 18 (3): 31.

Van Loon, Glastra Jan and J. Frederik. 1964. „Kiezen of delen." *Nederlands Juristenblad* 44: 1161–67.

Van Mierlo, Hans. 1968. De keuze van D'66.

Van Mil, F. 2013. Interview by C. Schuh.

Van Veldhuizen, Adriaan. 2013. "A grassroots sacred socialist history: Dutch social democrats (1894–1920)." In *Political Religion Beyond Totalitarianism*, edited by Joost Augusteijn, Patrick G. C. Dassen and Maartje J. Janse, 115–33. Hampshire: Palgrave Macmillan.

Van Weezel, Max and Michiel Zonneveld. 2002. *De Onttovering Van Paars: Een geschiedenis van de kabinetten-Kok*. Amsterdam: Van Gennep.

Varkevisser, Allan. 1998. "Een hartveroverend liberalisme." *Idee: tijdschrift van het Wetenschappelijk Bureau van D66* 19 (5): 25–7.

Waking Nomad [pseud.]. 2012a. "Thoughts of an Atheist Science Teacher." *PATAS Website*, October 6. http://patas.co/2012/10/thoughts-of-an-atheist-science-teacher/ (site discontinued).

Weber, Max. [1919] 2002. "Wissenschaft als Beruf." In *Max Weber: Schriften 1894–1922*, edited by Dirk Kaesler, 474–511. Stuttgart, Germany: Alfred Kröner Verlag.

———. [1920] 1986. *Gesammelte Aufsätze zur Religionssoziologie I*. Tübingen, Germany: Mohr Siebeck.

———. [1922] 1980a. "Erster Teil: Soziologische Kategorienlehre." In *Wirtschaft und Gesellschaft: Grundriß der verstehenden Soziologie*, edited by Johannes Winckelmann, 1–180. Tübingen, Germany: J.C.B. Mohr.

———. [1922] 1980b. "Zweiter Teil: Die Wirtschaft und die gesellschaftlichen Ordnungen und Mächte." In *Wirtschaft und Gesellschaft: Grundriß der verstehenden Soziologie*, based on edition by Johannes Winckelmann. Accessed www.zeno.org/Soziologie/M/Weber,+Max/Grundri%C3%9F+der+Soziologie/Wirtschaft+und+Gesellschaft. Tübingen Germany.

Weir, Todd H. 2014. *Secularism and Religion in Nineteenth-Century Germany: The Rise of the Fourth Confession*. Cambridge: Cambridge University Press.

———. 2015. "Germany and the New Global History of Secularism: Questioning the Postcolonial Genealogy." *The Germanic Review: Literature, Culture, Theory* 90 (1): 6–20.

Werron, Tobias. 2010. "Direkte Konflikte, indirekte Konkurrenzen. Unterscheidung und Vergleich zweier Formen des Kampfes." *Zeitschrift für Soziologie* 39 (4): 302–18.

Wessel-Tuinstra, Elida. 1985. "Het initiatiefontwerp Wessel-Tuinstra inzake euthanasie nader toegelicht." *idee'66* 6 (3): 77–81.

Weyers, Heleen. 2010. *Euthanasie: het proces van rechtsverandering*. Amsterdam: Amsterdam University Press.

Wiegele, Katharine L. 2005. *Investing in Miracles: El Shaddai and the Transformation of Popular Catholicism in the Philippines*. Honolulu: University of Hawai'i Press.

Wilfred, Felix. 2014. *The Oxford Handbook of Christianity in Asia*. Oxford: Oxford University Press.

Willander, Erika. 2013. "'Jag tror på något' Konstruktioner av tro och tilltro." *Sociologisk Forskning* 50 (2): 117–38.

———. 2015. "Religiositet och sekularisering." In *Sociologiska Perspektiv på Religion i Sverige*, edited by Mia Lövheim and Magdalena Nordin, 53–68. Malmö: Gleerups.

Wohlrab-Sahr, Monika and Marian Burchardt. 2012. "Multiple Secularities: Toward a Cultural Sociology of Secular Modernities." *Comparative Sociology* 11 (6): 875–909.

Yanis. 2013. Interview by S. Kind.

Yek Lai Fatt (PATAS). 2014. Interview by A. Blechschmidt.
Zenk, Thomas. 2012. "'Neuer Atheismus.' 'New Atheism' in Germany." *Approaching Religion* 2: 36–51.
Zuckerman, Phil. 2008. *Society without God: What the Least Religious Nations Can Tell Us about Contentment*. New York: New York University Press.
———. 2009. *Atheism and Secularity*, Volume 1 and 2. Santa Barbara: Praeger.
———. 2011. *Faith No More*. New York: Oxford University Press.
———. 2014. *Living the Secular Life: New Answers to Old Questions*. London: Penguin Books.
Zuckerman, Phil, Luke W. Galen and Frank L. Pasquale. 2016. *The Nonreligious*. New York: Oxford University Press.

Index

abortion *see* reproductive rights/reproductive health
agnosticism *see* methodological agnosticism
anti-revolutionary movement 110–11
antithesis 112–16, 128, 136, 154
areligious 7, 10, 12, 26, 30, 161
atheism 1, 12, 85–8, 97–9, 163; methodological (*see* methodological atheism); new 67, 92–5, 152, 158

borders 7–11, 13–18, 164–5
Bourdieu, Pierre 7–8, 11, 13–14, 16–19, 106–7, 119, 165
Bradlaugh, Charles 1, 6, 12, 164

Campbell, Colin D. 7–10, 17–18, 20, 25, 27, 29, 108, 164
ceremonies/ceremonial 4, 21, 36–7, 42, 44–7, 52–4, 57–67, 69–75, 147, 152, 159, 160
Christianity: Calvinism, Calvinist 105, 110–15, 135; Catholicism, Catholic 4, 78, 80–7, 102–3, 105, 121, 110–11, 147–8, 154–5 (*see also* Church, Catholic Church); Protestantism, Protestant 64, 80, 110–12, 121, 125–6, 151, 153–4
Church: Catholic Church 78, 80–2, 84–6, 102, 105, 147–8; Church of Sweden 21, 36–48, 66, 71, 145–7, 154–5, 160, 163; Dutch Reformed Church 110–11, 127
community: formation 22, 29, 31, 144; life stance 45, 47, 61, 146, 157, 161, 163; social 45–6, 49, 51–3, 67
competition 3, 14, 24–5, 150–1
conflict 23, 24–5, 67–9, 147, 148, 150

conservativism, conservative 18, 25, 110, 113, 153–5
cooperation 23–5, 95–8, 103, 152
criticism 1, 3, 42, 46, 51–3, 56–7, 68–71, 85–6, 102, 135, 154, 161

dialogue 19, 23, 26–7, 46–7, 103, 148, 155
differentiation 1, 5, 10, 13, 16–17, 29, 99–100, 104, 112, 115–16, 136, 165
disenchantment 119–22, 136, 158
diversity *see* nonreligion, diversity of
Dutch social liberal party (D66) 4–5, 105–36, 144–5, 149–51, 152–61, 163, 165

emancipation 1, 6, 49, 50, 54, 66, 69, 109, 115, 116–17, 119, 130, 148, 156–7
Engelke, Matthew 1–2, 12–13
enlightenment 22, 112–13, 128
epistemic-moral entanglement 22
equality (equal liberty) 22, 29, 31, 32, 40, 41, 49, 66, 106, 108, 123, 124–8, 135, 144, 149, 153–4, 156–7, 162, 163
eschatology 121
ethics *see* morality
euthanasia 35, 125–6

field: inter-field relations 15–16; political 5, 10, 16, 29, 56, 106, 107–9, 113, 117, 122, 124, 135; of power 15–16, 107, 165; religion-related surrounding (*Umfeld*) of religious field 2, 8, 11, 13–15, 16, 17, 19, 26, 144, 165; religious 4, 6–32, 49, 66, 70, 78, 84, 96, 103, 108, 109, 115, 127, 136, 144, 145–6, 160, 163, 164–5; religious-nonreligious field 17–18, 165; scientific 16, 160

Filipino Freethinkers 4, 77–104, 147, 160, 163
focus/foci 19, 21, 24, 26–8, 36, 68–70, 143, 146
freethought 84, 88, 111
French Revolution 109–10, 112

gender 5, 18, 22, 150, 153, 163, 165
Gruijters, Hans J.P.A. 117, 120–1

hegemony 4, 80–2, 147
Holyoake, George J. 1, 6, 12, 164
homology 12–13, 16, 108
homosexuality (homosexual) 116, 124–6, 157
humanism 9, 36; life stance 4, 26, 35–71, 145, 146–7, 151, 158–9, 161, 163, 164, 166; opinion-making 4, 35–71, 145–7, 162, 164–5; organized 21, 35–71, 98–9, 146
Humanisterna see Swedish Humanist Association (SHA)
human rights see universality

immanence (immanent) 42, 112, 120, 136, 149–50, 159, 161
India 2, 43, 78, 152, 158
indifference 1, 8, 17, 30–1, 118–19
individual liberty 3, 22, 106, 116–17, 124–8, 144, 149, 154
irreligion (irreligious) 8–10, 11, 16, 29, 108, 135–6, 150
Islam 40–3, 80, 95–6, 127–8, 154

Kuyper, Abraham 111–15, 128, 136, 138n21

law 5, 37–8, 43, 50, 66, 81, 85, 106–7, 126, 135, 149–50
Lee, Lois 2, 9–10, 95
liberalism (liberal) 109–16, 130–1, 149–51, 153–7, 160–1, 163–4
Loon, Glastra Jan Van 117–18, 119–20, 121, 129

methodological agnosticism 1, 6, 10, 12
methodological atheism 1, 6, 10, 12
Mierlo, Hans van 121–2, 129
milieu 20, 31, 78–9, 101–3, 145, 147, 151
mobilization 14, 24, 30, 46, 106–9, 118–19, 157, 163
modes of nonreligion see nonreligion

moral epistemic standpoint 5, 107, 128, 135, 162; see also epistemic-moral entanglement
morality/ethics 5–6, 8, 22, 25, 36, 42, 45–8, 52, 54, 66, 81, 83–4, 95, 100, 107, 111, 113–14, 118, 120–1, 123, 125–8, 130–1, 135, 147–8, 152, 154–5, 158, 159–60, 161–5
moving away from (religion-relatedness, religion-likeness) 1–2, 5–6, 8, 11–12, 15, 20, 22, 26, 28–31, 54, 69–70, 78, 91, 95, 99, 100, 103, 106–9, 114–15, 128, 132, 135–6, 144, 158, 161–2, 164, 165
multiculturalism (multicultural) 128, 151, 154
Muslims see Islam

Netherlands 4–5, 23, 29, 47–8, 105–36, 149–51, 154–5, 157–8, 161, 162, 165–6
neutrality (neutral) 2, 10, 51, 60, 61, 113, 131, 135
nonreligion: collective 78–9, 95–6, 103; diversity of 2–3, 5, 7, 143, 166; modes of 3, 5–6, 8, 17, 19–20, 29, 31–2, 77–9, 103, 143–4, 155, 164; NR 1 and NR 2 29–30, 161–2, 164; organized 78, 82–3, 102–4
normativity: religio-normativity 5, 18–19, 61, 143, 145, 152–5, 156

objectives 3, 21–3, 38, 56, 66, 144, 156, 161, 163, 164, 166

particularism, particularistic 48, 52, 107, 109–10, 115, 122, 125, 127, 131, 149
Philippine Atheists and Agnostics Society politics (PATAS) 4, 25, 77–104, 147–8, 153, 156–9, 162–3
Philippines 4, 25, 77–104, 147–9, 151, 154–5, 157–60, 163, 166
pillarization/depillarization 105–6, 109, 111, 115–16, 118, 119, 123, 149
pluralism 105–6, 115–16, 119, 135, 148–50, 157–8; worldview 31, 114, 123, 144
populism (populist) 127–8, 131, 134, 151, 164
postmodernism (postmodern) 43, 131, 146, 159, 160
pragmatism 117–18, 128–9, 159

Index

principles (principled) 112–14, 118, 129, 136, 151
private public divide (public, private) 42, 82, 88, 114, 120, 131, 149, 153, 156

Quack, Johannes 2, 8, 10, 22, 78, 158

realism 123, 159–60
relational approach/perspective 2–3, 10–19, 143–5, 164
relationality 8, 13, 106, 153; assemblages of 8, 11, 20, 26–7
relations 3, 7–34; kinds of 19, 23, 26–7, 69, 103, 144, 155, 161
relativism 21, 43, 68, 108, 131, 158, 160
religion: academic study of 1, 3, 12, 13; criticism of 1, 67, 86; differentiation from 1, 9; independence of 1–2; rejection of 8–9; religious others 1, 3, 17, 19–23, 31, 143, 160–1; transformation of 2, 15, 19, 165
religion-likeness (religion-like) *see* moving away from
religion-relatedness (religion-related) *see* moving away from
religious indifference *see* indifference
reproductive rights (abortion)/reproductive health 4, 35, 84–7, 124–5, 148–9, 154
responsibility 110, 118, 122–3, 149

same-sex marriage *see* homosexuality (homosexual)
secularity 1–6, 9–13, 16, 18–20, 21, 24–7, 30–1, 35–6, 39, 41–7, 49, 52–3, 55–6, 59, 62–3, 65–71, 82–6, 87, 91, 93, 95, 97, 103, 105–36, 145–6, 148, 149–54, 157–9, 160–3, 164–6
separation of religion and politics 42, 81, 110, 154, 162
separation of state and church 18, 35, 37–9, 65–6, 81, 85, 110, 125–7, 131, 135
sexuality 5, 18, 150, 153
socialism/Marxism 111–18, 121, 132–3, 136, 159, 161
spheres 13, 41, 107–8, 113, 115
state neutrality *see* separation of state and church
Sweden 3–4, 21, 23, 29, 35–71, 145–7, 151–2, 154–5, 157–8, 160, 163, 165–6; *see also* Church of Sweden
Swedish Humanist Association (SHA) 4, 35–71, 145–7, 151–4, 157, 159, 160, 163

Terlouw, Jan 129
themes 3, 7–8, 20–2, 26, 164, 166
Thorbecke, Johan Rudolf 109
truth 3, 22, 24–6, 29–30, 120, 158–60

unbelief 78, 111–14, 135, 153
universality 52, 68, 128, 158, 161–2; human rights 42, 52, 56, 68

values 3, 21–2, 35, 153–5, 166; humanist 45–6, 52–3, 70, 147
vision 112, 123, 128–32

worldview 10, 22–3, 28–9, 42, 107–8, 112–16, 148–50, 165; *see also* pluralism, worldview